CookingLight

fresh food *fast*

Cooking Light

fresh food *fast*

OXMOOR
HOUSE®

ISBN-13: 978-0-8487-3264-6
ISBN-10: 0-8487-3264-2
Library of Congress Control Number: 2008930049

Printed in the United States of America
First printing 2009

Be sure to check with your health-care provider
before making any changes in your diet.

Oxmoor House, Inc.

Editor in Chief: Nancy Fitzpatrick Wyatt
Executive Editor: Katherine M. Eakin
Art Director: Keith McPherson
Managing Editor: Allison Long Lowery

Cooking Light® Fresh Food Fast

Editor:	Heather Averett
Nutrition Editors:	Andrea C. Kirkland, M.S., R.D.; Rachel Quinlivan, R.D.
Project Editor:	Terri Laschober Robertson
Senior Designer:	Emily Albright Parrish
Copy Chief:	L. Amanda Owens
Director, Test Kitchens:	Elizabeth Tyler Austin
Assistant Director, Test Kitchens:	Julie Christopher
Test Kitchens Professionals:	Jane Chambliss; Patricia Michaud; Kathleen Royal Phillips; Catherine Crowell Steele; Ashley T. Strickland
Photography Director:	Jim Bathie
Senior Photo Stylist:	Kay E. Clarke
Associate Photo Stylist:	Katherine Eckert Coyne
Director of Production:	Laura Lockhart
Production Manager:	Terri Beste-Farley

Contributors

Compositor:	Rick Soldin
Copy Editor:	Carmine B. Loper
Proofreaders:	Jasmine Hodges, Norma Butterworth-McKittrick
Nutritional Analyses:	Kate Wheeler, R.D.
Indexer:	Mary Ann Laurens
Interns:	Anne-Harris Jones, Shea Staskowski
Food Stylists:	Ana Price Kelly, Debby Maugans
Photographers:	William Dickey, Beau Gustafson, Lee Harrelson
Photo Stylists:	Melanie J. Clarke
Recipe Developers:	Nancy Hughes, Lorrie Corvin

To order additional publications,
call 1–800–765–6400.

For more books to enrich your life,
visit **oxmoorhouse.com**

To search, savor, and share thousands of recipes,
visit **myrecipes.com**

Cooking Light®

Editor in Chief:	Mary Kay Culpepper
Executive Editor:	Billy R. Sims
Creative Director:	Susan Waldrip Dendy
Managing Editor:	Maelynn Cheung
Senior Editor:	Phillip Rhodes
Projects Editor:	Mary Simpson Creel, M.S., R.D.
Food Editor:	Ann Taylor Pittman
Associate Food Editors:	Timothy Q. Cebula; Kathy Kitchens Downie, R.D.; Julianna Grimes
Associate Editors:	Cindy Hatcher, Brandy Rushing
Test Kitchens Director:	Vanessa Taylor Johnson
Assistant Test Kitchens Director:	Tiffany Vickers
Senior Food Stylist:	Kellie Gerber Kelley
Test Kitchens Professionals:	Mary Drennen Ankar, SaBrina Bone, Mike Wilson
Art Director:	Maya Metz Logue
Associate Art Directors:	Fernande Bondarenko, J. Shay McNamee
Senior Designer:	Brigette Mayer
Senior Photographer:	Randy Mayor
Senior Photo Stylist:	Cindy Barr
Photo Stylists:	Jan Gautro, Leigh Ann Ross
Copy Chief:	Maria Parker Hopkins
Assistant Copy Chief:	Susan Roberts
Copy Editor:	Johannah Gilman Paiva
Copy Researcher:	Michelle Gibson Daniels
Production Manager:	Liz Rhoades
Production Editor:	Hazel R. Eddins
Cookinglight.com Editor:	Kim Cross
Cookinglight.com Intern:	Maggie Gordon
Administrative Coordinator:	Carol D. Johnson
Editorial Assistant:	Jason Horn

Welcome

Most cooks today want quick, reliable recipes their families and friends will love. That's why we've created ***Cooking Light*** *Fresh Food Fast,* a collection of over 280 incredibly flavorful 5-ingredient, 15-minute recipes. In these pages, you'll find the keys to getting dinner on the table in a snap, with short, fast recipes that are simultaneously nutrition-savvy and utterly delicious.

Each healthy recipe meets at least one of these two criteria: It requires five ingredients or less (excluding water, cooking spray, salt, pepper, and optional ingredients) or it can be whipped up in 15 minutes or less. And many fit the bill for both.

What's more, we share the smartest ways to make all your cooking sing. An example: In our Test Kitchens, we rely on the difference fresh seasonings can make in the taste of a tried-and-true dish. Take citrus such as lemon, lime, or orange: Even just a little squeeze can brighten the flavor of dressings and soups, add zip to fish and shellfish or desserts, and finish sauces and salsas to perfection.

Packed with chef-tested advice like that, ***Cooking Light*** *Fresh Food Fast* will guarantee that you'll serve the most fabulous meals ever—in a flash.

With more than 160 complete menus—with an appetizing photo of each—this book will convince you that it's an everyday pleasure to eat smart, be fit, and live well.

Mary Kay Culpepper
Editor in Chief

Contents

85

33

131

Reach for comfort with these simply sensational soups, perfected for fast preparation and incredible flavor. From Corn and Bacon Chowder featuring bits of sweet corn to veggie-rich Chicken-Vegetable Soup, these recipes yield healthy homemade soups in a hurry.

Always quick and satisfying, sandwiches, panini, burgers, and quesadillas will have your family preferring to eat in rather than dine out. Try burgers smothered with fruity Cranberry-Peach Chutney or Pear-Walnut Sandwiches piled high with the bounty of fall.

There's nothing quite like a salad to showcase fabulous seasonal produce and excite your taste buds. Turn to these dishes if you're craving a light, but nourishing lunch or dinner.

Only minutes in the making, no-fuss toss-and-serve pastas, veggie-loaded pizzas, and an abundance of protein-rich rice and grain options are just a few of the vegetarian meals that will entice the eye and delight the palate.

241

150

269

Fish and Shellfish, 186

Quick-cooking, healthful fish and seafood are ideal for any night of the week. Whether you stop by your local fish market on your way home from work or prefer to keep fillets in your freezer, these flavorful dishes come together in a flash.

Meats, 258

Aromatic seasonings and savory sauces enhance lean cuts of beef, pork, and lamb. From kid-friendly plates to easy, elegant entrées, this selection of meats will free you from your dinnertime rut and help you get hearty, family-pleasing food on the table fast.

Poultry, 308

From chicken tenders accompanied with Cajun-Creole Dipping Sauce to tender breasts dressed in simple, mouthwatering sauces and creams, here are our staff's no-hassle answers to that everyday question, "What's for dinner?"

soups

Creamy Avocado Soup with Tomato–Lump Crab Relish
Thai Coconut Shrimp Soup
Oriental Soup with Mushrooms, Bok Choy, and Shrimp
Cheese Tortellini and Vegetable Soup
Pan-Roasted Mushroom and Wild Rice Soup
Beefy Corn and Black Bean Chili
Caldillo
Posole
Spicy Poblano and Corn Soup
Corn and Bacon Chowder
Sweet Potato, Leek, and Ham Soup
Chicken-Vegetable Soup
Southwestern Chicken and White Bean Soup
Chicken Pasta Soup
Chicken-Escarole Soup
Smoked Turkey–Lentil Soup
Sausage and Barley Soup
Turkey Sausage–Gnocchi Soup

The simplicity of this soup allows the delicate, subtle flavor and luscious, velvety texture of the avocado to shine through.

Creamy Avocado Soup with Tomato–Lump Crab Relish

Prep: 9 minutes

2 ripe peeled avocados, coarsely chopped
2 cups fat-free, less-sodium chicken broth
1 (8-ounce) carton reduced-fat sour cream
2 tablespoons fresh lime juice
¼ teaspoon ground cumin
¼ teaspoon freshly ground black pepper
⅛ teaspoon salt
¼ pound fresh lump crabmeat, shell pieces removed
½ cup refrigerated prechopped tomato, onion, and bell pepper mix
Cilantro leaves (optional)

1. Combine first 7 ingredients in a blender or food processor; process until smooth. Chill soup until ready to serve.
2. Ladle soup into bowls. Combine crabmeat and tomato mixture in a small bowl. Spoon crabmeat mixture evenly on top of soup in each bowl. Garnish with cilantro leaves, if desired. Yield: 4 servings (serving size: 1 cup).

CALORIES 295 (69% from fat); FAT 23g (sat 6.8g, mono 9.7g, poly 2.1g); PROTEIN 12.6g; CARB 13.9g; FIBER 5.5g; CHOL 50mg; IRON 1.3mg; SODIUM 510mg; CALC 124mg

serve with

Minted Mango and Jicama Salad

Prep: 12 minutes

1 tablespoon fresh lime juice
2 tablespoons reduced-sugar orange marmalade
1 teaspoon minced peeled fresh ginger
1 tablespoon chopped fresh mint
1 sliced peeled ripe mango
1 cup (3 x ¼-inch) strips peeled jicama

1. Combine first 4 ingredients in a small bowl; stir well with a whisk.
2. Combine mango and jicama in a medium bowl. Drizzle juice mixture over mango mixture; toss gently to coat. Yield: 4 servings (serving size: about ½ cup).

CALORIES 59 (3% from fat); FAT 0.1g (sat 0g, mono 0.1g, poly 0g); PROTEIN 0.5g; CARB 14.9g; FIBER 2.5g; CHOL 0mg; IRON 0.3mg; SODIUM 3mg; CALC 10mg

Mangoes Nothing beats the aroma of a ripe, beautiful mango. Look for fruit with unblemished skin that is blushed with red. A mango is ready to eat when it becomes soft to the touch and very fragrant.

Freshly squeezed lime juice is the secret ingredient in this recipe. It balances and brightens the flavors and adds just the right amount of tartness to the soup.

Thai Coconut Shrimp Soup
Prep: 1 minute • Cook: 13 minutes

1 pound peeled and deveined large shrimp
1 tablespoon salt-free Thai seasoning (such as Frontier)
Cooking spray
1 cup refrigerated prechopped tricolor bell pepper
2½ cups fat-free, less-sodium chicken broth
1 tablespoon fish sauce
1 (13.5-ounce) can light coconut milk
1 tablespoon fresh lime juice
Chopped fresh cilantro (optional)

1. Sprinkle shrimp with Thai seasoning; toss well. Heat a Dutch oven over medium-high heat; coat pan and shrimp with cooking spray. Add shrimp to pan; sauté 2 minutes or until shrimp are almost done. Remove shrimp from pan; set aside. Coat pan with cooking spray; add bell pepper, and sauté 2 minutes.
2. Add chicken broth and fish sauce to bell pepper in pan; bring to a boil. Reduce heat; simmer 5 minutes. Stir in coconut milk and reserved shrimp. Cook 2 minutes or until thoroughly heated. Remove from heat; stir in lime juice. Stir in cilantro, if desired. Yield: 4 servings (serving size: 1¾ cups).

CALORIES 185 (27% from fat); FAT 6g (sat 4.5g, mono 0.2g, poly 0.4g); PROTEIN 21.6g; CARB 12.4g; FIBER 0.6g; CHOL 168mg; IRON 4.3mg; SODIUM 858mg; CALC 38mg

You can use most any greens in place of the baby bok choy, including spinach or napa (Chinese) cabbage.

Oriental Soup with Mushrooms, Bok Choy, and Shrimp
Prep: 3 minutes • Cook: 12 minutes

2 teaspoons dark sesame oil
Cooking spray
2 (3½-ounce) packages shiitake mushrooms, trimmed and thinly sliced
3 tablespoons chopped peeled fresh ginger
3 cups fat-free, less-sodium chicken broth
3 cups water
1 tablespoon low-sodium soy sauce
3 cups coarsely chopped baby bok choy
2 tablespoons sliced green onions
2 tablespoons chopped fresh cilantro
1 pound peeled and deveined shrimp
¼ cup fresh lime juice (about 3 limes)

1. Heat oil in a large Dutch oven coated with cooking spray over medium-high heat; sauté mushrooms and ginger 5 minutes or until liquid evaporates and mushrooms darken.
2. Add broth, 3 cups water, and soy sauce; bring mixture to a boil. Stir in bok choy and next 3 ingredients; cover, reduce heat, and simmer 3 minutes or until shrimp are done. Stir in lime juice just before serving. Yield: 6 servings (serving size: 1⅔ cups).

CALORIES 102 (20% from fat); FAT 2g (sat 0.4g, mono 0.1g, poly 0.3g); PROTEIN 15.1g; CARB 4.9g; FIBER 0.9g; CHOL 112mg; IRON 2.7mg; SODIUM 534mg; CALC 63mg

serve with
Sesame Wonton Crisps
Prep: 7 minutes • Cook: 5 minutes

2 teaspoons dark sesame oil
1 teaspoon water
18 wonton wrappers
Cooking spray
1 teaspoon sesame seeds
1 teaspoon black sesame seeds
¼ teaspoon salt
⅛ teaspoon five-spice powder

1. Preheat oven to 400°.
2. Combine sesame oil and 1 teaspoon water in a small bowl. Set aside.
3. Place wonton wrappers on a baking sheet coated with cooking spray. Brush evenly with oil mixture. Sprinkle evenly with sesame seeds, salt, and five-spice powder.
4. Bake at 400° for 5 minutes or until browned and crispy. Yield: 6 servings (serving size: 3 wonton crisps).

CALORIES 88 (25% from fat); FAT 2g (sat 0.3g, mono 0.1g, poly 0.3g); PROTEIN 2.6g; CARB 14.2g; FIBER 0.5g; CHOL 2mg; IRON 0.9mg; SODIUM 234mg; CALC 17mg

This hearty soup is reminiscent of the Italian classic minestrone. Though minestrone traditionally uses macaroni, we've substituted fresh cheese tortellini for better flavor and to speed preparation. Serve with a tossed spinach salad to round out the meal.

Cheese Tortellini and Vegetable Soup

Prep: 1 minute • Cook: 14 minutes

1 (14½-ounce) can diced tomatoes with garlic and onion, undrained
1 (11½-ounce) can condensed bean with bacon soup (such as Campbell's), undiluted
3 cups water
1 (16-ounce) package frozen Italian-style vegetables
¾ teaspoon dried Italian seasoning
¼ teaspoon freshly ground black pepper
½ (9-ounce) package fresh cheese tortellini
¼ cup grated Parmesan cheese

1. Combine first 6 ingredients in a 4-quart saucepan; cover and bring to a boil over high heat. Add pasta; reduce heat to medium. Cook, partially covered, 7 minutes or until pasta and vegetables are tender. Stir in cheese. Yield: 6 servings (serving size: 1⅓ cups).

CALORIES 201 (18% from fat); FAT 4g (sat 1.4g, mono 0.7g, poly 0.3g); PROTEIN 10.3g; CARB 31.3g; FIBER 5.4g; CHOL 11mg; IRON 2.1mg; SODIUM 920mg; CALC 66mg

The earthy flavor and meaty texture of mushrooms transforms a few simple ingredients into a mouthwatering soup. Use a packaged gourmet blend or any combination of cremini, shiitake, oyster, and button mushrooms.

Pan-Roasted Mushroom and Wild Rice Soup

Prep: 1 minute • Cook: 12 minutes

1 tablespoon olive oil
1 (4-ounce) package fresh gourmet-blend mushrooms
1 cup refrigerated prechopped celery, onion, and bell pepper mix
1 (2.75-ounce) package quick-cooking wild rice (such as Gourmet House)

1 (6-ounce) package light garlic-and-herb spreadable cheese wedges (such as The Laughing Cow)
2 cups 1% low-fat milk
½ teaspoon dried thyme
½ teaspoon freshly ground black pepper
¼ teaspoon salt

1. Heat oil in a large saucepan over medium-high heat. Add mushrooms and celery mixture; cook 6 to 7 minutes or until vegetables are browned, stirring occasionally.
2. While mushroom mixture cooks, prepare rice according to package directions, omitting salt and fat. Unwrap cheese; chop into bite-sized pieces.
3. Add milk, cheese, thyme, pepper, and salt to mushroom mixture, stirring well; bring to a boil. Reduce heat; cook 3 minutes or until cheese melts and soup thickens. Stir in rice. Cook 1 minute or until heated. Yield: 4 servings (serving size: 1 cup).

CALORIES 214 (37% from fat); FAT 9g (sat 3.4g, mono 2.9g, poly 0.6g); PROTEIN 14g; CARB 27.6g; FIBER 2.2g; CHOL 25mg; IRON 0.9mg; SODIUM 742mg; CALC 300mg

serve with
Mixed Greens and Raspberries with Hazelnuts and Raspberry Vinaigrette

Prep: 5 minutes

3 tablespoons white balsamic raspberry vinegar (such as Alessi)
2 tablespoons extra-virgin olive oil
1 tablespoon honey
1 tablespoon water
¼ teaspoon salt

⅛ teaspoon freshly ground black pepper
1 (5-ounce) package spring mix (such as Fresh Express)
1½ cups raspberries
4 tablespoons coarsely chopped hazelnuts, toasted

1. Whisk together first 6 ingredients in a large bowl. Add greens, tossing to coat.
2. Arrange salad on plates; top with raspberries and toasted hazelnuts. Yield: 4 servings (serving size: 1 cup salad, about ⅓ cup raspberries, and 1 tablespoon hazelnuts).

CALORIES 181 (64% from fat); FAT 13g (sat 2g, mono 8.3g, poly 1.7g); PROTEIN 2.9g; CARB 16.2g; FIBER 4.3g; CHOL 3mg; IRON 0.9mg; SODIUM 172mg; CALC 54mg

This dish has the flavor and aroma of a chili that has simmered all day—and only you have to know it hasn't. Dress it up with a dollop of sour cream and sliced green onions, and serve it with Cheesy Cheddar Corn Bread.

Beefy Corn and Black Bean Chili
Prep: 1 minute • Cook: 27 minutes

- 1 pound ground round
- 2 teaspoons salt-free chili powder blend (such as The Spice Hunter)
- 1 (14-ounce) package frozen seasoned corn and black beans (such as Pictsweet)
- 1 (14-ounce) can fat-free, less-sodium beef broth
- 1 (15-ounce) can seasoned tomato sauce for chili (such as Hunt's Family Favorites)

Reduced-fat sour cream (optional)
Sliced green onions (optional)

1. Combine beef and chili powder blend in a large Dutch oven. Cook 6 minutes over medium-high heat or until beef is browned, stirring to crumble. Drain and return to pan.
2. Stir in frozen corn mixture, broth, and tomato sauce; bring to a boil. Cover, reduce heat, and simmer 10 minutes. Uncover and simmer 5 minutes, stirring occasionally.
3. Ladle chili into bowls. Top each serving with sour cream and onions, if desired. Yield: 6 servings (serving size: about 1 cup).

CALORIES 193 (14% from fat); FAT 3g (sat 1g, mono 1g, poly 0.3g); PROTEIN 20g; CARB 20g; FIBER 3.4g; CHOL 40mg; IRON 2mg; SODIUM 825mg; CALC 0mg

serve with
Cheesy Cheddar Corn Bread
Prep: 4 minutes • Cook: 23 minutes

- 2 cups self-rising cornmeal mix (such as White Lily)
- 1¼ cups nonfat buttermilk
- ½ cup reduced-fat sour cream
- 1 large egg, lightly beaten
- ½ cup (2 ounces) reduced-fat shredded cheddar cheese

Butter-flavored cooking spray

1. Preheat oven to 425°.
2. Combine all ingredients except cooking spray in a large bowl. Pour batter into an 8-inch square baking pan coated with cooking spray. Bake at 425° for 20 minutes. Remove from oven; coat top of corn bread with cooking spray. Return to oven; bake 3 minutes or until a wooden pick inserted in center comes out clean and corn bread is golden. Serve warm, or cool completely in pan on a wire rack. Yield: 9 servings (serving size: 1 piece).

CALORIES 151 (27% from fat); FAT 5g (sat 2.1g, mono 0.2g, poly 0.1g); PROTEIN 6g; CARB 22.8g; FIBER 1.8g; CHOL 32mg; IRON 1.1mg; SODIUM 431mg; CALC 150mg

Serve this spicy stew with peeled orange slices sprinkled with cinnamon-sugar. Bottled cinnamon-sugar can be found on the spice aisle of your local supermarket.

Caldillo
Prep: 4 minutes • Cook: 45 minutes

1 pound boneless sirloin steak (about ½ inch thick), cut into bite-sized pieces
Cooking spray
1 (8-ounce) container refrigerated prechopped onion
3 cups water
2 (14½-ounce) cans diced tomatoes with zesty mild green chilies (such as Del Monte), undrained

1 teaspoon ground cumin
3 cups (½-inch) cubed unpeeled Yukon gold or red potato
¼ cup chopped fresh cilantro (optional)

1. Coat beef with cooking spray. Cook beef in a large Dutch oven coated with cooking spray over high heat 3 minutes; stir in onion. Cook 5 minutes or until liquid evaporates and beef and onion are browned.
2. Stir in 3 cups water, tomatoes, and cumin; cover and bring to a boil. Reduce heat to medium; simmer 20 minutes. Add potato; cover and simmer 10 minutes or until potato is tender. Remove from heat; stir in cilantro, if desired. Yield: 6 servings (serving size: 1⅓ cups).

CALORIES 165 (19% from fat); FAT 3g (sat 1.2g, mono 1.6g, poly 0.2g); PROTEIN 18.3g; CARB 15.5g; FIBER 3.2g; CHOL 28mg; IRON 2mg; SODIUM 595mg; CALC 59mg

The meat develops a rich, full-bodied flavor when it's cooked to a dark brown, so be sure not to stir the pork until it releases easily from the pan. Serve this fiery soup with warm flour tortillas.

Posole

Prep: 3 minutes • Cook: 30 minutes

Cooking spray
1 (1-pound) pork tenderloin, trimmed and cut into bite-sized pieces
2 teaspoons salt-free Southwest chipotle seasoning blend (such as Mrs. Dash)
1 (15.5-ounce) can white hominy, undrained

1 (14.5-ounce) can Mexican-style stewed tomatoes with jalapeño peppers and spices (such as Del Monte), undrained
1 cup water
¼ cup chopped fresh cilantro

1. Heat a large saucepan over medium-high heat. Coat pan with cooking spray. Sprinkle pork evenly with chipotle seasoning blend; coat evenly with cooking spray. Add pork to pan; cook 4 minutes or until browned. Stir in hominy, tomatoes, and 1 cup water. Bring to a boil; cover, reduce heat, and simmer 20 minutes or until pork is tender. Stir in cilantro. Yield: 4 servings (serving size: 1⅓ cups).

CALORIES 233 (17% from fat); FAT 5g (sat 1.4g, mono 1.9g, poly 0.8g); PROTEIN 24.4g; CARB 23g; FIBER 4.4g; CHOL 68mg; IRON 2.3mg; SODIUM 610mg; CALC 33mg

Cilantro Some call it cilantro; others call it coriander or even Chinese parsley. This native of southern Europe and the Middle East has a pungent flavor, with a faint undertone of anise. The leaves are often mistaken for flat-leaf parsley. One of the most versatile herbs, cilantro adds a distinctive taste to salsas, soups, stews, curries, and salads, as well as vegetable, fish, and chicken dishes.

While we prefer poblano chile peppers, you may substitute green chiles instead. Serve this soup with sliced tomatoes and tortillas.

Spicy Poblano and Corn Soup
Prep: 3 minutes • Cook: 10 minutes

1 (16-ounce) package frozen baby gold and white corn (such as Birds Eye), thawed and divided
2 cups fat-free milk, divided
4 poblano chiles, seeded and chopped (about 1 pound)

1 cup refrigerated prechopped onion
1 tablespoon water
¾ teaspoon salt
½ cup (2 ounces) reduced-fat shredded sharp cheddar cheese

1. Place 1 cup corn and 1½ cups milk in a Dutch oven. Bring mixture to a boil over medium heat.
2. Combine chopped chile, onion, and 1 tablespoon water in a microwave-safe bowl. Cover and microwave at HIGH 4 minutes.
3. Meanwhile, place 2 cups corn and ½ cup milk in a blender; process until smooth. Add pureed mixture to corn mixture in pan. Stir in chile mixture and salt, and cook 6 minutes over medium heat. Ladle soup into bowls, and top each serving with 2 tablespoons cheddar cheese. Yield: 4 servings (serving size: about 1⅓ cups soup and 2 tablespoons cheese).

CALORIES 239 (15% from fat); FAT 4g (sat 2.2g, mono 0.3g, poly 0.5g); PROTEIN 13.2g; CARB 42.3g; FIBER 4.9g; CHOL 13mg; IRON 1.5mg; SODIUM 633mg; CALC 275mg

Poblano Chiles The peak season for poblano chiles is summer and early fall. Ripe poblanos are reddish brown and sweeter than the green ones. Be sure to remove the seeds and membranes before cooking; that's where most of the heat-inducing capsaicin is found.

To capture the freshness of yellow jewel-like corn without the fuss of shucking ears or cutting kernels off the cob, use packages of frozen baby gold and white corn. This chowder is so wonderfully sweet with the frozen corn that our taste testers gave it our highest rating.

Corn and Bacon Chowder
Prep: 2 minutes • Cook: 14 minutes

2 bacon slices
½ cup refrigerated prechopped celery, onion, and bell pepper mix
2 (16-ounce) packages frozen baby gold and white corn, thawed and divided
2 cups 1% low-fat milk, divided

½ teaspoon salt
¼ teaspoon freshly ground black pepper
¾ cup (3 ounces) reduced-fat shredded extra-sharp cheddar cheese (such as Cracker Barrel)
Freshly ground black pepper (optional)

1. Cook bacon in a Dutch oven over medium heat until crisp. Remove bacon from pan; crumble and set aside. Add celery mixture and 1 package corn to drippings in pan; sauté 5 minutes or until vegetables are tender.
2. Place remaining 1 package corn and 1 cup milk in a blender, and process until smooth. Add pureed mixture to vegetables in pan; stir in remaining 1 cup milk, salt, black pepper, and cheese. Cook over medium heat (do not boil), stirring constantly, until cheese melts. Ladle chowder into bowls. Top each serving evenly with reserved crumbled bacon. Sprinkle with additional black pepper, if desired. Yield: 6 servings (serving size: 1 cup).

CALORIES 215 (24% from fat); FAT 6g (sat 3.1g, mono 1g, poly 0.6g); PROTEIN 10.8g; CARB 33.6g; FIBER 3.8g; CHOL 15mg; IRON 0.8mg; SODIUM 402mg; CALC 208mg

serve with
Tomato, Avocado, and Onion Salad
Prep: 7 minutes

3 small heirloom tomatoes, sliced
½ Vidalia or other sweet onion, vertically thinly sliced
½ cup coarsely chopped ripe peeled avocado (about ½ avocado)

1½ tablespoons thinly sliced fresh basil
2 tablespoons light Northern Italian salad dressing with basil and Romano (such as Ken's Steak House Lite)

1. Combine first 4 ingredients in a large bowl, tossing gently. Drizzle dressing evenly over salad; toss gently to coat. Yield: 6 servings (serving size: about ¾ cup).

CALORIES 46 (57% from fat); FAT 3g (sat 0.3g, mono 1.2g, poly 0.3g); PROTEIN 0.9g; CARB 5g; FIBER 1.5g; CHOL 0mg; IRON 0.3mg; SODIUM 61mg; CALC 16mg

Prechopped sweet potato is now available in most grocery stores. If you're unable to find it, peel and cube two small sweet potatoes to measure about 3 cups.

Sweet Potato, Leek, and Ham Soup

Prep: 6 minutes • Cook: 28 minutes

Olive oil-flavored cooking spray
1 cup diced cooked ham (such as Cumberland Gap)
1½ cups sliced leek (about 1 large)
2 tablespoons water (optional)
3 cups refrigerated cubed peeled sweet potato (such as Glory)
1 cup fat-free, less-sodium chicken broth
2 cups water
1 (5-ounce) can evaporated fat-free milk
¼ teaspoon freshly ground black pepper
Thinly sliced leek (optional)
Thinly sliced green onions (optional)

1. Heat a large Dutch oven over medium heat. Coat pan with cooking spray. Add ham; cook 3 to 4 minutes or until browned, stirring frequently. Remove ham from pan; set aside.

2. Add leek to pan; coat with cooking spray. Cook leek, covered, 5 minutes or until very tender, stirring occasionally. Add 2 tablespoons water to pan, if needed, to prevent burning.

3. Add sweet potato and next 4 ingredients, scraping pan to loosen browned bits; bring mixture to a boil. Cover, reduce heat, and simmer 15 minutes or until sweet potato is very tender. Place half of potato mixture in a blender or food processor. Remove center piece of blender lid (to allow steam to escape); secure blender lid on blender. Place a clean towel over opening in blender lid (to avoid splatters). Process until smooth. Pour puree into a large bowl. Repeat procedure with remaining mixture. Return pureed mixture to pan. Stir in ¾ cup reserved ham. Ladle soup into bowls; top servings evenly with ¼ cup reserved ham. Garnish with sliced leek and onions, if desired. Yield: 4 servings (serving size: about 1¼ cups).

CALORIES 193 (7% from fat); FAT 1g (sat 0.2g, mono 0g, poly 0.1g); PROTEIN 15.5g; CARB 29.2g; FIBER 3.6g; CHOL 26mg; IRON 2mg; SODIUM 625mg; CALC 153mg

If you use rotisserie chicken or refrigerated precooked chopped chicken, omit the salt because the processed products are higher in sodium than home-cooked unsalted chicken.

Chicken-Vegetable Soup

Prep: 1 minute • Cook: 14 minutes

1 (32-ounce) carton fat-free, less-sodium chicken broth
2½ cups diced cooked chicken breast
1 (8-ounce) container refrigerated prechopped celery, onion, and bell pepper mix
1 cup frozen sliced carrot
1 (14-ounce) package frozen baby potato and vegetable blend (such as Birds Eye)
1 teaspoon bottled minced roasted garlic
½ teaspoon dried Italian seasoning
½ teaspoon curry powder
½ teaspoon freshly ground black pepper
¼ teaspoon salt
1½ cups coarsely chopped fresh baby spinach
1 (12-ounce) can evaporated fat-free milk
Freshly ground black pepper (optional)

1. Bring first 4 ingredients to a boil in a covered large Dutch oven.
2. While broth mixture comes to a boil, place potato-vegetable blend in a microwave-safe bowl. Cover with heavy-duty plastic wrap; vent. Microwave at HIGH 5 minutes. While frozen vegetables cook, add garlic and next 4 ingredients to broth mixture; cover and continue to cook.
3. Using kitchen shears, snip cooked potato-vegetable blend into bite-sized pieces. Stir potato-vegetable blend, spinach, and milk into broth mixture. Cover and cook over high heat 5 minutes or until carrot is tender. Sprinkle with additional black pepper before serving, if desired. Yield: 6 servings (serving size: 1½ cups).

CALORIES 208 (10% from fat); FAT 2g (sat 0.6g, mono 0.7g, poly 0.5g); PROTEIN 25g; CARB 20g; FIBER 2.4g; CHOL 48mg; IRON 1.3mg; SODIUM 694mg; CALC 188mg

Baby Spinach Mild-flavored baby spinach gives this soup a boost of nutrients, including beta-carotene, potassium, and vitamin A.

We really like the extra zing of flavor from the fresh cilantro. It adds a nice burst of color to the dish as well. Simply toss some of the distinctive herb on top of the soup just before serving.

Southwestern Chicken and White Bean Soup

Prep: 2 minutes • Cook: 13 minutes

2 cups shredded cooked chicken breast
1 tablespoon 40%-less-sodium taco seasoning (such as Old El Paso)
Cooking spray
2 (14-ounce) cans fat-free, less-sodium chicken broth

1 (16-ounce) can cannellini beans or other white beans, rinsed and drained
½ cup green salsa
Light sour cream (optional)
Chopped fresh cilantro (optional)

1. Combine chicken and taco seasoning; toss well to coat. Heat a large saucepan over medium-high heat. Coat pan with cooking spray. Add chicken; sauté 2 minutes or until chicken is lightly browned. Add broth, scraping pan to loosen browned bits.
2. Place beans in a small bowl; mash until only a few whole beans remain. Add beans and salsa to pan, stirring well. Bring to a boil. Reduce heat; simmer 10 minutes or until slightly thick. Serve with sour cream and cilantro, if desired. Yield: 6 servings (serving size: 1 cup).

CALORIES 134 (19% from fat); FAT 3g (sat 0.5g, mono 0.6g, poly 0.5g); PROTEIN 18g; CARB 8.5g; FIBER 1.8g; CHOL 40mg; IRON 1.1mg; SODIUM 623mg; CALC 22mg

This quick twist on classic chicken noodle soup is loaded with fresh vegetables—carrots, celery, onion, and green bell pepper. You'll agree 100 percent that fresh is best.

Chicken Pasta Soup
Prep: 2 minutes • Cook: 22 minutes

Cooking spray
2 (6-ounce) skinless, boneless chicken breasts, cut into bite-sized pieces
1 (8-ounce) container refrigerated prechopped celery, onion, and bell pepper mix
1 cup matchstick-cut carrots
¼ teaspoon freshly ground black pepper
7 cups fat-free, less-sodium chicken broth
1 cup uncooked whole wheat rotini (corkscrew pasta)

1. Heat a Dutch oven over medium-high heat. Coat pan with cooking spray. Add chicken and next 3 ingredients; cook 6 minutes or until chicken begins to brown and vegetables are tender, stirring frequently. Add broth; bring to a boil. Add pasta, reduce heat to medium, and cook 8 minutes or until pasta is done. Yield: 6 servings (serving size: 1½ cups).

CALORIES 156 (14% from fat); FAT 3g (sat 0.6g, mono 0.6g, poly 0.4g); PROTEIN 20.4g; CARB 12.8g; FIBER 2.8g; CHOL 40mg; IRON 1.4mg; SODIUM 723mg; CALC 27mg

To cut down on time and keep cleanup to a minimum, use kitchen shears to easily chop tomatoes while they're still in the can.

Chicken-Escarole Soup
Prep: 1 minute • Cook: 14 minutes

1 (14½-ounce) can Italian-style stewed tomatoes, undrained and chopped
1 (14-ounce) can fat-free, less-sodium chicken broth

1 cup chopped cooked chicken breast
2 cups coarsely chopped escarole (about 1 small head)
2 teaspoons extra-virgin olive oil

1. Combine tomatoes and broth in a large saucepan. Cover and bring to a boil over high heat. Reduce heat to low; simmer 5 minutes. Add chicken, escarole, and oil; cook 5 minutes. Yield: 4 servings (serving size: 1 cup).

CALORIES 118 (27% from fat); FAT 4g (sat 0.7g, mono 2.1g, poly 0.6g); PROTEIN 13.5g; CARB 7.9g; FIBER 1.5g; CHOL 30mg; IRON 1.1mg; SODIUM 535mg; CALC 49mg

serve with
Salad-Filled Focaccia
Prep: 8 minutes

2½ cups mixed salad greens
⅓ cup refrigerated presliced red onion
3 tablespoons crumbled reduced-fat feta cheese
1 tablespoon fresh lemon juice

1 tablespoon extra-virgin olive oil
⅛ teaspoon crushed red pepper
1 (6-ounce) focaccia bread, cut in half horizontally

1. Combine first 6 ingredients in a large bowl, tossing well to coat.
2. Arrange salad on bottom half of loaf. Replace top half of loaf; cut crosswise into 4 equal portions. Yield: 4 servings (serving size: ¼ of filled focaccia).

CALORIES 170 (32% from fat); FAT 6g (sat 1.4g, mono 2.5g, poly 0.5g); PROTEIN 5.1g; CARB 25.2g; FIBER 1.3g; CHOL 4mg; IRON 1.5mg; SODIUM 347mg; CALC 36mg

Escarole This variety of endive is not as bitter as Belgian endive or curly endive. It has broad, bright green leaves that grow in loose heads. When purchasing escarole, look for fresh, crisp leaves without discoloration. Store escarole tightly wrapped in the refrigerator for up to three days.

Throw these ingredients into the slow cooker in the morning, and come home to a hearty and comforting meal without doing any further work. If you prefer to use dried oregano instead of the fresh, reduce the amount to ½ teaspoon. Dried herbs are very potent; a little goes a long way.

Smoked Turkey–Lentil Soup
Prep: 5 minutes • Cook: 8 hours

6 cups organic vegetable broth
1 (8-ounce) smoked turkey leg
½ pound dried lentils, rinsed and drained
1 (8-ounce) container refrigerated prechopped celery, onion, and bell pepper mix

2 teaspoons chopped fresh oregano
½ teaspoon freshly ground black pepper
Nonfat Greek yogurt (optional)
Oregano sprigs (optional)

1. Place first 6 ingredients in a 3- to 4-quart electric slow cooker. Cover and cook on LOW 8 to 10 hours or until lentils are tender and turkey falls off the bone.
2. Remove turkey leg from cooker. Remove and discard skin. Shred meat; return to cooker, discarding bone. Ladle soup into bowls; garnish with yogurt and oregano sprigs, if desired. Yield: 8 servings (serving size: 1 cup).

CALORIES 159 (16% from fat); FAT 3g (sat 0.6g, mono 0.7g, poly 0.5g); PROTEIN 12.7g; CARB 21.3g; FIBER 5g; CHOL 17mg; IRON 2.2mg; SODIUM 648mg; CALC 26mg

serve with
Fresh Lime and Oregano Spring Greens Salad
Prep: 7 minutes

1 garlic clove, minced
2 tablespoons water
1½ tablespoons extra-virgin olive oil
1 tablespoon fresh lime juice

1 teaspoon chopped fresh oregano
¼ teaspoon freshly ground black pepper
⅛ teaspoon salt
1 (5-ounce) package spring greens

1. Combine first 7 ingredients in a large bowl; stir well with a whisk. Add greens, and toss gently to coat. Yield: 4 servings (serving size: about 1 cup).

CALORIES 70 (84% from fat); FAT 7g (sat 1.4g, mono 4g, poly 0.5g); PROTEIN 1.3g; CARB 2.1g; FIBER 0.6g; CHOL 3mg; IRON 0.2mg; SODIUM 171mg; CALC 38mg

Fresh, delicate baby spinach doesn't hold up to hours of cooking, so it is added at the last minute. Pureeing the vegetables allows you to drastically cut cooking time while maintaining all the rich flavors of the vegetables.

Sausage and Barley Soup
Prep: 5 minutes • Cook: 18 minutes

Cooking spray
6 ounces turkey breakfast sausage
2½ cups frozen bell pepper stir-fry (such as Birds Eye)
2 cups water

1 (14½-ounce) can Italian-style stewed tomatoes, undrained and chopped
¼ cup uncooked quick-cooking barley
1 cup coarsely chopped fresh baby spinach

1. Heat a large saucepan over medium-high heat. Coat pan with cooking spray. Add sausage; cook 3 minutes or until browned. Remove from heat.
2. While sausage cooks, place stir-fry and 2 cups water in a blender; process until smooth. Add stir-fry puree, tomatoes, and barley to sausage in pan. Bring mixture to a boil over high heat; cover, reduce heat to low, and simmer 10 minutes. Stir in spinach; cook 1 minute or until spinach wilts. Yield: 4 servings (serving size: 1½ cups).

CALORIES 145 (24% from fat); FAT 4g (sat 1.5g, mono 1.2g, poly 0.5g); PROTEIN 9.9g; CARB 17.9g; FIBER 2.6g; CHOL 33mg; IRON 1.6mg; SODIUM 493mg; CALC 53mg

serve with
Asiago-Topped Garlic Bread
Prep: 6 minutes • Cook: 4 minutes

1 garlic clove, pressed
1 (6-ounce) whole wheat French bread baguette, cut in half lengthwise

1½ tablespoons light olive oil vinaigrette
½ teaspoon chopped fresh rosemary
¼ cup (1 ounce) finely grated Asiago cheese

1. Preheat broiler.
2. Spread garlic on cut sides of bread; brush evenly with vinaigrette. Top evenly with rosemary and cheese.
3. Broil 4 minutes or until cheese melts and bread is lightly browned. Cut into 8 pieces. Yield: 4 servings (serving size: 2 pieces).

CALORIES 138 (22% from fat); FAT 3g (sat 1.4g, mono 0.5g, poly 0.1g); PROTEIN 5.6g; CARB 20.2g; FIBER 0.7g; CHOL 7mg; IRON 1.1mg; SODIUM 283mg; CALC 70mg

Gnocchi are small, quick-cooking dumplings usually made from potatoes. Look for shelf-stable vacuum-packed packages of gnocchi with the dried pasta in your local supermarket. Serve this hearty main-dish soup with a crisp green salad.

Turkey Sausage–Gnocchi Soup

Prep: 1 minute • Cook: 14 minutes

1 (4.5-ounce) link hot turkey Italian sausage
2 cups water
1 (16-ounce) package vacuum-packed gnocchi (such as Bellino or Vigo)
1 (14-ounce) can fat-free, less-sodium beef broth
1 (14½-ounce) can Italian-style stewed tomatoes, undrained and chopped
½ cup (2 ounces) grated fresh Parmesan cheese

1. Remove casings from sausage. Cook sausage in a large Dutch oven over medium-high heat until sausage is browned, stirring to crumble.
2. Add 2 cups water and next 3 ingredients to pan; bring to a boil. Reduce heat, and simmer 4 to 5 minutes or until gnocchi float to the top of pan. Ladle soup into bowls; sprinkle each serving evenly with cheese. Yield: 7 servings (serving size: 1 cup soup and about 1 tablespoon cheese).

CALORIES 182 (21% from fat); FAT 4g (sat 1.7g, mono 0g, poly 0g); PROTEIN 10.5g; CARB 25.1g; FIBER 0.5g; CHOL 22mg; IRON 0.7mg; SODIUM 809mg; CALC 134mg

sandwiches

Pear-Walnut Sandwiches
Tofu Salad Sandwiches
Goat Cheese and Roasted Pepper Panini
Overstuffed Grilled Vegetable–Feta Sandwiches
Roasted Portobello Mushroom Sandwiches with Parmesan Mayonnaise
Open-Faced Smoked Salmon Sandwiches
Grilled Grouper Sandwiches with Tartar Sauce
Spicy Baja Beef Tortillas
Black and Blue Quesadillas
French Dip Sandwiches
Sloppy Skillet Beef Sandwiches
Mini Lamb Pitas with Minted Pea Hummus
Grilled Pork Sliders with Honey BBQ Sauce
Grilled Ham and Mango Quesadillas
Grilled Ham, Muenster, and Spinach Sandwiches
Prosciutto, Fontina, and Fig Panini
Grilled Chicken Reubens
Grilled BBQ Chicken Sandwiches with Spicy Avocado Spread
Grilled Chicken and Pineapple Sandwiches
Turkey Cobb Sandwiches
Turkey Antipasto Panini
Turkey Burgers with Cranberry-Peach Chutney

Crisp, ripe Bartlett pears and toasted walnuts from fall's harvest combine in these quick and tasty sandwiches. They pack nutrition and taste great for breakfast, lunch, or dinner. Pair them with Honey-Gingered Carrot Soup for a dynamic dinner duo.

Pear-Walnut Sandwiches
Prep: 15 minutes

½ cup (4 ounces) tub-style light cream cheese

8 (1.1-ounce) slices cinnamon-raisin bread, toasted

2 tablespoons finely chopped walnuts, toasted

2 Bartlett pears, cored and thinly sliced

1 cup alfalfa sprouts

1. Spread 1 tablespoon cream cheese evenly over each of 8 bread slices. Sprinkle ½ tablespoon walnuts evenly over each of 4 bread slices. Top each evenly with pear slices, sprouts, and 1 bread slice. Cut each sandwich in half diagonally. Yield: 4 servings (serving size: 1 sandwich).

CALORIES 335 (29% from fat); FAT 11g (sat 3.7g, mono 0.4g, poly 1.8g); PROTEIN 8.7g; CARB 52.2g; FIBER 5.9g; CHOL 15mg; IRON 2mg; SODIUM 363mg; CALC 56mg

serve with
Honey-Gingered Carrot Soup
Prep: 3 minutes • Cook: 12 minutes

3 cups fat-free, less-sodium chicken broth

2 (10-ounce) packages frozen sliced honey-glazed carrots (such as Green Giant), thawed

½ cup frozen chopped onion

1 tablespoon minced peeled fresh ginger

1 teaspoon grated orange rind

¼ teaspoon black pepper

Plain fat-free yogurt (optional)

Thyme sprigs (optional)

1. Combine first 6 ingredients in a large saucepan; bring to a boil. Reduce heat; simmer 2 minutes or until carrots are tender.

2. Place half of soup mixture in a blender or food processor. Remove center piece of blender lid (to allow steam to escape); secure blender lid on blender. Place a clean towel over opening in blender lid (to avoid splatters). Blend 30 seconds or until smooth. Pour pureed mixture into a large bowl. Repeat procedure with remaining soup mixture. Ladle soup into bowls; garnish with yogurt and thyme sprigs, if desired. Yield: 4 servings (serving size: 1¼ cups).

CALORIES 160 (21% from fat); FAT 4g (sat 0.6g, mono 0g, poly 0g); PROTEIN 3.7g; CARB 20.7g; FIBER 3.8g; CHOL 0mg; IRON 0.1mg; SODIUM 664mg; CALC 26mg

Toast the English muffins under a preheated broiler while preparing the filling. You can toast four muffins on a baking sheet in the same amount of time it takes to cook just one muffin in a toaster. Round out your meal with a handful of baked tortilla chips and a dill pickle spear.

Tofu Salad Sandwiches
Prep: 10 minutes

4 green leaf lettuce leaves
4 honey wheat double-fiber English muffins
    (such as Thomas' Hearty Grains), split
    and toasted

4 tomato slices
Tofu Salad
Freshly ground black pepper (optional)

1. Place 1 lettuce leaf on the bottom half of each English muffin; top each with 1 tomato slice. Spoon ⅓ cup Tofu Salad evenly over each tomato slice; sprinkle evenly with black pepper, if desired. Top sandwiches with remaining 4 muffin halves. Yield: 4 servings (serving size: 1 sandwich).

CALORIES 203 (28% from fat); FAT 6g (sat 0.5g, mono 0g, poly 0g); PROTEIN 9.5g; CARB 30.9g; FIBER 6.1g; CHOL 4mg; IRON 2.7mg; SODIUM 510mg; CALC 195mg

Tofu Salad
Prep: 5 minutes

8 ounces extra-firm tofu
¼ cup reduced-calorie salad dressing (such
    as Miracle Whip Light)
1 tablespoon dill pickle relish

1 teaspoon prepared mustard
⅛ teaspoon salt
⅛ teaspoon dried dill
⅛ teaspoon freshly ground black pepper

1. Press tofu between paper towels to remove excess moisture; cut into ¼-inch cubes.
2. Combine salad dressing and next 5 ingredients in a medium bowl, stirring until blended. Add half of tofu, mashing with the back of a large spoon. Add remaining tofu, stirring gently. Yield: 1⅓ cups (serving size: ⅓ cup).

CALORIES 88 (60% from fat); FAT 6g (sat 0.5g, mono 0g, poly 0g); PROTEIN 5.1g; CARB 3.8g; FIBER 0.8g; CHOL 4mg; IRON 1.1mg; SODIUM 287mg; CALC 109mg

The sweetness of roasted red bell peppers is an ideal foil to the pungency of the goat cheese and kalamata olives. Serve this hearty veggie sandwich with Melon Chillers.

Goat Cheese and Roasted Pepper Panini
Prep: 5 minutes • Cook: 6 minutes

1 (3-ounce) package goat cheese, softened
12 pitted kalamata olives, coarsely chopped
8 (2-ounce) slices sourdough bread
16 basil leaves

2 cups spring mix greens
1 cup bottled roasted red bell peppers
Cooking spray

1. Combine cheese and olives in a small bowl, stirring until well blended. Spread about 1 tablespoon cheese mixture evenly over each of 4 bread slices. Divide basil leaves, greens, and bell pepper into fourths; arrange evenly over cheese mixture on each bread slice. Top with remaining 4 bread slices.

2. Heat a large nonstick skillet over medium heat. Coat pan with cooking spray. Add sandwiches to pan. Cover with a sheet of foil; top with a heavy skillet. Cook 3 minutes or until lightly browned. Turn sandwiches over; replace foil and skillet. Cook 3 minutes or until golden. Yield: 4 servings (serving size: 1 sandwich).

CALORIES 477 (25% from fat); FAT 13g (sat 6.4g, mono 4.1g, poly 1.4g); PROTEIN 20.1g; CARB 69.3g; FIBER 3.8g; CHOL 22mg; IRON 4.9mg; SODIUM 1,198mg; CALC 174mg

serve with
Melon Chillers
Prep: 6 minutes

2 cups cubed fresh cantaloupe, frozen
⅓ cup orange juice
2 tablespoons fresh lime juice
¼ cup sugar
1 (12-ounce) can ginger ale, divided

1. Combine first 4 ingredients and ½ cup ginger ale in a blender; process until smooth. Add remaining ginger ale; process until smooth. Yield: 4 servings (serving size: about 1 cup).

CALORIES 116 (2% from fat); FAT 1g (sat 0.1g, mono 0g, poly 0.1g); PROTEIN 0.9g; CARB 29.2g; FIBER 0.1g; CHOL 0mg; IRON 0.4mg; SODIUM 19mg; CALC 13mg

Make sure your grill is nice and hot to create grill marks on the vegetables and bread.

Overstuffed Grilled Vegetable–Feta Sandwiches

Prep: 4 minutes • Cook: 11 minutes

1⅓ cups refrigerated presliced yellow squash and zucchini mix
4 (¼-inch-thick) slices red onion
Cooking spray
¾ cup grape tomatoes, halved
3 tablespoons light Northern Italian salad dressing with basil and Romano (such as Ken's Steak House Lite)

1 tablespoon chopped fresh basil
1 (8-ounce) loaf French bread, halved lengthwise
¾ cup (3 ounces) crumbled feta cheese

1. Prepare grill.
2. Coat squash mix and onion evenly with cooking spray. Place vegetables on grill rack; grill 4 minutes on each side or until crisp-tender and beginning to brown.
3. Place tomato in a medium bowl; add dressing and basil, tossing gently to coat. Add cooked vegetables to tomato mixture; toss well.
4. Coat cut sides of bread with cooking spray. Grill bread 1 minute on each side or until lightly toasted. Spoon vegetable mixture over bottom half of bread; sprinkle evenly with cheese. Top with remaining bread half. Press down lightly; cut crosswise into 4 equal pieces. Yield: 4 servings (serving size: 1 piece).

CALORIES 283 (25% from fat); FAT 8g (sat 3.5g, mono 1.2g, poly 0.7g); PROTEIN 11.6g; CARB 42.5g; FIBER 3.2g; CHOL 19mg; IRON 2.7mg; SODIUM 773mg; CALC 158mg

Red Onions Red onions contain more sugar than brown- or white-skinned onions and have a milder, sweeter flavor. They're best used in salads, on sandwiches, or in quick-cooking dishes, since they lose their jewel-toned purplish color when cooked a long time. When purchasing, look for onions with dry, clean, paper-thin skin, and be sure the onions are firm. Store in a dry, cool location.

Begin assembling these sandwiches while the mushrooms broil, and add the hot-from-the-oven mushrooms at the end. Spread leftover Parmesan Mayonnaise on any of your favorite deli meat sandwiches—it adds a fantastic burst of flavor.

Roasted Portobello Mushroom Sandwiches with Parmesan Mayonnaise

Prep: 7 minutes • Cook: 11 minutes

2 (6-ounce) packages presliced portobello mushrooms

12 sprays balsamic vinaigrette salad spritzer (such as Wish-Bone)

½ cup Parmesan Mayonnaise

8 (¾-ounce) slices crusty Chicago-style Italian bread (about ½ inch thick), toasted

1 (12-ounce) bottle roasted red bell peppers, drained

2 cups baby arugula

1. Preheat broiler.

2. Place mushrooms on a baking sheet; coat evenly with balsamic spritzer. Broil mushrooms 11 to 12 minutes or until browned and tender.

3. While mushrooms broil, spread 1 tablespoon Parmesan Mayonnaise over cut side of each bread slice; top each of 4 slices with about ⅔ cup bell pepper and ½ cup arugula. Arrange roasted mushrooms evenly over arugula. Top with remaining 4 bread slices. Yield: 4 servings (serving size: 1 sandwich).

CALORIES 276 (41% from fat); FAT 13g (sat 2.3g, mono 0.6g, poly 0.7g); PROTEIN 7.4g; CARB 32.4g; FIBER 2.8g; CHOL 13mg; IRON 2mg; SODIUM 806mg; CALC 88mg

Parmesan Mayonnaise

Prep: 3 minutes

½ cup light mayonnaise

1 garlic clove, pressed

2 tablespoons grated Parmesan cheese

2 tablespoons minced red onion

¼ teaspoon black pepper

1. Combine all ingredients in a small bowl, stirring until well blended. Yield: ⅔ cup (serving size: about 1 tablespoon).

CALORIES 46 (82% from fat); FAT 4g (sat 0.8g, mono 0.1g, poly 0g); PROTEIN 0.5g; CARB 1.4g; FIBER 0.1g; CHOL 5mg; IRON 0.1mg; SODIUM 111mg; CALC 13mg

Served with a mixed green salad, this light salmon sandwich is perfect for a warm summer's day. Low in calories and rich in protein, alfalfa sprouts crown this sandwich with lots of vitamins and minerals—particularly vitamin C.

Open-Faced Smoked Salmon Sandwiches
Prep: 9 minutes

Dill Cream Cheese Spread
4 (1-ounce) slices pumpernickel bread, toasted

4 ounces thinly sliced smoked salmon
8 (¼-inch-thick) slices red onion
1 cup alfalfa sprouts

1. Spread 1 tablespoon Dill Cream Cheese Spread over each of 4 bread slices. Top each with 1 ounce salmon, 2 onion slices, and ¼ cup sprouts. Yield: 4 servings (serving size: 1 sandwich).

CALORIES 176 (24% from fat); FAT 5g (sat 1.9g, mono 0.9g, poly 0.7g); PROTEIN 10.7g; CARB 23.6g; FIBER 3.6g; CHOL 14mg; IRON 1.4mg; SODIUM 568mg; CALC 66mg

Dill Cream Cheese Spread
Prep: 3 minutes

¼ cup (2 ounces) tub-style light chive-and-onion cream cheese

2 teaspoons chopped fresh dill
2 teaspoons capers, rinsed

1. Combine all ingredients in a bowl, stirring until well blended. Yield: ¼ cup (serving size: 1 tablespoon).

CALORIES 30 (67% from fat); FAT 2g (sat 1.5g, mono 0g, poly 0g); PROTEIN 1.5g; CARB 1.1g; FIBER 0.1g; CHOL 8mg; IRON 0mg; SODIUM 128mg; CALC 21mg

Grouper is a white-meat fish that is well suited for the grill. If you can't find grouper, use sea bass or mahimahi. Look for fish that is free of blemishes, has a fresh smell, and has flesh that springs back when touched. Serve these fish sandwiches with fresh seasonal cherries and pineapple to add bright color and tart flavor to your meal.

Grilled Grouper Sandwiches with Tartar Sauce

Prep: 6 minutes • Cook: 6 minutes

4 (6-ounce) grouper fillets (about 1½ inches thick)
2 teaspoons olive oil
¼ teaspoon salt
¼ teaspoon black pepper
Cooking spray
Tartar Sauce
4 (1.8-ounce) white wheat hamburger buns
4 green leaf lettuce leaves

1. Prepare grill.
2. Brush fillets evenly with olive oil; sprinkle evenly with salt and pepper. Place fillets on grill rack coated with cooking spray; grill 3 to 4 minutes on each side or until fish flakes easily when tested with a fork.
3. While fish cooks, prepare Tartar Sauce. Spread about 2½ tablespoons Tartar Sauce over cut sides of each bun; place 1 lettuce leaf on bottom half of each bun. Top lettuce with fish; top with remaining bun halves. Yield: 4 servings (serving size: 1 sandwich).

CALORIES 388 (37% from fat); FAT 16g (sat 2.8g, mono 2g, poly 1.9g); PROTEIN 38.5g; CARB 26.3g; FIBER 5.5g; CHOL 73mg; IRON 4.6mg; SODIUM 783mg; CALC 311mg

Tartar Sauce

Prep: 4 minutes

½ cup light mayonnaise
2 tablespoons chopped green onions
1 tablespoon sweet pickle relish
1½ teaspoons capers, drained
1½ teaspoons fresh lemon juice
½ teaspoon Worcestershire sauce

1. Combine all ingredients in a small bowl, stirring with a whisk until well blended. Yield: ⅔ cup (serving size: about 1 tablespoon).

CALORIES 43 (84% from fat); FAT 4g (sat 0.6g, mono 0g, poly 0g); PROTEIN 0.1g; CARB 1.8g; FIBER 0.1g; CHOL 4mg; IRON 0.1mg; SODIUM 124mg; CALC 2mg

These "open-faced wraps" get their kick from the adobo sauce in canned chipotle chiles. Quench the heat with a refreshing Cranberry-Açai Spritzer. Research on the health-promoting abilities of açai berries shows promise because they are rich in antioxidants, phytochemicals, anti-inflammatory substances, vitamins, and minerals.

Spicy Baja Beef Tortillas

Prep: 12 minutes

¼ cup light sour cream
1 tablespoon adobo sauce from canned chipotle chiles in adobo sauce (reserve chiles for another use)
4 (6-inch) low-fat whole wheat tortillas
5 cups gourmet salad greens

6 ounces thinly sliced low-sodium deli roast beef (such as Boar's Head)
1 cup refrigerated prechopped tomato
⅓ cup mild pickled banana pepper rings
1 ripe peeled avocado, coarsely chopped

1. Combine ¼ cup sour cream and adobo sauce in a small bowl, stirring well. Place 1 tortilla on each of 4 plates. Spread 1 tablespoon sour cream mixture over each tortilla. Top each evenly with salad greens; arrange beef over greens.
2. Combine tomato, pepper rings, and avocado in a medium bowl; toss gently. Top beef evenly with tomato mixture. Yield: 4 servings (serving size: 1 tortilla).

CALORIES 284 (42% from fat); FAT 13.1g (sat 3.5g, mono 4.8g, poly 1g); PROTEIN 16.9g; CARB 26.4g; FIBER 6.1g; CHOL 25mg; IRON 3.2mg; SODIUM 352mg; CALC 103mg

serve with
Cranberry-Açai Spritzer

Prep: 4 minutes

2 cups cranberry juice
1 (10.5-ounce) bottle organic açai juice blend (such as Sambazon Original Blend)
1 tablespoon fresh lime juice
1 (12-ounce) can diet ginger ale
2 cups crushed ice (optional)
4 lime slices (optional)

1. Combine first 3 ingredients in a 1½-quart pitcher. Slowly add ginger ale. Serve over ice, and garnish with lime slices, if desired. Yield: 4 servings (serving size: about 1 cup).

CALORIES 108 (9% from fat); FAT 1g (sat 0.3g, mono 0g, poly 0.1g); PROTEIN 0.3g; CARB 24.9g; FIBER 0.5g; CHOL 0mg; IRON 0.3mg; SODIUM 31mg; CALC 14mg

A sweet and salty flavor combination is always a huge hit, and the blue cheese and balsamic glaze in these beefy quesadillas is no exception. Pair with Mixed Greens with Lime Vinaigrette for a sensational meal.

Black and Blue Quesadillas
Prep: 5 minutes • Cook: 11 minutes

Cooking spray
⅓ cup thinly sliced red onion
4 (8-inch) fat-free flour tortillas
½ pound thinly sliced low-sodium deli roast beef (such as Boar's Head)

2 tablespoons crumbled blue cheese
4 teaspoons balsamic glaze (such as Gia Russa)

1. Heat a large nonstick skillet over medium heat. Coat pan with cooking spray. Add onion; sauté 3 to 4 minutes or until tender and lightly browned. Remove from heat.
2. Top half of each tortilla evenly with beef, onion, and cheese. Fold tortillas in half.
3. Return pan to heat. Coat pan and both sides of quesadillas evenly with cooking spray. Place 2 quesadillas in pan; cook 2 to 3 minutes on each side or until browned. Repeat procedure with remaining quesadillas. Cut each quesadilla into 4 wedges; drizzle with 1 teaspoon glaze. Yield: 4 servings (serving size: 1 quesadilla).

CALORIES 233 (17% from fat); FAT 4g (sat 1.8g, mono 0.3g, poly 0g); PROTEIN 20.3g; CARB 27.9g; FIBER 2.3g; CHOL 33.5mg; IRON 1.5mg; SODIUM 484mg; CALC 26mg

serve with
Mixed Greens with Lime Vinaigrette
Prep: 7 minutes

2 tablespoons white wine vinegar
1 tablespoon olive oil
½ teaspoon grated lime rind
¼ teaspoon freshly ground black pepper

⅛ teaspoon salt
6 cups mixed baby greens
1 peeled avocado, cut into 8 slices
1 cup cherry tomatoes, halved

1. Combine first 5 ingredients in a small bowl, stirring well with a whisk.
2. Arrange greens evenly on plates. Top evenly with avocado and tomato. Drizzle evenly with dressing. Yield: 4 servings (serving size: 1½ cups mixed greens, 2 slices avocado, and ¼ cup tomato).

CALORIES 177 (75% from fat); FAT 15g (sat 3.7g, mono 7.3g, poly 1.5g); PROTEIN 4.9g; CARB 9.6g; FIBER 4.7g; CHOL 10mg; IRON 1.2mg; SODIUM 154mg; CALC 108mg

Deglazing the pan with a couple of tablespoons of water while cooking the onions speeds up the browning process. The result is a "shortcut" caramelized onion that adds maximum flavor to this deli classic.

French Dip Sandwiches

Prep: 3 minutes • Cook: 12 minutes

1 medium Vidalia or other sweet onion, peeled and thinly sliced
Cooking spray
2 teaspoons salt-free onion and herb seasoning blend, divided
½ cup plus 2 tablespoons water

1 cup fat-free, less-sodium beef broth
12 ounces very thinly sliced low-sodium deli roast beef (such as Boar's Head)
4 (2½-ounce) hoagie rolls, split lengthwise
4 (0.8-ounce) slices reduced-fat Swiss cheese, torn in half

1. Preheat oven to 500°.
2. Heat a large nonstick skillet over high heat; add onion. Coat onion with cooking spray; stir in ½ teaspoon seasoning blend. Sauté 11 to 12 minutes or until onion is tender and golden brown. While onion cooks, add 2 tablespoons water at a time; cook each time until liquid evaporates, scraping pan to loosen browned bits.
3. While onion cooks, combine broth and remaining 1½ teaspoons seasoning blend in a medium saucepan; cook over medium heat until hot. Remove pan from heat; add beef, pushing beef down into liquid until covered. Let stand 5 minutes.
4. While beef stands, place hoagie rolls, cut sides up, on a baking sheet. Bake at 500° for 4 minutes or until bread is lightly toasted.
5. Remove beef from broth, allowing excess broth to drip back into pan; reserve broth. Arrange beef evenly over bottom halves of rolls; top evenly with onion, cheese slices, and remaining bread halves. Serve with warm broth for dipping. Yield: 4 servings (serving size: 1 sandwich and 2 tablespoons broth).

CALORIES 395 (22% from fat); FAT 10g (sat 4.5g, mono 0g, poly 1g); PROTEIN 37.4g; CARB 42.2g; FIBER 2.7g; CHOL 46mg; IRON 2.4mg; SODIUM 683mg; CALC 219mg

serve with
Creamy Ranch-Style Coleslaw

Prep: 7 minutes

⅓ cup light mayonnaise
¼ cup nonfat buttermilk
1 teaspoon salt-free onion and herb seasoning blend (such as Mrs. Dash)

¼ teaspoon salt
⅛ teaspoon black pepper
4 cups packaged coleslaw

1. Combine first 5 ingredients in a bowl, stirring well with a whisk. Pour dressing over slaw; toss well. Chill until ready to serve. Yield: 4 servings (serving size: 1 cup).

CALORIES 85 (71% from fat); FAT 7g (sat 1.3g, mono 0g, poly 0g); PROTEIN 1.1g; CARB 4.8g; FIBER 1g; CHOL 6.8mg; IRON 0.2mg; SODIUM 328mg; CALC 39mg

Add color, crunch, and—most importantly—convenience to this weeknight family favorite with prechopped yellow, red, and green bell pepper.

Sloppy Skillet Beef Sandwiches
Prep: 2 minutes • Cook: 15 minutes

Cooking spray
1 pound lean ground beef
1 cup refrigerated prechopped tricolor bell pepper
½ cup frozen whole-kernel corn

1 (14.5-ounce) can Mexican-style stewed tomatoes with jalapeño peppers and spices, undrained
¼ cup plus 2 tablespoons ketchup
4 (1½-ounce) whole wheat hamburger buns

1. Heat a large nonstick skillet over medium-high heat. Coat pan with cooking spray. Add beef and bell pepper; sauté 5 minutes or until meat is browned, stirring to crumble. Drain well; return meat mixture to pan. Add corn, tomatoes, and ketchup; cook 9 minutes or to desired consistency. Serve on hamburger buns. Yield: 4 servings (serving size: 1 cup beef and 1 bun).

CALORIES 382 (29% from fat); FAT 13g (sat 4.5g, mono 5g, poly 1.5g); PROTEIN 29.1g; CARB 41.2g; FIBER 6.1g; CHOL 41mg; IRON 4.1mg; SODIUM 864mg; CALC 79mg

serve with
Sweet and Tangy Mustard Coleslaw
Prep: 5 minutes

2 tablespoons sugar
1 tablespoon canola oil
1 tablespoon cider vinegar
1 tablespoon prepared mustard
¼ teaspoon salt

4 cups packaged cabbage-and-carrot coleslaw
½ cup refrigerated prechopped tricolor bell pepper

1. Combine first 5 ingredients in a large bowl; stir well with a whisk. Add coleslaw and bell pepper; toss gently to coat. Yield: 4 servings (serving size: 1 cup).

CALORIES 75 (44% from fat); FAT 4g (sat 0.3g, mono 2.2g, poly 1.1g); PROTEIN 0.8g; CARB 9.9g; FIBER 1.4g; CHOL 0mg; IRON 0.3mg; SODIUM 196mg; CALC 24mg

Nothing says spring like these pita pockets loaded with delicate lamb and colorful Minted Pea Hummus. Green peas contribute bold color and are especially high in vitamin K, which helps protect against osteoporosis. Add fresh fruit as a side dish, and you've got a wonderfully healthy meal. Use leftover hummus as a refreshing and vibrant veggie dip. It also goes well with Greek-Style Pita Chips (recipe on page 106).

Mini Lamb Pitas with Minted Pea Hummus

Prep: 9 minutes • Cook: 12 minutes • Other: 5 minutes

1 pound lean ground lamb
¼ cup (1 ounce) crumbled reduced-fat feta cheese
¼ teaspoon ground cumin
¼ teaspoon freshly ground black pepper
Cooking spray

8 (1-ounce) miniature whole wheat pitas (such as Toufayan Mini Pitettes)
½ cup Minted Pea Hummus
Red onion slices (optional)
Alfalfa sprouts (optional)
Cucumber slices (optional)

1. Prepare grill.
2. Combine first 4 ingredients. Divide mixture into 4 equal portions, shaping each into a ½-inch-thick patty.
3. Place patties on a grill rack coated with cooking spray; grill 6 minutes on each side or until a thermometer registers 165°. Remove from grill; let stand 5 minutes. Cut each patty in half. Split each pita in half horizontally, cutting to, but not through, opposite side. Spread 1 tablespoon Minted Pea Hummus on bottom half of each pita, and top with half of 1 patty. Add onion, sprouts, and cucumber, if desired. Yield: 4 servings (serving size: 2 stuffed pitas).

CALORIES 391 (38% from fat); FAT 17g (sat 6.9g, mono 6.7g, poly 1.1g); PROTEIN 27.4g; CARB 33.9g; FIBER 4g; CHOL 77mg; IRON 3.7mg; SODIUM 354mg; CALC 84mg

Minted Pea Hummus

Prep: 3 minutes

2 cups frozen petite green peas, thawed
2 garlic cloves
½ cup mint leaves

1½ teaspoons olive oil
1 teaspoon water
¼ teaspoon salt

1. Place all ingredients in a blender or food processor; process until smooth. Yield: 1¼ cups (serving size: 1 tablespoon).

CALORIES 15 (24% from fat); FAT 0.5g (sat 0.1g, mono 0.3g, poly 0.1g); PROTEIN 0.7g; CARB 2.1g; FIBER 0.8g; CHOL 0mg; IRON 0.4mg; SODIUM 60mg; CALC 5mg

Crisp on the outside, soft on the inside, Herbed Sweet Potato Fries are the perfect side to pair with a barbecue pork sandwich. We guarantee you can't eat just one. And that's a good thing: Sweet potatoes are rich in beta carotene, vitamin C, and vitamin E.

Grilled Pork Sliders with Honey BBQ Sauce

Prep: 5 minutes • Cook: 24 minutes • Other: 5 minutes

½ cup bottled barbecue sauce (such as Sticky Fingers Memphis Original)
2 tablespoons dark rum (such as Myers's)
2 tablespoons honey
1 (1-pound) pork tenderloin, trimmed
Cooking spray
4 (1.8-ounce) white wheat hamburger buns

1. Prepare grill.
2. Combine barbecue sauce, rum, and honey in a medium saucepan; bring to a boil. Cook 2 minutes or until reduced to ½ cup. Reserve ¼ cup sauce for serving. Use remaining ¼ cup sauce for basting.
3. Place pork on grill rack coated with cooking spray; grill 8 minutes. Turn and baste pork with sauce; cook 8 minutes. Turn and baste with sauce. Cook 4 minutes or until a thermometer registers 160° (slightly pink). Let stand 5 minutes; cut into thin slices.
4. Place buns, cut sides down, on grill rack; toast 1 minute. Place 3 ounces pork on bottom half of each bun. Spoon 1 tablespoon sauce over each serving; top with remaining halves of buns. Yield: 4 servings (serving size: 1 sandwich).

CALORIES 319 (17% from fat); FAT 6g (sat 1.8g, mono 1.5g, poly 1.4g); PROTEIN 27.6g; CARB 39.2g; FIBER 5.1g; CHOL 63mg; IRON 4mg; SODIUM 520mg; CALC 261mg

serve with
Herbed Sweet Potato Fries

Prep: 3 minutes • Cook: 14 minutes

2 cups frozen sweet potato fries (such as Alexia)
Cooking spray
1 teaspoon chopped fresh thyme
1 teaspoon chopped fresh rosemary
¼ teaspoon salt
¼ teaspoon freshly ground black pepper

1. Preheat oven to 425°.
2. Arrange fries in a single layer on a rimmed baking sheet coated with cooking spray. Coat fries evenly with cooking spray; sprinkle remaining ingredients evenly over fries, tossing to coat.
3. Bake at 425° for 14 minutes or until golden. Yield: 4 servings (serving size: ½ cup).

CALORIES 86 (36% from fat); FAT 3g (sat 0.3g, mono 0g, poly 0g); PROTEIN 1.2g; CARB 13.8g; FIBER 1.8g; CHOL 0mg; IRON 0.5mg; SODIUM 225mg; CALC 25mg

Exotic mango chutney teams up with queso fresco and shaved deli ham in these grilled quesadillas. Queso fresco, which literally translates as "fresh cheese," is a soft, moist, and mild Mexican cheese; try it sprinkled over enchiladas, soups, or salads.

Grilled Ham and Mango Quesadillas
Prep: 5 minutes • Cook: 4 minutes

½ cup mango chutney (such as Sun Brand)
4 (8-inch) multigrain tortillas (such as Tumaro's)
8 ounces shaved lower-sodium deli ham (such as Boar's Head)

½ cup (2 ounces) crumbled queso fresco
3 tablespoons chopped green onions
Cooking spray

1. Prepare grill.
2. Spread 2 tablespoons mango chutney over half of each tortilla. Top evenly with ham, cheese, and onions. Fold tortillas in half.
3. Place quesadillas on a grill rack coated with cooking spray over medium-high heat. Grill 2 to 3 minutes on each side or until golden and cheese melts. Cut each quesadilla into 4 wedges. Yield: 4 servings (serving size: 1 quesadilla).

CALORIES 287 (19% from fat); FAT 6g (sat 1.6g, mono 0.8g, poly 0.1g); PROTEIN 20.9g; CARB 35g; FIBER 8.1g; CHOL 35mg; IRON 1.7mg; SODIUM 882mg; CALC 171mg

serve with
Sweet Broccoli Slaw with Cranberries
Prep: 4 minutes

¼ cup light sweet Vidalia onion dressing (such as Ken's Steak House Lite)
2 teaspoons cider vinegar
3 cups packaged broccoli coleslaw

1 cup chopped Gala apple (about ½ pound)
¼ cup dried cranberries
2 tablespoons chopped pecans, toasted (optional)

1. Combine dressing and cider vinegar in a large bowl, stirring with a whisk. Add coleslaw, apple, and cranberries; toss well to coat. Top evenly with pecans, if desired. Yield: 4 servings (serving size: about ¾ cup).

CALORIES 137 (34% from fat); FAT 5g (sat 0.6g, mono 1.5g, poly 0.8g); PROTEIN 2.2g; CARB 21.9g; FIBER 3g; CHOL 0mg; IRON 0.6mg; SODIUM 78mg; CALC 92mg

Spinach offers a vitamin-rich alternative to lettuce in this sandwich. Chowchow is a mustard-flavored mixed vegetable and pickle relish available on the condiment aisle. Often served alongside pork and cooked greens, here it adds a subtle tang that complements the ham and spinach.

Grilled Ham, Muenster, and Spinach Sandwiches
Prep: 7 minutes • Cook: 4 minutes

8 (¾-ounce) slices crusty Chicago-style Italian bread (about ½ inch thick), toasted
8 ounces thinly sliced lower-sodium deli ham (such as Boar's Head)
4 (1-ounce) slices reduced-sodium Muenster cheese (such as Alpine Lace)
2 cups fresh baby spinach
¼ cup mild chowchow (such as Braswell's)
Cooking spray

1. Layer each of 4 bread slices with 2 ounces ham, 1 slice Muenster cheese, ½ cup baby spinach, 1 tablespoon chowchow, and 1 bread slice.
2. Heat a large nonstick skillet over medium-high heat. Coat sandwiches with cooking spray; add to pan. Cook 2 minutes on each side or until browned and cheese melts. Cut sandwiches in half, if desired. Serve immediately. Yield: 4 servings (serving size: 1 sandwich).

CALORIES 315 (31% from fat); FAT 11g (sat 5.8g, mono 2.8g, poly 0.8g); PROTEIN 20.8g; CARB 32.4g; FIBER 1.7g; CHOL 53mg; IRON 2.1mg; SODIUM 821mg; CALC 245mg

serve with
Green Apple Waldorf Salad
Prep: 11 minutes

2 large Granny Smith apples, chopped
¼ cup sweetened dried cranberries
¼ cup light mayonnaise
1 tablespoon fresh lemon juice
⅛ teaspoon salt
2½ tablespoons chopped walnuts, toasted

1. Combine first 5 ingredients in a medium bowl; sprinkle evenly with walnuts. Cover and chill until ready to serve. Yield: 4 servings (serving size: 1 cup).

CALORIES 145 (50% from fat); FAT 8g (sat 1.3g, mono 0.4g, poly 2.2g); PROTEIN 1g; CARB 19.6g; FIBER 2.5g; CHOL 5mg; IRON 0.4mg; SODIUM 194mg; CALC 10mg

Granny Smith Apples Extend your search for the famously tart, fiber-rich Granny Smith apples beyond the produce aisle of your supermarket. Check out roadside stands and farmers' markets. Look for apples that are firm, vibrantly colored, and free from bruises. They should smell fresh, not musty. Skins should be tight and smooth. Braeburn, Fuji, or Gala apples can be substituted, if desired.

If you don't have a panini grill, place sandwiches in a grill pan or large nonstick skillet coated with cooking spray over medium heat. Cover sandwiches with foil, and top with a heavy skillet. Cook 2 to 3 minutes on each side or until golden brown.

Prosciutto, Fontina, and Fig Panini
Prep: 7 minutes • Cook: 3 minutes

8 (0.9-ounce) slices crusty Chicago-style Italian bread
4 ounces very thinly sliced prosciutto
1¼ cups (4 ounces) shredded fontina cheese
½ cup baby arugula leaves
¼ cup fig preserves
Olive oil-flavored cooking spray

1. Preheat panini grill.
2. Top each of 4 bread slices evenly with prosciutto, fontina cheese, and arugula. Spread 1 tablespoon fig preserves evenly over 1 side of each of remaining 4 bread slices; top sandwiches with remaining bread slices. Coat outsides of sandwiches with cooking spray. Place sandwiches on panini grill; cook 3 to 4 minutes or until golden and cheese is melted. Cut panini in half before serving, if desired. Yield: 4 servings (serving size: 1 sandwich).

CALORIES 345 (34% from fat); FAT 13g (sat 6.8g, mono 4.1g, poly 1.6g); PROTEIN 18.2g; CARB 37.1g; FIBER 1.4g; CHOL 50mg; IRON 2mg; SODIUM 951mg; CALC 202mg

serve with
Balsamic Mixed Greens with Strawberries
Prep: 7 minutes

1 tablespoon balsamic vinegar
2 teaspoons extra-virgin olive oil
1 teaspoon honey
¼ teaspoon freshly ground black pepper
1½ cups sliced strawberries
2½ cups mixed baby greens
2 tablespoons chopped walnuts, toasted

1. Combine first 4 ingredients in a small bowl; stir well with a whisk.
2. Combine strawberries and mixed greens, tossing gently. Pour dressing over greens mixture, tossing gently to coat. Arrange salad evenly on each of 4 plates; top each serving with ½ tablespoon walnuts. Yield: 4 servings (serving size: 1 cup salad and ½ tablespoon walnuts).

CALORIES 98 (57% from fat); FAT 6g (sat 1.3g, mono 2.2g, poly 1.9g); PROTEIN 2.9g; CARB 9.2g; FIBER 2.2g; CHOL 4mg; IRON 0.7mg; SODIUM 33mg; CALC 55mg

Freshen up a chicken Reuben with this homemade coleslaw. It will have your family—like our Test Kitchens staff—asking for more. Melon Salad with Lavender Honey Dressing makes a perfect accompaniment.

Grilled Chicken Reubens
Prep: 9 minutes • Cook: 3 minutes

2 cups packaged angel hair coleslaw
2 tablespoons light mayonnaise
2 tablespoons chili sauce (such as Heinz) or ketchup
1 teaspoon dill pickle relish
8 (1-ounce) slices rye and pumpernickel swirled bread (such as Pepperidge Farms)

2 cups shredded cooked chicken breast
4 (⅞-ounce) slices reduced-fat Jarlsberg cheese
2 tablespoons yogurt-based spread (such as Brummel and Brown), divided

1. Combine first 4 ingredients in a medium bowl; toss well to coat.
2. Spoon coleslaw evenly onto each of 4 bread slices; top each evenly with chicken and cheese. Top with remaining 4 bread slices.
3. Heat a large nonstick skillet over medium heat. While skillet heats, spread ¾ teaspoon yogurt spread evenly over 1 side of each sandwich. Place sandwiches in skillet, spread sides down. Cook 2 to 3 minutes or until lightly browned. While sandwiches cook, spread tops of sandwiches evenly with remaining yogurt spread. Turn sandwiches over; cook 1 to 2 minutes or until lightly browned and cheese melts. Cut sandwiches in half before serving, if desired. Yield: 4 servings (serving size: 1 sandwich).

CALORIES 412 (28% from fat); FAT 13g (sat 3.9g, mono 0.9g, poly 0.5g); PROTEIN 35.1g; CARB 34.7g; FIBER 2.7g; CHOL 62mg; IRON 2.9mg; SODIUM 856mg; CALC 272mg

serve with
Melon Salad with Lavender Honey Dressing
Prep: 4 minutes

1 tablespoon chopped fresh mint
1 tablespoon fresh lime juice

1 teaspoon lavender honey
2 cups mixed melon

1. Combine first 3 ingredients in a small bowl. Pour dressing over melon, tossing to coat. Yield: 4 servings (serving size: ½ cup).

CALORIES 34 (5% from fat); FAT 0.1g (sat 0g, mono 0g, poly 0.1g); PROTEIN 0.7g; CARB 8.4g; FIBER 0.1g; CHOL 0mg; IRON 0.2mg; SODIUM 13mg; CALC 9mg

The Spicy Avocado Spread is bursting with flavor, but if time is short, use prepared guacamole or a few slices of fresh avocado to still enjoy the benefits of the avocado's healthful plant fats. Serve with baked potato chips. If you prefer your bun toasted, place it on the grill during the last minute of cooking.

Grilled BBQ Chicken Sandwiches with Spicy Avocado Spread
Prep: 2 minutes • Cook: 6 minutes

4   (3-ounce) skinless, boneless chicken breast cutlets
¼   cup barbecue sauce (such as Sticky Fingers Memphis Original)
Cooking spray
4   (0.7-ounce) slices 2% reduced-fat sharp cheddar cheese

Green leaf lettuce leaves (optional)
Tomato slices (optional)
4   (1.8-ounce) white wheat hamburger buns
Spicy Avocado Spread

1. Preheat grill.
2. Brush both sides of chicken with barbecue sauce. Place chicken on grill rack coated with cooking spray. Grill 3 to 4 minutes on each side or until chicken is done, placing 1 cheese slice on each chicken breast during last minute of cooking.
3. Place lettuce and tomato on bottom half of each bun, if desired; add 1 chicken breast. Top each with about 2½ tablespoons Spicy Avocado Spread. Place remaining bun halves on top. Yield: 4 servings (serving size: 1 sandwich and about 2½ tablespoons Spicy Avocado Spread).

CALORIES 368 (39% from fat); FAT 16g (sat 5g, mono 5.1g, poly 2.3g); PROTEIN 31.9g; CARB 31.8g; FIBER 7.8g; CHOL 64mg; IRON 3.9mg; SODIUM 678mg; CALC 423mg

Spicy Avocado Spread
Prep: 6 minutes

1   ripe peeled avocado, coarsely mashed
1   tablespoon minced jalapeño pepper
1   tablespoon minced red onion
1½   tablespoons fresh lime juice

1   garlic clove, pressed
2   teaspoons minced fresh cilantro
⅛   teaspoon salt

1. Combine all ingredients in a small bowl, stirring well. Yield: ½ cup plus 3 tablespoons (serving size: 1 tablespoon).

CALORIES 31 (81% from fat); FAT 3g (sat 0.5g, mono 1.8g, poly 0.4g); PROTEIN 0.4g; CARB 1.8g; FIBER 1g; CHOL 0mg; IRON 0.2mg; SODIUM 28mg; CALC 3mg

Tickle your palate with a taste of the tropics. Pineapple has a natural juiciness that gives this sandwich an irresistible taste. The fruit also offers a healthy reason for indulging: It's a high source of vitamin C.

Grilled Chicken and Pineapple Sandwiches

Prep: 6 minutes • Cook: 10 minutes

4   (6-ounce) skinless, boneless chicken
     breast halves
½   teaspoon salt
¼   teaspoon freshly ground black pepper
Cooking spray
¼   cup fresh lime juice (about 2 limes)

4   (½-inch-thick) slices fresh pineapple
4   (1.5-ounce) whole wheat hamburger buns,
     toasted
Light mayonnaise (optional)
4   large basil leaves

1. Prepare grill.
2. Sprinkle chicken evenly with salt and pepper. Place chicken on grill rack coated with cooking spray; grill 5 to 6 minutes on each side or until done, brushing occasionally with lime juice. Grill pineapple 2 to 3 minutes on each side or until browned.
3. Spread mayonnaise on bottom halves of buns, if desired. Top each with 1 chicken breast half, 1 pineapple slice, 1 basil leaf, and 1 bun top. Serve immediately. Yield: 4 servings (serving size: 1 sandwich).

CALORIES 333 (11% from fat); FAT 4g (sat 0.9g, mono 1g, poly 1.4g); PROTEIN 43.4g; CARB 30.5g; FIBER 4.1g; CHOL 99mg; IRON 2.5mg; SODIUM 608mg; CALC 75mg

serve with
Guilt-Free Piña Coladas

Prep: 9 minutes

⅓   cup fat-free sweetened condensed milk
⅓   cup thawed orange-pineapple-apple juice
     concentrate, undiluted
1   (21-ounce) package frozen diced pineapple
½   cup white rum
¼   teaspoon coconut extract
Pineapple wedges (optional)

1. Combine half of each ingredient except pineapple wedges in a blender; process until smooth. Pour into a pitcher. Repeat procedure. Pour into glasses, and garnish with pineapple wedges, if desired. Serve immediately. Yield: 4 servings (serving size: about ¾ cup).

CALORIES 263 (1% from fat); FAT 0.1g (sat 0g, mono 0g, poly 0.1g); PROTEIN 2.8g; CARB 47.1g; FIBER 2.1g; CHOL 3mg; IRON 0.4mg; SODIUM 30mg; CALC 86mg

Bookend the traditional ingredients of a Cobb salad with two slices of fresh wheat bread, and you've got a flavorful Turkey Cobb Sandwich. As an added convenience, you can now purchase boiled eggs at your supermarket. If you can't find them in your local store, hard-cook your own a day ahead. It will make preparation for this recipe quick and easy. Serve the sandwich with waffle-cut carrot chips.

Turkey Cobb Sandwiches
Prep: 10 minutes

2 tablespoons reduced-fat mayonnaise
8 (1-ounce) slices double-fiber wheat bread (such as Nature's Own), toasted
4 small green leaf lettuce leaves
4 tomato slices

6 ounces shaved deli turkey
1 peeled avocado, sliced
4 precooked bacon slices
2 hard-cooked large eggs, sliced

1. Spread ½ tablespoon mayonnaise evenly over each of 4 bread slices. Layer each evenly with lettuce and remaining ingredients. Top with remaining 4 bread slices. Cut each sandwich in half diagonally. Yield: 4 servings (serving size: 1 sandwich).

CALORIES 319 (42% from fat); FAT 14.9g (sat 2.7g, mono 5.9g, poly 1.9g); PROTEIN 22.1g; CARB 32.1g; FIBER 12.9g; CHOL 126mg; IRON 3.5mg; SODIUM 712mg; CALC 25mg

Serve with fresh cherries and an Italian Berry Float to top off your meal. If you don't have a panini grill, refer to page 78 for directions on preparing this sandwich using a stove-top method.

Turkey Antipasto Panini

Prep: 7 minutes • Cook: 3 minutes

2 tablespoons reduced-fat mayonnaise
8 (0.9-ounce) slices crusty Chicago-style Italian bread
8 ounces shaved lower-sodium deli turkey (such as Boar's Head)
1 (6-ounce) jar quartered marinated artichoke hearts, drained and coarsely chopped
½ cup moist sun-dried tomato halves, packed without oil and sliced
½ cup sliced bottled roasted red bell peppers
12 basil leaves
4 (1-ounce) slices reduced-fat provolone cheese (such as Alpine Lace)
Cooking spray

1. Preheat panini grill.
2. Spread mayonnaise evenly over each bread slice. Top each of 4 bread slices evenly with turkey, artichokes, tomato, bell pepper, basil leaves, and cheese. Top with remaining bread slices. Coat both sides of sandwiches with cooking spray.
3. Place sandwiches on panini grill. Grill 3 to 4 minutes or until bread is browned and cheese melts. Cut panini in half before serving, if desired. Yield: 4 servings (serving size: 1 sandwich).

CALORIES 361 (24% from fat); FAT 10g (sat 3.5g, mono 0.4g, poly 1.2g); PROTEIN 26.9g; CARB 39.8g; FIBER 4.5g; CHOL 35mg; IRON 3.1mg; SODIUM 1,087mg; CALC 83mg

serve with
Italian Berry Float

Prep: 5 minutes

2 cups blood orange or lemon sorbet
2 cups mixed berries (such as raspberries, strawberries, blackberries, and blueberries)
2 cups Prosecco or other sparkling wine
Mint sprigs

1. Place ½ cup sorbet in each of 4 glasses. Arrange ½ cup berries evenly around sorbet in each glass. Pour ½ cup Prosecco over berries in each glass; garnish with mint sprigs. Serve immediately. Yield: 4 servings (serving size: 1 float).

CALORIES 203 (1% from fat); FAT 0.3g (sat 0g, mono 0g, poly 0.2g); PROTEIN 0.6g; CARB 30.4g; FIBER 2.7g; CHOL 0mg; IRON 0.4mg; SODIUM 34mg; CALC 13mg

Enjoy the flavors of Thanksgiving all year long in this dressed-up turkey burger. Purchase ground turkey breast versus ground turkey—the white meat is much lower in calories and fat. Try grilling the burgers for an added boost of flavor. Serve with vegetable chips and red grapes.

Turkey Burgers with Cranberry-Peach Chutney
Prep: 5 minutes • Cook: 6 minutes

1 pound ground turkey breast	Cooking spray
1 large egg white	4 lettuce leaves
¼ teaspoon salt	4 (1½-ounce) whole wheat hamburger buns
¼ teaspoon freshly ground black pepper	Cranberry-Peach Chutney

1. Combine turkey and next 3 ingredients. Divide turkey mixture into 4 equal portions, shaping each into a ½-inch-thick patty.
2. Heat a large nonstick skillet over medium heat; coat pan with cooking spray. Add patties; cook 3 to 4 minutes on each side or until a thermometer registers 165°.
3. Place 1 lettuce leaf on bottom half of each bun; top each with 1 burger. Spread 2 tablespoons Cranberry-Peach Chutney on inside of each bun top; place each on top of 1 burger. Yield: 4 servings (serving size: 1 burger).

CALORIES 342 (27% from fat); FAT 10g (sat 2.9g, mono 0.5g, poly 1g); PROTEIN 28.2g; CARB 35.8g; FIBER 3.6g; CHOL 71mg; IRON 2.8mg; SODIUM 447mg; CALC 92mg

Cranberry-Peach Chutney
Prep: 4 minutes

⅓ cup prepared cranberry chutney	1 tablespoon finely chopped green onions
⅓ cup finely chopped peaches	

1. Combine all ingredients in a small bowl, stirring well to blend. Yield: ½ cup (serving size: 1 tablespoon).

CALORIES 30 (1% from fat); FAT 0g (sat 0g, mono 0g, poly 0g); PROTEIN 0.1g; CARB 6.7g; FIBER 0.1g; CHOL 0mg; IRON 0.3mg; SODIUM 1mg; CALC 1mg

salads

Fresh Vegetable and Tortelloni Pasta Salad
Taco Salad with Cilantro-Lime Vinaigrette
Couscous, Sweet Potato, and Black Soybean Salad
Chop Cobb Salad
Grilled Salmon and Grapefruit Salad with Blood Orange Vinaigrette
Salmon, Asparagus, and Orzo Salad with Lemon-Dill Vinaigrette
Mediterranean Tuna Salad
Crab, Lemon, and Avocado Salad
Roast Beef, Beet, and Arugula Salad with Orange Vinaigrette
Steak Salad with Creamy Horseradish Dressing
Spinach Salad with Grilled Pork Tenderloin and Nectarines
Prosciutto and Spicy Green Olive Pasta Salad
Chicken Salad with Roasted Peppers
Curried Chicken-Rice Salad
Greek Salad Bowl
Chicken BLT Salad with Creamy Avocado–Horned Melon Dressing
Asian Chicken Salad with Sweet and Spicy Wasabi Dressing
Chicken and Spring Greens with Açai Dressing
Chicken, Bean, and Blue Cheese Pasta Salad with Sun-Dried Tomato Vinaigrette
Asian Chicken, Noodle, and Sugar Snap Pea Salad
Feta-Chicken Couscous Salad with Basil
Chicken, Edamame, and Rice Salad
Chicken Bulgur Salad
Chicken Caesar Salad
Grilled Duck Breast Salad with Champagne-Honey Vinaigrette

With tortelloni, asparagus, and baby spinach, this pasta salad is great for a picnic or a light weekday lunch. Serve it with Tomato and Basil Soup or with fresh fruit, such as watermelon or strawberries.

Fresh Vegetable and Tortelloni Pasta Salad
Prep: 1 minute • Cook: 12 minutes

1 (9-ounce) package fresh rainbow five-cheese tortelloni (such as Monterey Pasta Company)
2 cups (1-inch) sliced asparagus (about ½ pound)
2 teaspoons olive oil
2 garlic cloves, minced

1 (6-ounce) package fresh baby spinach
¼ teaspoon salt
¼ teaspoon freshly ground black pepper
2 teaspoons fresh lemon juice
3 tablespoons shaved fresh Parmesan cheese
3 tablespoons pine nuts, toasted

1. Prepare tortelloni according to package directions, omitting salt and fat. Add asparagus during last 3 minutes of cooking. Drain pasta and asparagus; rinse with cold water.
2. While pasta cooks, heat oil in a large nonstick skillet over medium heat. Add garlic; sauté 1 minute. Add spinach, salt, and pepper; cook 2 minutes or until spinach wilts.
3. Combine pasta mixture and spinach mixture in a large bowl. Add lemon juice; toss gently to coat. Top servings evenly with cheese and nuts. Yield: 3 servings (serving size: about 1⅓ cups pasta salad, 1 tablespoon cheese, and 1 tablespoon nuts).

CALORIES 407 (39% from fat); FAT 18g (sat 5.7g, mono 3.8g, poly 3.2g); PROTEIN 19.3g; CARB 44.6g; FIBER 5.6g; CHOL 48mg; IRON 4.7mg; SODIUM 750mg; CALC 368mg

serve with
Tomato and Basil Soup
Prep: 1 minute • Cook: 7 minutes • Other: 3 minutes

1 (14½-ounce) can Italian-style stewed tomatoes, undrained
1 (14-ounce) can fat-free, less-sodium chicken broth

1 teaspoon sugar
2 tablespoons chopped fresh basil
1 tablespoon extra-virgin olive oil

1. Place tomatoes in a medium saucepan. Using kitchen shears, snip tomatoes until coarsely chopped. Stir in broth and sugar. Bring to a boil; cover, reduce heat, and simmer 5 minutes. Remove from heat; stir in basil and oil. Let soup stand 3 minutes. Ladle soup into bowls. Yield: 3 servings (serving size: 1 cup).

CALORIES 95 (45% from fat); FAT 5g (sat 0.7g, mono 3.7g, poly 0.3g); PROTEIN 3.2g; CARB 11.1g; FIBER 1.2g; CHOL 0mg; IRON 0.9mg; SODIUM 673mg; CALC 48mg

An ice-cold beer is all you need to complete the meal with this main-dish salad that's topped with a zesty cilantro-lime dressing. The mushrooms add meaty texture and flavor. Try rolling up the salad mixture in iceberg lettuce leaves for a quick-and-easy variation.

Taco Salad with Cilantro-Lime Vinaigrette
Prep: 5 minutes • Cook: 5 minutes

Cooking spray
1 (8-ounce) package presliced mushrooms
2 cups refrigerated meatless fat-free crumbles (such as Lightlife Smart Ground)
2 teaspoons 40%-less-sodium taco seasoning
1 (8-ounce) package shredded iceberg lettuce

1 cup (⅛-inch-thick) slices red onion
Fresh salsa (optional)
Cilantro-Lime Vinaigrette
Preshredded reduced-fat Mexican blend cheese (optional)
16 light restaurant-style tortilla chips (such as Tostitos)

1. Heat a large nonstick skillet over medium-high heat. Coat pan with cooking spray. Add mushrooms; sauté 3 minutes or until lightly browned. Add crumbles and taco seasoning. Cook 2 minutes or until thoroughly heated; set aside.
2. Layer lettuce, onion, and crumbles mixture evenly on each of 4 plates. Top with salsa, if desired; drizzle evenly with Cilantro-Lime Vinaigrette. Top with cheese, if desired. Serve each salad with tortilla chips. Yield: 4 servings (serving size: 1½ cups taco salad, about 1 tablespoon dressing, and 4 chips).

CALORIES 198 (50% from fat); FAT 11g (sat 1.5g, mono 5.8g, poly 2.5g); PROTEIN 11.7g; CARB 16.7g; FIBER 4.3g; CHOL 0mg; IRON 2.3mg; SODIUM 328mg; CALC 35mg

Cilantro-Lime Vinaigrette
Prep: 6 minutes

2 tablespoons finely chopped fresh cilantro
3 tablespoons red wine vinegar
2 tablespoons olive oil

1 teaspoon grated lime rind
1 teaspoon fresh minced garlic

1. Combine all ingredients, stirring well with a whisk. Yield: ⅓ cup (serving size: about 1 tablespoon).

CALORIES 69 (100% from fat); FAT 8g (sat 1.1g, mono 5.5g, poly 0.8g); PROTEIN 0.1g; CARB 0.3g; FIBER 0.1g; CHOL 0mg; IRON 0.1mg; SODIUM 1mg; CALC 2mg

Choose this lime-basil-infused salad—with chunks of beta-carotene-laced sweet potatoes and tender, high-fiber, protein-rich black soybeans—for a healthy meatless main dish you can have on the table in 15 minutes.

Couscous, Sweet Potato, and Black Soybean Salad
Prep: 5 minutes • Cook: 5 minutes • Other: 5 minutes

¾ cup water
⅔ cup wheat couscous
1 (16-ounce) package refrigerated cubed peeled sweet potato (such as Glory)
¼ cup fat-free lime-basil vinaigrette (such as Maple Grove Farms)
½ teaspoon freshly ground black pepper
¼ teaspoon salt

1 (15-ounce) can no-salt-added black soybeans (such as Eden Organic), rinsed and drained
2 cups baby spinach
5 tablespoons crumbled reduced-fat feta cheese
3 green onions, chopped

1. Bring ¾ cup water to boil in a medium saucepan; gradually stir in couscous. Remove from heat; cover and let stand 5 minutes. Fluff with a fork.
2. While couscous stands, place sweet potato on a microwave-safe plate. Microwave at HIGH 5 minutes or until tender.
3. Combine vinaigrette, pepper, and salt in a large bowl; stir well with a whisk. Add couscous, sweet potato, soybeans, and spinach; toss gently to coat. Top each serving with cheese; sprinkle evenly with onions. Yield: 5 servings (serving size: about 1⅓ cups couscous salad and 1 tablespoon cheese).

CALORIES 228 (17% from fat); FAT 4g (sat 1.1g, mono 0.7g, poly 1.7g); PROTEIN 10.5g; CARB 39.8g; FIBER 7.3g; CHOL 3mg; IRON 2.4mg; SODIUM 287mg; CALC 102mg

Homemade bread cubes, which bake in the oven while you prepare the other ingredients, are worth the extra effort—though you may use a commercial fat-free crouton instead.

Chop Cobb Salad

Prep: 8 minutes • Cook: 12 minutes • Other: 2 minutes

4 ounces whole-grain Italian bread, cut into ½-inch cubes
Cooking spray
5 hard-cooked large eggs
1 (12-ounce) package American-style mixed salad greens (such as Fresh Express)
1 (16-ounce) can chickpeas (garbanzo beans), rinsed and drained
1 cup refrigerated prechopped green bell pepper
½ cup refrigerated prechopped red onion
½ cup light ranch dressing (such as Naturally Fresh)
⅓ cup (1.3 ounces) crumbled blue cheese
Freshly ground black pepper

1. Arrange bread cubes in a single layer on a large baking sheet; lightly coat bread cubes with cooking spray. Place baking sheet in oven while preheating to 350°. Bake bread cubes 12 minutes or until firm. Remove from oven, and cool on a wire rack 2 minutes.

2. While bread cubes bake, cut eggs in half lengthwise; remove and reserve 3 yolks for another use. Chop remaining egg whites and yolks.

3. Combine chopped egg, salad greens, and next 3 ingredients in a large bowl. Add bread cubes; toss gently. Divide salad evenly on each of 5 plates. Combine dressing and cheese in a small bowl. Drizzle evenly over each salad; toss well. Sprinkle with freshly ground black pepper. Yield: 5 servings (serving size: about 2 cups salad and about 1½ tablespoons dressing).

CALORIES 291 (35% from fat); FAT 11g (sat 2.9g, mono 1.8g, poly 1.1g); PROTEIN 13.4g; CARB 33.4g; FIBER 5.7g; CHOL 85mg; IRON 2.9mg; SODIUM 688mg; CALC 147mg

Bell Peppers A quick, crunchy addition to any salad, prechopped bell pepper is now widely available in the produce section of most supermarkets. If you prefer to chop your own, buy a pepper that feels heavy for its size—a sign of thick, juicy flesh—and that has bright, glossy skin that's free of spots and wrinkles. Store bell peppers in a plastic bag in the refrigerator up to a week.

A generous portion of tender, flaky salmon tops this vitamin C–packed salad. To speed preparation, use a jar of fresh red grapefruit sections and bottled blood orange juice. Prepare the Blood Orange Vinaigrette while the salmon and onion are on the grill.

Grilled Salmon and Grapefruit Salad with Blood Orange Vinaigrette

Prep: 11 minutes • Cook: 10 minutes

2 (6-ounce) salmon fillets (1 to 1¼ inches thick)
½ teaspoon salt
¼ teaspoon freshly ground black pepper
1 large Vidalia or other sweet onion, cut into ½-inch-thick slices

Cooking spray
8 cups mixed baby salad greens
1 (24-ounce) jar red grapefruit sections (such as Del Monte), drained
Blood Orange Vinaigrette

1. Prepare grill.

2. Sprinkle fillets with salt and pepper. Coat fillets and onion slices with cooking spray. Place fish and onion on grill rack coated with cooking spray. Cover and grill 5 minutes on each side or until fish flakes easily when tested with a fork and onion is tender.

3. Cut onion into bite-sized chunks; break fish into chunks. Place 2 cups salad greens on each of 4 serving plates; arrange grapefruit sections, onion, and fish evenly over greens on each plate. Drizzle Blood Orange Vinaigrette evenly over salads. Yield: 4 servings (serving size: 2 cups greens, ½ cup grapefruit, about ⅓ cup onion, 2 ounces fish, and about 3 tablespoons Blood Orange Vinaigrette).

CALORIES 319 (28% from fat); FAT 10g (sat 2.1g, mono 5.3g, poly 2.1g); PROTEIN 21.2g; CARB 35.8g; FIBER 2.5g; CHOL 43mg; IRON 2.5mg; SODIUM 493mg; CALC 69mg

Blood Orange Vinaigrette

Prep: 4 minutes

⅓ cup blood orange juice
1 tablespoon minced shallots
2 tablespoons honey
1 tablespoon olive oil

1 teaspoon Dijon mustard
⅛ teaspoon salt
⅛ teaspoon freshly ground black pepper

1. Combine all ingredients in a small bowl, stirring well with a whisk. Yield: ⅔ cup plus 1 tablespoon (serving size: about 3 tablespoons).

CALORIES 75 (42% from fat); FAT 4g (sat 0.5g, mono 2.5g, poly 0.5g); PROTEIN 0.2g; CARB 11.6g; FIBER 0.1g; CHOL 0mg; IRON 0.1mg; SODIUM 103mg; CALC 4mg

This savory salad epitomizes the concept of fresh food fast. It's quick and easy and loaded with flavorful ingredients such as crisp-tender asparagus, perfectly cooked pink salmon, red onion, and a refreshing lemon juice–based vinaigrette. It received our highest Test Kitchens rating.

Salmon, Asparagus, and Orzo Salad with Lemon-Dill Vinaigrette

Prep: 3 minutes • Cook: 18 minutes

6 cups water
1 pound asparagus, trimmed and cut into 3-inch pieces
1 cup uncooked orzo (rice-shaped pasta)
1 (1¼-pound) skinless salmon fillet
¼ teaspoon salt
¼ teaspoon freshly ground black pepper
Cooking spray
¼ cup thinly sliced red onion
Lemon-Dill Vinaigrette

1. Preheat broiler.
2. Bring 6 cups water to a boil in a large saucepan. Add asparagus; cook 3 minutes or until crisp-tender. Remove asparagus from water with tongs or a slotted spoon, reserving water in pan. Plunge asparagus into ice water; drain and set aside.
3. Return reserved water to a boil. Add orzo, and cook according to package directions, omitting salt and fat.
4. While orzo cooks, sprinkle fillet evenly with salt and pepper. Place fish on a foil-lined broiler pan coated with cooking spray. Broil 5 minutes or until fish flakes easily when tested with a fork or until desired degree of doneness. Using 2 forks, break fish into large chunks. Combine fish, orzo, asparagus, onion, and Lemon-Dill Vinaigrette in a large bowl; toss gently to coat. Yield: 6 servings (serving size: about 1¼ cups).

CALORIES 310 (32% from fat); FAT 11g (sat 3.2g, mono 4.7g, poly 2g); PROTEIN 26g; CARB 24.6g; FIBER 2.2g; CHOL 56mg; IRON 1.4mg; SODIUM 333mg; CALC 67mg

Lemon-Dill Vinaigrette

Prep: 6 minutes

⅓ cup (1.3 ounces) crumbled feta cheese
1 tablespoon chopped fresh dill
3 tablespoons fresh lemon juice
2 teaspoons extra-virgin olive oil
¼ teaspoon salt
¼ teaspoon freshly ground black pepper

1. Combine all ingredients in a small bowl, stirring well with a whisk. Yield: ⅓ cup (serving size: about 1 tablespoon).

CALORIES 43 (80% from fat); FAT 4g (sat 1.7g, mono 1.8g, poly 0.2g); PROTEIN 1.4g; CARB 1.2g; FIBER 0.1g; CHOL 8mg; IRON 0.1mg; SODIUM 214mg; CALC 48mg

This Mediterranean-style salad spotlights albacore tuna—a fish that is rich in omega-3 fatty acids. Serve the salad over sliced summer tomatoes with Greek-Style Pita Chips, or stuff the salad in a pita with shredded lettuce for lunch on the go.

Mediterranean Tuna Salad
Prep: 11 minutes

1 (12-ounce) can albacore tuna in water, drained and flaked into large chunks
½ cup thinly sliced red onion
2 celery stalks, thinly sliced
2 tablespoons coarsely chopped pitted kalamata olives

2½ tablespoons fresh lemon juice
1 tablespoon olive oil
¼ teaspoon freshly ground black pepper
⅛ teaspoon kosher salt
2 large tomatoes, sliced

1. Combine first 4 ingredients in a medium bowl. Add lemon juice and next 3 ingredients; toss gently to combine. Serve salad over sliced tomatoes. Yield: 3 servings (serving size: 1 cup tuna salad and 2 tomato slices).

CALORIES 203 (36% from fat); FAT 8g (sat 1g, mono 4.6g, poly 1g); PROTEIN 24.9g; CARB 9.1g; FIBER 2.3g; CHOL 39mg; IRON 0.5mg; SODIUM 593mg; CALC 31mg

serve with
Greek-Style Pita Chips
Prep: 7 minutes • Cook: 7 minutes

2 (6-inch) pitas
Olive oil-flavored cooking spray

½ teaspoon dried Greek seasoning

1. Preheat oven to 400°.
2. Cut each pita into 8 wedges. Separate each wedge into 2 triangles. Place triangles in a single layer on a large baking sheet. Coat top sides of triangles with cooking spray; sprinkle evenly with seasoning.
3. Bake at 400° for 7 to 8 minutes or until crisp and lightly browned; cool. Yield: 4 servings (serving size: 8 chips).

CALORIES 80 (0% from fat); FAT 0g (sat 0g, mono 0g, poly 0g); PROTEIN 3.5g; CARB 16.5g; FIBER 0.5g; CHOL 0mg; IRON 1.4mg; SODIUM 201mg; CALC 20mg

The two-step simplicity of this glorious salad highlights the appetizing colors and textures of delicate lump crabmeat, creamy avocado, and freshly squeezed lemon juice. Serve with chilled slices of watermelon for a light meal.

Crab, Lemon, and Avocado Salad
Prep: 12 minutes

3½ tablespoons fresh lemon juice
1½ tablespoons extra-virgin olive oil
½ teaspoon salt
⅛ teaspoon freshly ground black pepper
1 pound lump crabmeat, drained and shell pieces removed

½ cup finely chopped green onions
1 diced peeled avocado
8 red leaf lettuce leaves

1. Combine first 4 ingredients, stirring well with a whisk.
2. Place crabmeat, onions, and avocado in a medium bowl. Add lemon juice mixture; toss gently to coat. Serve over lettuce leaves. Yield: 4 servings (serving size: about 1 cup salad and 2 lettuce leaves).

CALORIES 257 (50% from fat); FAT 14g (sat 2.2g, mono 9.1g, poly 1.9g); PROTEIN 25.9g; CARB 7g; FIBER 3g; CHOL 83mg; IRON 1.2mg; SODIUM 714mg; CALC 82mg

Avocados You can purchase avocados at your local supermarket year-round. Look for fruit that is firm, yet gives when gently squeezed. If it's still hard, it's not ready to be eaten. You may refrigerate ripe avocados until you're ready to use them, but only for a few days.

Sweet beets marry well with the peppery bite of arugula in this roast beef salad, while a citrusy vinaigrette provides a bright counterpoint to the richness of the meat, goat cheese, and pine nuts.

Roast Beef, Beet, and Arugula Salad with Orange Vinaigrette

Prep: 8 minutes • Cook: 8 minutes

3 small beets, trimmed	½ cup (2 ounces) crumbled goat cheese
8 cups loosely packed arugula	2 tablespoons pine nuts, toasted
Orange Vinaigrette	
1 (4-ounce) slice low-sodium deli roast beef (about ¼ inch thick), cut into strips	

1. Place beets in a microwave-safe bowl; add enough water to come halfway up sides of bowl. Cover with plastic wrap; vent. Microwave at HIGH 8 minutes or until tender; drain and cool. Peel and slice into wedges.

2. While beets cook, combine arugula and Orange Vinaigrette, tossing gently to coat. Arrange arugula mixture evenly on each of 4 plates. Top evenly with beef, beets, cheese, and nuts. Yield: 4 servings (serving size: about 1½ cups arugula salad, 1 ounce beef, 3 beet wedges, 2 tablespoons cheese, and ½ tablespoon nuts).

CALORIES 226 (62% from fat); FAT 16g (sat 4.6g, mono 6.7g, poly 2.4g); PROTEIN 13.4g; CARB 10.4g; FIBER 2.6g; CHOL 26mg; IRON 2.4mg; SODIUM 234mg; CALC 120mg

Orange Vinaigrette

Prep: 8 minutes

1 orange	2 teaspoons Dijon mustard
2 tablespoons white wine vinegar	¼ teaspoon sugar
1 tablespoon minced shallots	2 tablespoons olive oil

1. Grate 1 teaspoon orange rind; squeeze 2 tablespoons juice from orange over a bowl.

2. Combine orange rind and juice, white wine vinegar, and next 3 ingredients in a small bowl, stirring well with a whisk. Slowly add oil, stirring well with a whisk. Yield: ⅓ cup (serving size: about 1 tablespoon).

CALORIES 52 (88% from fat); FAT 5g (sat 0.7g, mono 3.7g, poly 0.5g); PROTEIN 0.1g; CARB 1.6g; FIBER 0.1g; CHOL 0mg; IRON 0.1mg; SODIUM 46mg; CALC 2mg

Beets When selecting beets, buy small to medium globes with stems and leaves attached. You will usually find about three beets per bunch. The skins should be smooth, firm, and void of soft spots. Be sure to wear disposable latex gloves when handling the beets to protect your hands from staining.

Have a steak house–style dinner at home with this tangy, horseradish-seasoned salad boasting melt-in-your-mouth beef tenderloin slices, juicy ruby-red cherry tomatoes, and crunchy cucumber. Pair with warm breadsticks.

Steak Salad with Creamy Horseradish Dressing
Prep: 6 minutes • Cook: 10 minutes • Other: 10 minutes

2 (6-ounce) beef tenderloin steaks, trimmed (about ¾ to 1 inch thick)
¼ teaspoon salt
¼ teaspoon freshly ground black pepper
Cooking spray

1 (6.5-ounce) package sweet butter lettuce blend
1 cup cherry tomatoes, halved
½ cup thinly sliced English cucumber
Creamy Horseradish Dressing

1. Prepare grill.
2. Sprinkle steaks evenly with salt and pepper. Place steaks on grill rack coated with cooking spray; grill 5 minutes on each side or until desired degree of doneness. Let stand 10 minutes before slicing.
3. While steak stands, combine lettuce, tomato, and cucumber in a large bowl; divide evenly among 4 plates. Top salads with steak slices. Drizzle evenly with Creamy Horseradish Dressing. Yield: 4 servings (serving size: 2 cups salad, about 2 ounces steak, and about 3 tablespoons dressing).

CALORIES 203 (46% from fat); FAT 10g (sat 5.4g, mono 1.9g, poly 0.2g); PROTEIN 19.6g; CARB 7.9g; FIBER 1.5g; CHOL 68mg; IRON 1.3mg; SODIUM 79mg; CALC 96mg

Creamy Horseradish Dressing
Prep: 7 minutes

¾ cup reduced-fat sour cream
¼ cup chopped red onion
2 teaspoons chopped fresh chives

2½ teaspoons prepared horseradish
½ teaspoon fresh lemon juice
¼ teaspoon freshly ground black pepper

1. Combine all ingredients in a small bowl. Stir until well blended; chill, if desired. Yield: about ¾ cup (serving size: 1 tablespoon).

CALORIES 26 (66% from fat); FAT 2g (sat 1.2g, mono 0g, poly 0g); PROTEIN 0.8g; CARB 1.5g; FIBER 0.1g; CHOL 8mg; IRON 0mg; SODIUM 13mg; CALC 27mg

Grilling heightens the sweetness and flavor of the nectarines. Because they have such thin skins, nectarines don't require peeling for this dish. However, you may substitute fresh peeled peaches if you prefer.

Spinach Salad with Grilled Pork Tenderloin and Nectarines

Prep: 6 minutes • Cook: 10 minutes • Other: 10 minutes

1 (1-pound) peppercorn-flavored pork tenderloin, trimmed	2 (6-ounce) packages fresh baby spinach
3 nectarines, halved	¼ cup light balsamic vinaigrette
Cooking spray	¼ cup (1 ounce) crumbled feta cheese
	Freshly ground black pepper (optional)

1. Prepare grill.

2. Cut pork horizontally through center of meat, cutting to, but not through, other side using a sharp knife; open flat as you would a book. Place pork and nectarine halves, cut sides down, on grill rack coated with cooking spray. Grill pork 5 minutes on each side or until a thermometer registers 160°. Grill nectarine halves 4 to 5 minutes on each side or until thoroughly heated. Remove pork and nectarine halves from grill. Let pork rest 10 minutes.

3. Cut nectarine halves into slices. Thinly slice pork. Combine spinach and vinaigrette in a large bowl; toss gently to coat.

4. Divide spinach mixture evenly on each of 6 plates. Top each serving evenly with nectarine slices and pork slices. Sprinkle with cheese. Sprinkle evenly with pepper, if desired. Yield: 6 servings (serving size: 1⅔ cups spinach salad, ½ nectarine, about 2 ounces pork, and 2 teaspoons cheese).

CALORIES 169 (31% from fat); FAT 6g (sat 2g, mono 1.5g, poly 0.9g); PROTEIN 16g; CARB 15.8g; FIBER 3.9g; CHOL 41mg; IRON 2.9mg; SODIUM 766mg; CALC 86mg

Nectarines Think of nectarines and peaches as fraternal twins. Nectarines have a smooth skin, while the skin of peaches is covered with a soft fuzz. Otherwise, the two fruits are indistinguishable and can be used interchangeably in recipes. The meat of clingstone nectarines and peaches adheres to the pits. These varieties are available early in the season. Freestone varieties—in which the pit easily pulls away from the fruit—begin to ripen mid-season (late June to early July).

Prosciutto is an Italian ham that's air-cured with salt and seasonings pressed into the densely textured meat. The best prosciutto sold in the United States comes from the Parma area of Italy; it is made from larger pork legs than American prosciutto and is aged longer. Serve this pasta salad with cantaloupe slices—a common partner for prosciutto—to cap off your meal.

Prosciutto and Spicy Green Olive Pasta Salad
Prep: 11 minutes • Cook: 14 minutes

1¾ cups uncooked multigrain penne
2 cups baby spinach
8 jalapeño-stuffed green olives, sliced
2 ounces thinly sliced prosciutto, chopped
2 tablespoons chopped fresh oregano
1 tablespoon extra-virgin olive oil
½ cup (2 ounces) crumbled reduced-fat feta cheese

1. Cook pasta according to package directions, omitting salt and fat. Drain and rinse with cold water.
2. While pasta cooks, combine spinach and next 4 ingredients in a large bowl. Add pasta and cheese; toss well. Yield: 4 servings (serving size: about 1½ cups).

CALORIES 235 (36% from fat); FAT 9g (sat 2.3g, mono 3.8g, poly 1.9g); PROTEIN 12g; CARB 32.6g; FIBER 5.2g; CHOL 13mg; IRON 2.1mg; SODIUM 585mg; CALC 83mg

Oregano To keep the potent flavor of oregano fresh for up to a week, trim about ¼ inch from the stem and rinse with cold water. Loosely wrap the herb in a damp paper towel, and then seal in a zip-top plastic bag filled with air. Keep it refrigerated, and check on it daily to make sure it is maintaining its freshness.

It's a snap to stir together this tasty salad when you use prechopped bell pepper, celery, and onion, which are now widely available in most produce departments.

Chicken Salad with Roasted Peppers
Prep: 10 minutes

2 cups chopped cooked chicken breast (about ¾ pound)
½ cup refrigerated prechopped green bell pepper
½ cup refrigerated prediced celery
½ cup dried cranberries
½ cup chopped bottled roasted red bell peppers
¼ cup refrigerated prechopped red onion
¼ cup chopped pecans, toasted
¼ cup light mayonnaise
2 teaspoons low-sodium soy sauce
¼ teaspoon crushed red pepper

1. Combine all ingredients in a medium bowl; toss well. Cover and chill until ready to serve. Yield: 4 servings (serving size: 1 cup).

CALORIES 280 (43% from fat); FAT 13g (sat 2.2g, mono 4.1g, poly 2.4g); PROTEIN 23g; CARB 17.5g; FIBER 2.3g; CHOL 65mg; IRON 1.1mg; SODIUM 333mg; CALC 26mg

serve with
Cantaloupe with Balsamic Berries and Cream
Prep: 8 minutes

12 (5-inch) slices cantaloupe
2 cups vanilla bean light ice cream (such as Edy's)
1 cup fresh raspberries
2 tablespoons balsamic glaze (such as Gia Russa)

1. Arrange 3 slices cantaloupe on each of 4 dessert plates; top each with ice cream and raspberries. Drizzle balsamic glaze over each serving. Yield: 4 servings (serving size: 3 slices cantaloupe, ½ cup ice cream, ¼ cup raspberries, and 1½ teaspoons balsamic glaze).

CALORIES 174 (20% from fat); FAT 4g (sat 2.1g, mono 0g, poly 0.2g); PROTEIN 4.4g; CARB 32.6g; FIBER 2g; CHOL 20mg; IRON 0.5mg; SODIUM 71mg; CALC 79mg

Crisp Gala apple and crunchy celery give this nutrient-rich salad an extra dimension of tantalizing texture and color. An excellent source of vitamin C, celery helps strengthen the immune system.

Curried Chicken-Rice Salad
Prep: 8 minutes • Cook: 3½ minutes • Other: 8 minutes

1 (10-ounce) package frozen microwaveable brown rice (such as Birds Eye)
1 cup vanilla fat-free yogurt
1 teaspoon curry powder
¼ teaspoon salt
3 cups chopped cooked chicken breast (about 1 pound)

1½ cups chopped Gala apple (about 1 medium)
½ cup chopped celery
¼ cup cherry-flavored sweetened dried cranberries (such as Craisins)
Green leaf lettuce leaves (optional)

1. Prepare rice according to package directions. Spread rice in a shallow pan; place in freezer 8 to 10 minutes.
2. While rice chills, combine yogurt, curry powder, and salt in a large bowl. Add chicken and next 3 ingredients to yogurt mixture, stirring until coated.
3. Stir chilled rice into chicken mixture. Spoon chicken salad onto lettuce leaves, if desired. Yield: 6 servings (serving size: 1 cup).

CALORIES 238 (11% from fat); FAT 3g (sat 0.8g, mono 1g, poly 0.7g); PROTEIN 25.3g; CARB 26.5g; FIBER 1.9g; CHOL 60mg; IRON 1mg; SODIUM 187mg; CALC 97mg

Crispy thin breadsticks such as grissini or low-fat crackers would make an ideal accompaniment to this flavor-packed Mediterranean salad. Check the hearts of palm and artichoke hearts labels carefully if you are watching your sodium intake; sodium levels vary greatly among brands.

Greek Salad Bowl
Prep: 12 minutes

8 cups torn romaine lettuce
2 cups chopped cooked chicken breast (about ¾ pound)
1 (14-ounce) can hearts of palm (such as Vigo), drained and sliced
1 (14-ounce) can quartered artichoke hearts (such as Vigo), drained

1 cup grape tomatoes, halved
½ cup pitted kalamata olives, halved
½ cup thinly sliced red onion
⅓ cup light Greek vinaigrette with oregano and feta cheese (such as Good Seasons)

1. Combine all ingredients in a large bowl; toss well to coat. Serve immediately. Yield: 6 servings (serving size: 2 cups).

CALORIES 182 (38% from fat); FAT 8g (sat 1.4g, mono 3.7g, poly 2.1g); PROTEIN 18.1g; CARB 11.1g; FIBER 3.2g; CHOL 40mg; IRON 3.4mg; SODIUM 695mg; CALC 67mg

Romaine Romaine leaves grow in heads and range in color from dark-green outer leaves to a yellowish-green heart in the center. Baby romaine leaves, which are available prewashed in packages, offer the same pleasing, slightly bitter flavor of regular romaine. But stick with the full-sized version for the signature crunch that comes from a romaine leaf's succulent center vein.

The horned melon lends subtle cucumber flavor and creaminess to this crisp, colorful chicken BLT salad. You may store the remaining Creamy Avocado-Horned Melon Dressing in the refrigerator up to three days.

Chicken BLT Salad with Creamy Avocado–Horned Melon Dressing
Prep: 7 minutes

3 cups sliced cooked chicken breast (about 1 pound)
1 tomato, cut into wedges
1 (10-ounce) package romaine salad

¾ cup Creamy Avocado-Horned Melon Dressing
3 center-cut bacon slices, cooked and crumbled

1. Combine first 3 ingredients in a large bowl; toss well. Drizzle Creamy Avocado–Horned Melon Dressing over salad; top with bacon. Yield: 6 servings (serving size: about 1¾ cups).

CALORIES 184 (34% from fat); FAT 7g (sat 1.8g, mono 3.1g, poly 1.3g); PROTEIN 24.5g; CARB 5.8g; FIBER 2.9g; CHOL 63mg; IRON 1.5mg; SODIUM 186mg; CALC 42mg

Creamy Avocado–Horned Melon Dressing
Prep: 8 minutes

1 horned melon
1 small ripe peeled avocado
1 small garlic clove
¼ cup low-fat buttermilk

2 tablespoons fresh lemon juice
2 tablespoons water
¼ teaspoon salt
¼ teaspoon freshly ground black pepper

1. Cut horned melon in half lengthwise; scoop out pulp. Place pulp in a fine sieve over a bowl. Press pulp with the back of a spoon to extract juice; discard juice. Place pulp and remaining ingredients in a blender or food processor; process until smooth. Store in an airtight container in the refrigerator up to 3 days. Yield: 1¼ cups (serving size: 1 tablespoon).

CALORIES 21 (69% from fat); FAT 2g (sat 0.3g, mono 0.9g, poly 0.3g); PROTEIN 0.5g; CARB 1.7g; FIBER 0.8g; CHOL 0mg; IRON 0.1mg; SODIUM 33mg; CALC 7mg

Horned Melons Also known as kiwano melons, horned melons grow in New Zealand and are now commonly found in many grocery stores. They have a yellow-orange spiked exterior and a green jellylike flesh similar in flavor to that of the cucumber. The fruit has broad applications in savory and sweet dishes. Strain out the seeds, and use the pulp in salad dressings, soups, sauces, or sorbet.

Don't be shy about using the wasabi powder—
the dressing is full of flavor, not heat. Rotisserie chicken
works well for this salad, although any shredded cooked
chicken will do.

Asian Chicken Salad with Sweet and Spicy Wasabi Dressing

Prep: 10 minutes

2 tablespoons rice vinegar
2 tablespoons maple syrup
2 tablespoons olive oil
¾ teaspoon wasabi powder (dried Japanese horseradish)
¼ teaspoon salt
⅛ teaspoon freshly ground black pepper

1 (11.4-ounce) package Asian supreme salad mix (such as Fresh Express)
1 (8¼-ounce) can mandarin oranges in light syrup, drained
2 cups shredded cooked chicken breast (about ¾ pound)
1 diagonally cut green onion

1. Combine first 6 ingredients in a large bowl; stir well with a whisk.
2. Add salad mix to vinegar mixture, reserving wonton strips for topping and sesame-orange dressing for another use. Add oranges and chicken; toss gently to coat. Top evenly with onion and reserved wonton strips. Yield: 4 servings (serving size: about 1½ cups salad and 3 wonton strips).

CALORIES 316 (40% from fat); FAT 14g (sat 3.6g, mono 5.9g, poly 1.6g); PROTEIN 25.3g; CARB 23.5g; FIBER 2.5g; CHOL 67mg; IRON 1.5mg; SODIUM 279mg; CALC 100mg

The açai berry is considered to be a superfood high in antioxidants, amino acids, and essential fatty acids. Some even say that the berry—the fruit of a palm tree native to tropical parts of Central and South America—is one of the most nutritious foods in the world. Serve this salad with multigrain crispbreads such as those made by Wasa.

Chicken and Spring Greens with Açai Dressing

Prep: 6 minutes

8 cups mixed baby salad greens	½ cup red onion slices
2 cups chopped cooked chicken breast (about ¾ pound)	¼ cup chopped pecans, toasted
	¾ cup Açai Dressing

1. Arrange 2 cups salad greens on each of 4 plates. Top each evenly with chicken, onion slices, and pecans. Drizzle 3 tablespoons dressing over each salad. Yield: 4 servings (serving size: 2 cups greens, ½ cup chicken, about 5 onion slices, 1 tablespoon pecans, and 3 tablespoons dressing).

CALORIES 293 (43% from fat); FAT 14g (sat 1.7g, mono 7.2g, poly 3.9g); PROTEIN 24.5g; CARB 18.5g; FIBER 3.8g; CHOL 60mg; IRON 2.5mg; SODIUM 81mg; CALC 87mg

Açai Dressing

Prep: 4 minutes

½ cup açai juice blend (such as Sambazon Original Blend)	3 tablespoons rice vinegar
3 tablespoons sugar	1½ tablespoons canola oil
1½ tablespoons grated orange rind	¼ teaspoon crushed red pepper

1. Combine all ingredients in a small bowl, stirring well with a whisk. Yield: ¾ cup (serving size: 3 tablespoons).

CALORIES 100 (50% from fat); FAT 6g (sat 0.5g, mono 3.1g, poly 1.6g); PROTEIN 0.1g; CARB 12.8g; FIBER 0.5g; CHOL 0mg; IRON 0.1mg; SODIUM 1mg; CALC 8mg

Asparagus will work in place of the green beans, but be sure to cook the asparagus spears only 1 to 2 minutes or until crisp-tender.

Chicken, Bean, and Blue Cheese Pasta Salad with Sun-Dried Tomato Vinaigrette
Prep: 6 minutes • Cook: 16 minutes

1½ cups uncooked rotini (corkscrew pasta)	¼ cup (1 ounce) crumbled blue cheese
1½ cups (2-inch) cut green beans (about 6 ounces)	¼ cup Sun-Dried Tomato Vinaigrette
2 cups diced cooked chicken breast (about ¾ pound)	

1. Cook pasta according to package directions, omitting salt and fat. Add beans during last 5 minutes of cooking. Drain pasta and beans; rinse with cold water until cool.

2. Combine pasta mixture and remaining ingredients; toss gently to coat. Yield: 4 servings (serving size: 1 cup).

CALORIES 315 (25% from fat); FAT 9g (sat 2.7g, mono 3.9g, poly 1.1g); PROTEIN 28.8g; CARB 30.1g; FIBER 2.8g; CHOL 65mg; IRON 2.5mg; SODIUM 192mg; CALC 75mg

Sun-Dried Tomato Vinaigrette
Prep: 4 minutes

2 tablespoons balsamic vinegar	1 tablespoon chopped fresh basil
1 tablespoon olive oil	1 tablespoon chopped red onion
1 tablespoon water	
2 tablespoons chopped sun-dried tomatoes, packed without oil	

1. Combine first 3 ingredients in a small bowl, stirring well with a whisk. Stir in tomatoes, basil, and onion. Yield: ¼ cup (serving size: 1 tablespoon).

CALORIES 43 (75% from fat); FAT 4g (sat 0.5g, mono 2.5g, poly 0.5g); PROTEIN 0.3g; CARB 2.6g; FIBER 0.3g; CHOL 0mg; IRON 0.2mg; SODIUM 37mg; CALC 6mg

For extra crunch, serve this Asian noodle salad over a bed of shredded napa (Chinese) cabbage. Look for toasted sesame seeds on the spice aisle of your supermarket.

Asian Chicken, Noodle, and Snap Pea Salad
Prep: 12 minutes • Cook: 6 minutes

3 ounces uncooked soba (buckwheat noodles)
1 (8-ounce) package sugar snap peas
1 red bell pepper, thinly sliced
3 cups shredded lemon-pepper rotisserie chicken

½ cup light sesame-ginger dressing (such as Newman's Own)
Toasted sesame seeds (such as McCormick) (optional)
Sliced green onions (optional)
Shredded napa (Chinese) cabbage (optional)

1. Prepare soba according to package directions. Drain.
2. While soba cooks, microwave peas in package at HIGH 1 minute. Rinse peas under cold water. Combine soba, peas, and next 3 ingredients in a large bowl; toss to combine. Garnish with sesame seeds and onions, if desired. Serve over cabbage, if desired. Yield: 4 servings (serving size: 1½ cups).

CALORIES 333 (21% from fat); FAT 8g (sat 1.7g, mono 2.3g, poly 1.6g); PROTEIN 35.2g; CARB 27.8g; FIBER 3.1g; CHOL 92mg; IRON 2.5mg; SODIUM 640mg; CALC 65mg

Serve this salad with crispbreads and red pepper hummus for a light summer meal.

Feta-Chicken Couscous Salad with Basil
Prep: 9 minutes • Cook: 2 minutes • Other: 5 minutes

1¼ cups water
⅔ cup uncooked whole wheat couscous
1 cup diced cooked chicken breast (such as Tyson)
¼ cup chopped fresh basil
3 tablespoons capers, rinsed and drained

1 tablespoon extra-virgin olive oil
1 teaspoon grated lemon rind
1 tablespoon fresh lemon juice
2 cups mixed baby salad greens
¼ cup (1 ounce) crumbled reduced-fat feta cheese

1. Bring 1¼ cups water to a boil in a medium saucepan. Add couscous; cover and let stand 5 minutes.
2. While couscous stands, combine chicken and next 5 ingredients in a large bowl, tossing gently to coat.
3. Fluff couscous with a fork. Add couscous, salad greens, and cheese to chicken mixture; toss gently to coat. Yield: 4 servings (serving size: 1 cup).

CALORIES 208 (31% from fat); FAT 7g (sat 1.8g, mono 2.9g, poly 0.8g); PROTEIN 17.2g; CARB 20.7g; FIBER 2.7g; CHOL 33mg; IRON 1.1mg; SODIUM 366mg; CALC 56mg

Lemons Whether using juice, lemon zest (rind), or slices, the acidity of lemon adds to the final balance of flavor in all types of food, from savory to sweet. Look for lemons with smooth, brightly colored skin that are heavy for their size. Store up to 2 to 3 weeks in the refrigerator. Allow lemons to come to room temperature before juicing to ensure that you get the most juice from each lemon.

The distinct and powerful taste combination of fresh ginger and mint lends a burst of flavor to this main-dish salad.

Chicken, Edamame, and Rice Salad
Prep: 11 minutes • Cook: 5 minutes • Other: 2 minutes

1 (8.8-ounce) pouch microwaveable cooked long-grain rice (such as Uncle Ben's Original Ready Rice)
1¼ cups frozen shelled edamame (green soybeans)
3 tablespoons water
1 cup diced cooked chicken breast

2 tablespoons chopped fresh mint
1 tablespoon grated peeled fresh ginger
2 tablespoons rice vinegar
1 tablespoon canola oil
¼ teaspoon salt
4 radicchio leaves

1. Microwave rice according to package directions. Set aside; keep warm.
2. Combine edamame and 3 tablespoons water in a small bowl. Cover with plastic wrap. Microwave at HIGH 3 minutes. Let stand 2 minutes; drain.
3. Combine rice, edamame, chicken, and next 5 ingredients in a large bowl; toss to coat. Serve over radicchio. Yield: 4 servings (serving size: about ¾ cup salad and 1 radicchio leaf).

CALORIES 235 (31% from fat); FAT 8g (sat 0.6g, mono 2.5g, poly 1.3g); PROTEIN 16.6g; CARB 23.5g; FIBER 2.4g; CHOL 30mg; IRON 1.6mg; SODIUM 399mg; CALC 49mg

serve with
Green Tea–Kiwi and Mango Smoothie
Prep: 15 minutes

2½ cups frozen diced mango
¾ cup vanilla fat-free yogurt, divided
¼ cup honey, divided
2 tablespoons water
½ teaspoon grated lime rind

3 ripe kiwifruit, peeled and quartered
2 cups ice cubes
½ cup packed baby spinach
2 tablespoons bottled green tea
Kiwifruit slices (optional)

1. Place mango, ½ cup yogurt, 2 tablespoons honey, 2 tablespoons water, and lime rind in a blender; process until smooth, stirring occasionally. Divide mango mixture into each of 4 serving glasses; place glasses in freezer.
2. Rinse blender container. Place ¼ cup yogurt, 2 tablespoons honey, kiwifruit, and next 3 ingredients in blender; process until smooth, stirring occasionally. Gently spoon green tea–kiwi mixture onto mango mixture in reserved glasses, working carefully around inside of each glass to create a clean horizontal line. Garnish with kiwifruit slices, and stir to combine flavors, if desired. Serve immediately. Yield: 4 servings (serving size: 1 cup).

CALORIES 234 (2% from fat); FAT 0.4g (sat 0.1g, mono 0.1g, poly 0.2g); PROTEIN 3.2g; CARB 59.3g; FIBER 2.8g; CHOL 1mg; IRON 0.5mg; SODIUM 58mg; CALC 107mg

Reminiscent of tabbouleh, this Lebanese-inspired dish is a smart choice if you want to incorporate more fiber into your diet. Bulgur—wheat berries that have been steamed, dried, and ground—is the basis of many salads in the Middle East. Serve this salad with warmed whole wheat pita bread.

Chicken Bulgur Salad

Prep: 3 minutes • Cook: 11 minutes

1   cup water
½   cup uncooked quick-cooking bulgur
1½ cups cubed cooked chicken breast (about ½ pound)
1   cup finely chopped fresh parsley
1   (14-ounce) can quartered artichoke hearts, drained and coarsely chopped

1   cup grape tomatoes, halved
⅓   cup light Northern Italian salad dressing with basil and Romano (such as Ken's Steak House Lite)
2   tablespoons fresh lemon juice

1. Bring 1 cup water to a boil in a medium saucepan; stir in bulgur. Return to a boil; reduce heat, cover, and simmer 8 minutes or until liquid is absorbed. Drain bulgur, and rinse with cold water; drain well.
2. Combine chicken and remaining ingredients in a large bowl, tossing to coat. Add bulgur; toss gently to coat. Yield: 4 servings (serving size: 1¼ cups).

CALORIES 228 (23% from fat); FAT 6g (sat 1g, mono 1g, poly 0.5g); PROTEIN 21.2g; CARB 22.8g; FIBER 4.5g; CHOL 45mg; IRON 3mg; SODIUM 435mg; CALC 56mg

Parsley No refrigerator should be without parsley. It's the workhorse of the herb world and can go in just about every dish you cook. Parsley's mild, grassy taste doesn't overpower the other ingredients. Flat-leaf parsley is preferred for cooking because it stands up better to heat and has more flavor, while the more decorative curly parsley is used mostly for garnishing.

For an easy addition to this salad, place baguette slices on the grill while you're cooking the chicken. Grill the bread slices for 2 minutes on each side; then rub the slices with the cut side of a halved garlic clove.

Chicken Caesar Salad
Prep: 3 minutes • Cook: 4 minutes

Caesar Dressing, divided
3 (4-ounce) chicken cutlets
Cooking spray
1 (10-ounce) package romaine salad

2 tomatoes, cut into wedges
¼ cup (1 ounce) grated fresh Parmesan cheese

1. Prepare grill to medium-high heat.
2. While grill heats, prepare Caesar Dressing. Reserve ⅓ cup dressing in a separate bowl; set aside.
3. Place chicken on grill rack coated with cooking spray over medium-high heat. Grill 2 to 3 minutes on each side or until done, basting frequently with remaining dressing. Remove from grill. Cool slightly; slice.
4. Combine chicken, reserved ⅓ cup dressing, lettuce, and tomato in a large bowl; toss gently to coat. Divide salad evenly among each of 4 bowls. Sprinkle each serving with 1 tablespoon cheese. Yield: 4 servings (serving size: 2½ cups).

CALORIES 225 (42% from fat); FAT 11g (sat 2.4g, mono 0.7g, poly 0.4g); PROTEIN 23.6g; CARB 9g; FIBER 2.6g; CHOL 68mg; IRON 1.8mg; SODIUM 446mg; CALC 114mg

Caesar Dressing
Prep: 5 minutes

6 tablespoons light mayonnaise
3 tablespoons fresh lemon juice
1½ tablespoons water
1½ teaspoons anchovy paste

3 large garlic cloves, minced
1 teaspoon dried oregano
½ teaspoon freshly ground black pepper

1. Combine all ingredients in a small bowl, stirring well with a whisk. Yield: about ⅔ cup (serving size: about 1 tablespoon).

CALORIES 33 (79% from fat); FAT 3g (sat 0.5g, mono 0g, poly 0g); PROTEIN 0.2g; CARB 1.5g; FIBER 0.1g; CHOL 6mg; IRON 0.1mg; SODIUM 112mg; CALC 5mg

Fresh cherries add a wonderful accent to this elegantly easy salad. A good rule of thumb for sweet, dark cherries: the darker the fruit, the sweeter it is.

Grilled Duck Breast Salad with Champagne-Honey Vinaigrette

Prep: 5 minutes • Cook: 8 minutes • Other: 4 minutes

4 (6-ounce) boneless duck breast halves, skinned
¼ teaspoon salt
¼ teaspoon freshly ground black pepper
Cooking spray

1 (5-ounce) package herb salad mix
1½ cups pitted and halved cherries
¼ cup (1 ounce) crumbled blue cheese
¼ cup sliced almonds, toasted
Champagne-Honey Vinaigrette

1. Prepare grill to medium-high heat.

2. Sprinkle duck evenly with salt and pepper. Place on grill rack coated with cooking spray. Cook 4 minutes on each side or until desired degree of doneness; let stand 4 minutes. While duck grills, prepare Champagne-Honey Vinaigrette.

3. Slice duck breast thinly across the grain. Divide salad mix evenly on each of 4 plates. Top each serving with duck, cherries, blue cheese, and almonds. Drizzle Champagne-Honey Vinaigrette evenly over each serving. Yield: 4 servings (serving size: about 1½ cups salad mix, 2 ounces duck, about ⅓ cup cherries, 1 tablespoon cheese, 1 tablespoon almonds, and about 1 tablespoon Champagne-Honey Vinaigrette).

CALORIES 296 (49% from fat); FAT 16g (sat 3.9g, mono 9g, poly 1.9g); PROTEIN 22.2g; CARB 17.9g; FIBER 3.4g; CHOL 72mg; IRON 7.1mg; SODIUM 655mg; CALC 131mg

Champagne-Honey Vinaigrette

Prep: 2 minutes

2 tablespoons extra-virgin olive oil
2 tablespoons champagne vinegar
1 tablespoon honey

½ teaspoon salt
⅛ teaspoon freshly ground black pepper

1. Combine all ingredients in a small bowl; stir well with a whisk. Yield: ⅓ cup (serving size: about 1 tablespoon).

CALORIES 62 (77% from fat); FAT 5g (sat 0.7g, mono 4.1g, poly 0.5g); PROTEIN 0g; CARB 3.8g; FIBER 0g; CHOL 0mg; IRON 0mg; SODIUM 219mg; CALC 1mg

Cherries Open the stone-fruit season in late May with cherries. They do not ripen after harvest, so once picked, their flavor is set. Store fresh cherries for up to a week in the refrigerator in a bowl lined with paper towels. A cherry pitter is the most efficient way to remove the pits, but you can also use a small knife. Wear disposable latex gloves to avoid staining your fingers.

meatless main

Grape, Blue Cheese, and Walnut Pizza
Grilled Heirloom Tomato and Goat Cheese Pizza
Roasted Vegetable Pizza
Garden Scrambled Eggs
Porcini-Parmesan Frittata
Mediterranean-Style Frittata
Black Bean and Corn–Topped Potatoes
Refried Bean Poblanos with Cheese
Portobello and Black Bean Quesadillas
Spicy Vegetable Fried Rice
Creamy Butternut Squash Risotto
Taco Beans and Rice
Southwestern Rice and Veggie Cakes
Grain and Vegetable–Stuffed Portobello Mushrooms
Asiago Tortellini
Roasted Vegetable Pasta
Sweet Grape Tomato and White Bean Pasta
Ravioli with Sun-Dried Tomato Cream Sauce
Rosemary and White Bean Pasta
Vietnamese Noodle-Vegetable Toss

We made our own balsamic syrup for this unique thin-crust pizza, but you can substitute bottled balsamic glaze found in the vinegar section of your supermarket. This recipe can easily be doubled to serve two.

Grape, Blue Cheese, and Walnut Pizza
Prep: 4 minutes • Cook: 10 minutes

1 (2.8-ounce) whole wheat flatbread (such as Flatout Harvest Wheat)
¾ cup seedless red grapes, halved
2 tablespoons crumbled blue cheese
2 tablespoons chopped walnuts, toasted
2 tablespoons balsamic vinegar
1 cup arugula leaves

1. Preheat oven to 375°.
2. Place flatbread on rack in oven; bake at 375° for 3 minutes or until lightly browned. Remove flatbread from oven; top with grapes, cheese, and walnuts. Place flatbread back on rack in oven; bake 5 minutes or until cheese melts and crust is browned.
3. While pizza bakes, bring vinegar to a boil in a small saucepan. Boil 1 minute or until vinegar thickens and reduces to about ½ tablespoon. Top pizza with arugula; drizzle with balsamic syrup. Serve immediately. Yield: 1 serving (serving size: 1 pizza).

CALORIES 479 (32% from fat); FAT 17g (sat 3.2g, mono 2g, poly 6g); PROTEIN 18.3g; CARB 66g; FIBER 6.2g; CHOL 13mg; IRON 3.2mg; SODIUM 682mg; CALC 157mg

Grapes One cup of grapes has almost as much fiber as a slice of whole wheat toast, a good amount of potassium, just a trace of fat, and a little more than 100 calories. But this fruit's most potent benefits lie in the phytonutrients found within grape skins of all colors, which may help prevent several kinds of cancer and heart disease.

Heirloom tomatoes are remarkably flavorful and colorful compared with their grocery store counterparts. They vary from red to orange, gold, taxi yellow, nearly white, pink, purplish black, and green. Some are even multicolored, such as Mr. Stripey, which we used here. Your choice of tomato will shine in this simple pizza.

Grilled Heirloom Tomato and Goat Cheese Pizza

Prep: 11 minutes • Cook: 4 minutes

1 (13.8-ounce) can refrigerated pizza crust dough
Cooking spray
1 garlic clove, halved
1 large heirloom tomato, seeded and chopped (about 10 ounces)
½ cup (2 ounces) shredded part-skim mozzarella cheese
¾ cup (3 ounces) crumbled herbed goat cheese

1. Prepare grill to medium heat.
2. Unroll dough onto a large baking sheet coated with cooking spray; pat dough into a 12 x 9–inch rectangle. Lightly coat dough with cooking spray.
3. Place dough on grill rack coated with cooking spray; grill 1 minute or until lightly browned. Turn crust over. Rub with garlic; sprinkle with tomato and cheeses. Close grill lid; grill 3 minutes. Serve immediately. Yield: 6 servings (serving size: 1 slice).

CALORIES 242 (29% from fat); FAT 8g (sat 4.4g, mono 1.4g, poly 0.2g); PROTEIN 10.7g; CARB 33.1g; FIBER 0.4g; CHOL 17mg; IRON 2.2mg; SODIUM 590mg; CALC 107mg

serve with
Peanut Butter–Chocolate Banana Split

Prep: 7 minutes • Cook: 1 minute

¼ cup plus 2 tablespoons chocolate syrup
1½ tablespoons reduced-fat peanut butter
3 bananas, cut in half lengthwise
3 cups vanilla bean light ice cream (such as Edy's)
3 tablespoons chopped unsalted peanuts

1. Combine chocolate syrup and peanut butter in a 1-cup glass measure. Microwave at HIGH 40 seconds or until peanut butter melts. Stir until smooth.
2. Cut each banana half crosswise into 2 pieces. Arrange 2 banana pieces in each of 6 dessert dishes; top banana with ice cream and hot chocolate sauce. Sprinkle with peanuts. Serve immediately. Yield: 6 servings (serving size: 2 pieces banana, ½ cup ice cream, about 1½ tablespoons chocolate sauce, and 1½ teaspoons peanuts).

CALORIES 255 (26% from fat); FAT 7g (sat 2.6g, mono 1.1g, poly 0.7g); PROTEIN 6g; CARB 44.9g; FIBER 2.1g; CHOL 20mg; IRON 0.6mg; SODIUM 82mg; CALC 62mg

Roast the grape tomatoes and zucchini ahead, and refrigerate. Use the mixture as a topping for this hearty pizza or as a side dish for grilled chicken or fish.

Roasted Vegetable Pizza
Prep: 3 minutes • Cook: 12 minutes

1 (10-ounce) Italian cheese-flavored thin pizza crust (such as Boboli)
⅓ cup commercial pesto
3 cups Roasted Zucchini and Tomatoes

1 cup (4 ounces) preshredded part-skim mozzarella cheese
2 tablespoons grated fresh Parmesan cheese

1. Preheat oven to 500°. Place pizza crust on rack in oven while preheating, and heat 5 minutes.
2. Remove crust from oven; place on an ungreased baking sheet. Spread pesto evenly over crust. Top with Roasted Zucchini and Tomatoes; sprinkle evenly with cheeses. Bake at 500° for 7 minutes or until cheeses melt. Yield: 6 servings (serving size: 1 slice).

CALORIES 309 (43% from fat); FAT 15g (sat 4.9g, mono 6.1g, poly 3.4g); PROTEIN 13.6g; CARB 31.8g; FIBER 3g; CHOL 17mg; IRON 2.3mg; SODIUM 629mg; CALC 277mg

Roasted Zucchini and Tomatoes
Prep: 4 minutes • Cook: 18 minutes

1 (8-ounce) container refrigerated prechopped red onion
2 medium zucchini, coarsely chopped
1 cup grape tomatoes

2 teaspoons olive oil
¼ teaspoon salt
¼ teaspoon black pepper
1 tablespoon chopped fresh basil

1. Preheat oven to 500°.
2. Combine first 6 ingredients; toss well. Place on a large rimmed baking sheet. Bake at 500° for 18 minutes or until vegetables are tender and lightly browned, stirring after 12 minutes. Add basil to roasted vegetables; toss gently. Yield: 3 cups (serving size: ½ cup).

CALORIES 44 (37% from fat); FAT 2g (sat 0.3g, mono 1.1g, poly 0.3g); PROTEIN 1.5g; CARB 6.8g; FIBER 1.7g; CHOL 0mg; IRON 0.4mg; SODIUM 106mg; CALC 22mg

Bring garden freshness to your table with these veggie-laden scrambled eggs. Red tomato, juicy onion, and green bell pepper perk up this traditional breakfast dish.

Garden Scrambled Eggs
Prep: 5 minutes • Cook: 5 minutes

Butter-flavored cooking spray
¾ cup refrigerated prechopped tomato, onion, and bell pepper mix
4 large eggs
4 large egg whites

2 tablespoons chopped fresh parsley
6 tablespoons reduced-fat sour cream
1 tablespoon Dijon mustard
Dash of salt
Dash of black pepper

1. Heat a large nonstick skillet over medium heat. Coat pan with cooking spray; add tomato mixture. Coat vegetables with cooking spray; cook 3 minutes or until vegetables are tender, stirring often.
2. While vegetables cook, combine eggs, egg whites, and remaining ingredients in a medium bowl, stirring with a whisk.
3. Add egg mixture to pan; cook over medium heat 2 minutes. Do not stir until mixture begins to set on bottom. Draw a heat-resistant spatula through egg mixture to form large curds. Do not stir constantly. Egg mixture is done when thickened, but still moist. Serve immediately. Yield: 4 servings.

CALORIES 133 (54% from fat); FAT 8g (sat 3.3g, mono 2.7g, poly 0.8g); PROTEIN 11g; CARB 4.3g; FIBER 0.5g; CHOL 220mg; IRON 1.2mg; SODIUM 263mg; CALC 59mg

serve with
Garlic-Roasted Potatoes
Prep: 5 minutes • Cook: 20 minutes

1 pound small red potatoes (about 8 potatoes)
1 teaspoon olive oil
¼ teaspoon salt

¼ teaspoon garlic powder
¼ teaspoon black pepper
Butter-flavored cooking spray

1. Preheat oven to 450°.
2. Scrub potatoes; cut each into 8 wedges. Place wedges in a large bowl. Drizzle with oil; toss well. Sprinkle with salt, garlic powder, and pepper; toss until potatoes are evenly coated with spices. Arrange wedges in a single layer on a large rimmed baking sheet coated with cooking spray.
3. Bake at 450° for 20 minutes or until browned. Yield: 4 servings (serving size: ¾ cup).

CALORIES 92 (15% from fat); FAT 2g (sat 0.2g, mono 0.8g, poly 0.2g); PROTEIN 2.2g; CARB 18.2g; FIBER 2g; CHOL 0mg; IRON 0.8mg; SODIUM 152mg; CALC 12mg

Porcini mushrooms have a smooth, meaty
texture when hydrated. Their pungent, woodsy taste gives
extraordinary depth of flavor to this frittata.

Porcini-Parmesan Frittata

Prep: 10 minutes • Cook: 9 minutes • Other: 2 minutes

2 cups dried porcini mushrooms (about 2 ounces)
6 large egg whites
4 large eggs
½ teaspoon salt
¼ teaspoon freshly ground black pepper
½ cup preshredded Parmesan cheese
1 tablespoon olive oil
Minced fresh chives (optional)

1. Preheat broiler.
2. Place mushrooms in a large ovenproof skillet. Cover mushrooms with cold water; let stand 2 minutes. Drain. Return mushrooms to skillet. Cover with cold water; bring to a boil. Drain. Pat mushrooms dry with a paper towel.
3. Combine egg whites and next 3 ingredients in a large bowl, stirring well with a whisk. Stir in mushrooms and cheese.
4. Heat oil in pan over medium-high heat. Add egg mixture; cook 3 minutes or until slightly set. Broil 3 minutes or until eggs are completely set and browned. Cut frittata into 4 wedges. Garnish with chives, if desired. Yield: 4 servings (serving size: 1 wedge).

CALORIES 209 (49% from fat); FAT 11g (sat 3.8g, mono 5.3g, poly 1.3g); PROTEIN 18.2g; CARB 6.5g; FIBER 2.7g; CHOL 219mg; IRON 3mg; SODIUM 613mg; CALC 156mg

serve with
Caprese Salad with Heirloom Tomatoes

Prep: 9 minutes

2 tablespoons white balsamic vinegar
1 tablespoon olive oil
12 (¼-inch-thick) slices heirloom tomato (about 3 tomatoes)
¼ pound fresh mozzarella cheese, cut into 12 slices
12 large fresh basil leaves

1. Combine vinegar and oil, stirring well with a whisk.
2. Place 1 tomato slice on each of 4 plates. Top each with 1 cheese slice and 1 basil leaf. Repeat layers twice, ending with basil leaves. Drizzle evenly with vinaigrette. Yield: 4 servings (serving size: 3 tomato slices, 1 ounce cheese, 3 basil leaves, and about 2 teaspoons vinaigrette).

CALORIES 138 (65% from fat); FAT 10g (sat 4.6g, mono 2.5g, poly 0.6g); PROTEIN 5.9g; CARB 6.8g; FIBER 1.2g; CHOL 22mg; IRON 0.5mg; SODIUM 45mg; CALC 174mg

The deep green of the spinach in the frittata and the bright red of the Herb-Crusted Broiled Tomatoes create a vibrant combination for a vitamin-packed brunch. To speed up prep time, prepare the tomatoes while the frittata broils.

Mediterranean-Style Frittata
Prep: 8 minutes • Cook: 6 minutes

2 teaspoons olive oil
¾ cup packed baby spinach
2 green onions
4 large egg whites
6 large eggs

⅓ cup (1.3 ounces) crumbled feta cheese with basil and sun-dried tomatoes
2 teaspoons salt-free Greek seasoning (such as Cavender's)
¼ teaspoon salt

1. Preheat broiler.
2. Heat oil in a 10-inch ovenproof skillet over medium heat. While oil heats, coarsely chop spinach and finely chop onions. Combine egg whites, eggs, cheese, Greek seasoning, and salt in a large bowl; stir well with a whisk. Add spinach and onions, stirring well.
3. Add egg mixture to pan; cook until edges begin to set, about 2 minutes. Gently lift edge of egg mixture, tilting pan to allow uncooked egg mixture to come in contact with pan. Cook 2 minutes or until egg mixture is almost set.
4. Broil 2 to 3 minutes or until center is set. Transfer the frittata to a serving platter immediately; cut into 4 wedges. Yield: 4 servings (serving size: 1 wedge).

CALORIES 178 (62% from fat); FAT 12g (sat 4g, mono 4.5g, poly 1.4g); PROTEIN 15.7g; CARB 2.2g; FIBER 0.6g; CHOL 326mg; IRON 1.7mg; SODIUM 438mg; CALC 86mg

serve with
Herb-Crusted Broiled Tomatoes
Prep: 4 minutes • Cook: 3 minutes

¼ cup whole wheat panko (Japanese breadcrumbs)
2 tablespoons grated Parmesan cheese
1 teaspoon dried Italian seasoning
½ teaspoon black pepper

¼ teaspoon seasoned salt
1 teaspoon unsalted butter, melted
2 tomatoes, cut in half horizontally
Cooking spray

1. Preheat broiler.
2. Combine first 5 ingredients in a small bowl. Stir butter into breadcrumb mixture. Place tomato halves on a rimmed baking sheet coated with cooking spray. Sprinkle breadcrumb mixture evenly over tomato halves. Broil 3 to 4 minutes or until topping is golden. Serve immediately. Yield: 4 servings (serving size: 1 tomato half).

CALORIES 48 (36% from fat); FAT 2g (sat 1.1g, mono 0.5g, poly 0.1g); PROTEIN 2.3g; CARB 6.2g; FIBER 1.3g; CHOL 5mg; IRON 0.4mg; SODIUM 135mg; CALC 35mg

Also enjoy this bountiful Southwestern-style topping with baked tortilla chips. When corn is in season, feel free to substitute fresh sweet corn kernels for frozen.

Black Bean and Corn–Topped Potatoes
Prep: 4 minutes • Cook: 10 minutes

4 (6-ounce) baking potatoes
Cooking spray
½ cup chopped onion
2 garlic cloves, minced
1 teaspoon ground cumin
½ teaspoon chili powder
1 (15-ounce) can no-salt-added black beans
   (such as Eden Organic), rinsed and drained

1½ cups frozen whole-kernel corn
1½ cups fresh salsa
¼ cup (1 ounce) reduced-fat shredded
   cheddar-Jack cheese (such as Cabot)
¼ cup chopped fresh cilantro

1. Pierce potatoes with a fork; arrange in a circle on paper towels in microwave oven. Microwave at HIGH 10 minutes, turning and rearranging potatoes after 5 minutes.
2. While potatoes cook, heat a large nonstick skillet over medium-high heat. Coat pan with cooking spray. Add onion and next 3 ingredients; sauté 3 minutes. Reduce heat to low. Add beans, corn, and salsa; cook 4 minutes or until thoroughly heated.
3. Split potatoes lengthwise, cutting to, but not through, other side. Fluff with a fork. Spoon about 1 cup bean mixture over each potato. Top each serving evenly with cheese and cilantro. Yield: 4 servings (serving size: 1 potato, 1 cup bean mixture, 1 tablespoon cheese, and 1 tablespoon cilantro).

CALORIES 332 (8% from fat); FAT 3g (sat 1.7g, mono 0.1g, poly 0.3g); PROTEIN 11g; CARB 64.1g; FIBER 9g; CHOL 7mg; IRON 3.5mg; SODIUM 308mg; CALC 106mg

Poblano chiles grown in a hot, dry climate can be more intense than others, so the spiciness of this dish depends on the heat of your peppers.

Refried Bean Poblanos with Cheese
Prep: 2 minutes • Cook: 6 minutes

4 medium poblano chiles, halved and seeded
1 (16-ounce) can fat-free refried beans
1 (8.8-ounce) pouch microwaveable cooked long-grain rice (such as Uncle Ben's Original Ready Rice)
½ cup picante sauce

1 cup (4 ounces) preshredded reduced-fat 4-cheese Mexican blend cheese
Chopped fresh cilantro (optional)

1. Place chile halves, cut sides up, on a round microwave-safe plate. Cover with wax paper; microwave at HIGH 3 minutes.
2. While chiles cook, combine beans, rice, and picante sauce in a medium bowl, stirring well. Spoon bean mixture evenly into chile halves. Cover with wax paper; microwave at HIGH 2 minutes. Uncover chiles, sprinkle each half with 2 tablespoons cheese, and microwave at HIGH 1 to 2 minutes or until cheese melts. Sprinkle evenly with cilantro, if desired. Yield: 4 servings (serving size: 2 stuffed chile halves).

CALORIES 303 (19% from fat); FAT 6g (sat 3.1g, mono 0g, poly 0.1g); PROTEIN 17g; CARB 45.4g; FIBER 7.7g; CHOL 10mg; IRON 0.7mg; SODIUM 960mg; CALC 232mg

serve with
Creamy Chipotle Wedge Salad
Prep: 5 minutes

½ cup light ranch dressing (such as Naturally Fresh)
1 chipotle chile, canned in adobo sauce

1 green onion, cut into 2-inch pieces
½ head iceberg lettuce, cored and quartered

1. Place first 3 ingredients in a blender; process until smooth. Serve over lettuce wedges. Yield: 4 servings (serving size: 1 lettuce wedge and 2½ tablespoons dressing).

CALORIES 90 (70% from fat); FAT 7g (sat 0.6g, mono 1.2g, poly 5.1g); PROTEIN 1g; CARB 5.8g; FIBER 1.2g; CHOL 8mg; IRON 0.5mg; SODIUM 338mg; CALC 23mg

Sautéed portobellos are delicious in ragouts; as a topping for polenta or pizza; or as a filling for fajitas, tacos, or quesadillas. The portobello mushroom stands up to the robust flavors in these quesadillas, all the while preserving its own steaklike texture.

Portobello and Black Bean Quesadillas

Prep: 1 minute • Cook: 14 minutes

4 (8-inch) fat-free flour tortillas
Butter-flavored cooking spray
2 (4½-inch) portobello caps, chopped
2 tablespoons light balsamic vinaigrette
1 cup no-salt-added black beans, rinsed and drained
1 (2-ounce) jar diced pimiento, drained
1 cup (4 ounces) preshredded reduced-fat 4-cheese Mexican blend cheese
¼ cup thinly sliced green onions
Salsa (optional)
Chopped fresh cilantro (optional)

1. Stack tortillas; microwave at HIGH 1 minute. Leave in microwave to keep warm while preparing filling.

2. Heat a large nonstick skillet over medium-high heat. Coat pan with cooking spray. Add mushrooms; sauté 2 minutes or until tender. Add vinaigrette, beans, and pimiento; cook 1 to 2 minutes, stirring constantly, or until liquid evaporates. Mash bean mixture slightly with a potato masher.

3. Spoon about ⅓ cup bean mixture onto each tortilla. Sprinkle evenly with cheese and onions. Fold tortillas in half.

4. Wipe skillet with paper towels; heat over medium heat. Coat pan with cooking spray. Place 2 quesadillas in pan; cook 2 to 3 minutes on each side or until golden and cheese melts. Repeat with remaining 2 quesadillas. Cut each quesadilla into 3 wedges. Serve immediately with salsa and cilantro, if desired. Yield: 4 servings (serving size: 3 wedges).

CALORIES 251 (32% from fat); FAT 9g (sat 3.7g, mono 0.8g, poly 1.8g); PROTEIN 18.9g; CARB 25.8g; FIBER 7.5g; CHOL 10mg; IRON 2.3mg; SODIUM 695mg; CALC 318mg

Portobellos Let a cremini grow a few days longer, and you end up with a portobello. This flying saucer–shaped mushroom, which often measures from three to six inches across, is firm, meaty, and intensely flavorful.

The crushed red pepper adds a hint of heat to this Asian favorite. If you're sensitive to spices, simply omit it.

Spicy Vegetable Fried Rice

Prep: 2 minutes • Cook: 9 minutes

1½ cups frozen broccoli stir-fry (such as Birds Eye)
1 cup frozen shelled edamame (green soybeans)
Cooking spray
½ cup egg substitute
2 teaspoons dark sesame oil
2 teaspoons bottled minced garlic
¼ teaspoon crushed red pepper
2 (8.8-ounce) pouches microwaveable cooked brown rice (such as Uncle Ben's Whole Grain Brown Ready Rice)
2½ tablespoons low-sodium soy sauce
Toasted sesame seeds (optional)
Sliced green onions (optional)

1. Combine broccoli stir-fry and edamame in a microwave-safe bowl. Microwave at HIGH 2 minutes or until thawed; set aside.
2. While vegetables thaw, heat a large nonstick skillet over medium-high heat; coat pan with cooking spray. Add egg substitute; cook 2 minutes, stirring frequently, until scrambled. Remove from pan. Wipe pan with paper towels.
3. Heat sesame oil in pan over medium-high heat; add garlic and crushed red pepper. Cook 1 minute or until fragrant. Stir in vegetables and rice; cook 2 minutes or until thoroughly heated. Stir in soy sauce and reserved egg. Garnish with sesame seeds and onions, if desired. Yield: 4 servings (serving size: about 1⅓ cups).

CALORIES 289 (24% from fat); FAT 8g (sat 0.8g, mono 3.6g, poly 2.9g); PROTEIN 11.5g; CARB 42.6g; FIBER 4g; CHOL 0mg; IRON 2mg; SODIUM 447mg; CALC 35mg

serve with
Broiled Pineapple

Prep: 6 minutes • Cook: 6 minutes

1 cored fresh pineapple, cut into 8 slices
2 tablespoons butter, melted
½ cup packed brown sugar
⅓ cup flaked sweetened coconut

1. Preheat broiler.
2. Place pineapple slices on a jelly-roll pan. Drizzle with butter; sprinkle with sugar. Broil 4 minutes or until sugar melts. Sprinkle coconut over pineapple; broil 2 minutes or until coconut is toasted. Yield: 4 servings (serving size: 2 slices).

CALORIES 239 (29% from fat); FAT 8g (sat 5.2g, mono 1.6g, poly 0.3g); PROTEIN 0.9g; CARB 45g; FIBER 2.3g; CHOL 15mg; IRON 1mg; SODIUM 70mg; CALC 41mg

This soul-satisfying risotto is cooked in the microwave, but no one would ever guess.

Creamy Butternut Squash Risotto
Prep: 3 minutes • Cook: 20 minutes • Other: 5 minutes

1¼ cups uncooked Arborio rice or other medium-grain rice
2 teaspoons olive oil
2½ cups fat-free, less-sodium chicken broth
1 cup water
1 (12-ounce) package frozen pureed butternut squash (such as McKenzie's)

¼ teaspoon salt
¼ teaspoon freshly ground black pepper
6 tablespoons grated fresh Parmesan cheese
Grated fresh Parmesan cheese (optional)
Thyme sprigs (optional)

1. Combine rice and oil in a 1½-quart microwave-safe dish, stirring to coat. Microwave, uncovered, at HIGH 3 minutes.
2. Add broth and 1 cup water to rice mixture; microwave, uncovered, at HIGH 9 minutes. Stir well; microwave, uncovered, at HIGH 6 minutes. Remove from microwave; let stand 5 minutes or until all liquid is absorbed.
3. While risotto stands, heat squash in microwave at HIGH 2 minutes or until warm. Add squash, salt, pepper, and cheese to risotto. Stir well to combine. Garnish with additional cheese and thyme sprigs, if desired. Yield: 4 servings (serving size: 1¼ cups).

CALORIES 326 (20% from fat); FAT 7g (sat 2g, mono 2.3g, poly 0.4g); PROTEIN 10.5g; CARB 55.9g; FIBER 3.3g; CHOL 7mg; IRON 0.8mg; SODIUM 814mg; CALC 98mg

serve with
Roasted Brussels Sprouts with Balsamic Glaze
Prep: 4 minutes • Cook: 15 minutes

1 pound Brussels sprouts, trimmed and halved lengthwise
1 tablespoon olive oil
¼ teaspoon salt
¼ teaspoon freshly ground black pepper

Cooking spray
1 tablespoon balsamic glaze (such as Gia Russa)
1 teaspoon water

1. Preheat oven to 450°.
2. Combine Brussels sprouts and next 3 ingredients on a jelly-roll pan coated with cooking spray. Bake at 450° for 15 minutes or until Brussels sprouts are tender and browned, stirring occasionally.
3. Combine balsamic glaze and 1 teaspoon water. Drizzle evenly over Brussels sprouts. Yield: 4 servings (serving size: ¾ cup).

CALORIES 82 (42% from fat); FAT 4g (sat 0.6g, mono 2.5g, poly 0.7g); PROTEIN 3.5g; CARB 11g; FIBER 3.9g; CHOL 0mg; IRON 1.4mg; SODIUM 173mg; CALC 43mg

We call for ready-to-eat brown rice, but if you have leftover brown rice, this is the perfect time to use it. Grill some summer squash, which is at its peak from June through late August, for a fresh side to this Mexican-style dish.

Taco Beans and Rice

Prep: 2 minutes • Cook: 12 minutes

1 tablespoon olive oil
1½ cups refrigerated prechopped tricolor bell pepper
1 cup refrigerated prechopped onion
1 (16-ounce) can dark red kidney beans, rinsed and drained
1 (1.25-ounce) package 40%-less-sodium taco seasoning mix, divided

1 (8.8-ounce) pouch microwaveable cooked brown rice (such as Uncle Ben's Whole Grain Brown Ready Rice)
½ cup (2 ounces) reduced-fat shredded sharp cheddar cheese

1. Heat oil in a large nonstick skillet over medium-high heat; add bell pepper and onion. Cook 7 minutes or until lightly browned, stirring often. Stir in beans; cook 1 minute or until thoroughly heated. Remove from heat; stir in half package of seasoning mix.
2. Place rice in a medium bowl; heat according to package directions. Add remaining half of seasoning mix to rice, stirring well to combine. Spoon bean mixture over rice; sprinkle evenly with cheese. Yield: 4 servings (serving size: 6 tablespoons rice, about ¾ cup bean mixture, and 2 tablespoons cheese).

CALORIES 286 (28% from fat); FAT 9g (sat 2.8g, mono 4.4g, poly 1.5g); PROTEIN 10.2g; CARB 40.7g; FIBER 5.3g; CHOL 10mg; IRON 1.4mg; SODIUM 830mg; CALC 137mg

serve with
Yellow Squash Melt

Prep: 2 minutes • Cook: 6 minutes

2 yellow squash, halved lengthwise
Cooking spray
¼ teaspoon salt

⅓ cup (1.3 ounces) shredded 50%-less-fat pepper-Jack cheese

1. Prepare grill.
2. Lightly coat squash with cooking spray; sprinkle evenly with salt. Place squash on grill rack coated with cooking spray; grill 3 to 4 minutes on each side or until almost tender.
3. Place squash, cut sides up, on a serving plate; sprinkle evenly with cheese. Serve immediately. Yield: 4 servings (serving size: 1 squash half).

CALORIES 45 (40% from fat); FAT 2g (sat 1.4g, mono 0g, poly 0.1g); PROTEIN 3.5g; CARB 3.3g; FIBER 1.1g; CHOL 7mg; IRON 0.3mg; SODIUM 207mg; CALC 15mg

Not only does the cheese add flavor to this dish, but it also helps hold the cakes together; the thicker the shred of cheese, the better.

Southwestern Rice and Veggie Cakes
Prep: 7 minutes • Cook: 8 minutes

2 (8.5-ounce) pouches Santa Fe microwaveable cooked whole grain rice medley (such as Uncle Ben's Santa Fe Ready Rice)
4 egg whites, lightly beaten
1 cup (3 ounces) double-fiber breadcrumbs (about 2 slices)
¾ cup (3 ounces) preshredded reduced-fat 4-cheese Mexican blend cheese (such as Sargento) or shredded 50%-less-fat jalapeño cheddar (such as Cabot)

Cooking spray
½ cup light sour cream
2 teaspoons fresh lime juice
¼ teaspoon chili powder
Chopped fresh cilantro (optional)

1. Heat a large nonstick skillet over medium-high heat. While skillet heats, combine first 4 ingredients in a large bowl; mix well. Divide mixture into 8 equal portions, shaping each into a 2-inch patty.
2. Coat pan with cooking spray. Add 4 patties to pan; cook 3 minutes. Carefully turn patties over; cook 1 minute or until lightly browned. Repeat procedure with remaining 4 patties. While patties cook, combine sour cream, lime juice, and chili powder in a small bowl.
3. Arrange cakes on a serving platter. Top each with sour cream mixture. Garnish with cilantro, if desired. Yield: 4 servings (serving size: 2 rice cakes and 2 tablespoons sour cream mixture).

CALORIES 349 (28% from fat); FAT 11g (sat 3.8g, mono 4.5g, poly 1.8g); PROTEIN 19.2g; CARB 47.7g; FIBER 7.3g; CHOL 25mg; IRON 2.2mg; SODIUM 851mg; CALC 321mg

serve with
Spicy Tricolor Pepper Stir-Fry
Prep: 4 minutes • Cook: 6 minutes

2 teaspoons canola oil
3 bell peppers (1 each of red, yellow, and green), cut into strips

1 teaspoon bottled minced garlic
¼ teaspoon crushed red pepper
¼ teaspoon salt

1. Heat a large nonstick skillet over medium-high heat; add oil. Add peppers, garlic, and crushed red pepper. Stir-fry 4 minutes or until crisp-tender; sprinkle evenly with salt. Yield: 4 servings (serving size: ¾ cup).

CALORIES 46 (53% from fat); FAT 3g (sat 0.2g, mono 1.4g, poly 0.8g); PROTEIN 0.9g; CARB 5.4g; FIBER 1.4g; CHOL 0mg; IRON 0.4mg; SODIUM 148mg; CALC 9mg

Meatless Main **171**

Serve these generously stuffed mushrooms with Broiled Asparagus with Lemon. Put dinner on the table even more quickly by broiling the asparagus and portobellos simultaneously on the same baking sheet.

Grain and Vegetable–Stuffed Portobello Mushrooms

Prep: 5 minutes • Cook: 7 minutes

4 (5-inch) portobello caps
Cooking spray
1 garlic clove, minced
1 cup refrigerated prechopped tomato, onion, and bell pepper mix
1 (8.5-ounce) pouch microwaveable cooked vegetable harvest whole grain rice medley (such as Uncle Ben's Vegetable Harvest Ready Rice)
1 cup (4 ounces) shredded Italian cheese blend, divided
2 teaspoons Worcestershire sauce
¼ teaspoon salt
¼ teaspoon freshly ground black pepper

1. Preheat broiler.
2. Remove brown gills from the undersides of mushrooms using a spoon; discard gills. Place mushrooms, gill sides down, on a foil-lined baking sheet coated with cooking spray. Broil 4 minutes.
3. While mushrooms broil, heat a nonstick skillet over medium heat. Coat pan with cooking spray. Add garlic and tomato mixture to pan. Sauté 2 minutes; remove from heat. Stir in rice, ¾ cup cheese, and Worcestershire sauce.
4. Turn mushrooms over; sprinkle evenly with salt and pepper. Divide rice mixture evenly among mushrooms; sprinkle evenly with ¼ cup cheese. Broil 3 minutes or until cheese melts. Yield: 4 servings (serving size: 1 stuffed mushroom).

CALORIES 220 (31% from fat); FAT 8g (sat 3.5g, mono 2.7g, poly 1.2g); PROTEIN 12g; CARB 25.7g; FIBER 4g; CHOL 20mg; IRON 1.4mg; SODIUM 681mg; CALC 227mg

serve with
Broiled Asparagus with Lemon

Prep: 3 minutes • Cook: 3 minutes

1 pound asparagus, trimmed
1 garlic clove, minced
½ teaspoon grated lemon rind
½ teaspoon olive oil
⅛ teaspoon salt
⅛ teaspoon freshly ground black pepper
Cooking spray

1. Preheat broiler.
2. Combine all ingredients except cooking spray in a large bowl or dish; toss gently to coat.
3. Place asparagus on a foil-lined baking sheet coated with cooking spray. Broil 3 minutes or until desired degree of doneness. Yield: 4 servings (serving size: ¼ pound asparagus).

CALORIES 21 (30% from fat); FAT 1g (sat 0.1g, mono 0.4g, poly 0.1g); PROTEIN 1.4g; CARB 2.7g; FIBER 1.3g; CHOL 0mg; IRON 1.3mg; SODIUM 74mg; CALC 16mg

When boiling water for the pasta, start with hot tap water and cover the pot with a lid. This is a surefire way to speed up your cook time. Serve this pasta dish with Black Pepper–Garlic Flatbread to soak up the basil-infused broth.

Asiago Tortellini
Prep: 5 minutes • Cook: 13 minutes

1 (9-ounce) package fresh three-cheese tortellini
1 (14-ounce) can fat-free, less-sodium chicken broth
2 plum tomatoes, chopped
¼ cup chopped fresh basil
½ cup (2 ounces) shaved fresh Asiago cheese
Basil leaves (optional)
Freshly ground black pepper (optional)

1. Cook pasta according to package directions, omitting salt and fat; drain.
2. While pasta cooks, combine broth and tomato in a medium saucepan; bring to a boil. Remove from heat; stir in basil. Cover and let broth mixture stand until pasta is done. Add drained pasta to broth mixture. Ladle soup into shallow bowls; sprinkle each serving with cheese. Garnish with basil leaves and pepper, if desired. Yield: 4 servings (serving size: 1 cup soup and 2 tablespoons cheese).

CALORIES 267 (29% from fat); FAT 9g (sat 4.1g, mono 0g, poly 0.1g); PROTEIN 12.7g; CARB 34.8g; FIBER 2.3g; CHOL 32mg; IRON 0.2mg; SODIUM 676mg; CALC 106mg

serve with
Black Pepper–Garlic Flatbread
Prep: 4 minutes • Cook: 15 minutes

2 garlic cloves, minced
1 tablespoon minced fresh oregano
1½ teaspoons coarsely ground black pepper
¼ teaspoon kosher salt
1 (13.8-ounce) can refrigerated pizza crust dough
Cooking spray

1. Preheat oven to 400°.
2. Combine first 4 ingredients in a small bowl. Unroll dough onto a baking sheet coated with cooking spray; form into a 12 x 9–inch rectangle. Lightly coat top of dough with cooking spray; sprinkle evenly with garlic mixture.
3. Bake at 400° for 15 minutes or until golden. Cool flatbread; cut into 6 slices. Yield: 6 servings (serving size: 1 slice).

CALORIES 164 (11% from fat); FAT 2g (sat 0.5g, mono 0g, poly 0g); PROTEIN 5.2g; CARB 31.8g; FIBER 0.2g; CHOL 0mg; IRON 1.9mg; SODIUM 550mg; CALC 7mg

This aromatic, colorful, and delicious pasta will please your senses of smell, sight, and taste. You'll hardly be able to wait to sit down and eat.

Roasted Vegetable Pasta
Prep: 9 minutes • Cook: 15 minutes

3 cups (8 ounces) uncooked farfalle (bow tie pasta)
2 cups Roasted Vegetables
1 cup frozen petite green peas, thawed
¼ cup chopped fresh parsley
¼ cup (1½ ounces) thinly shaved fresh Parmesan cheese

1. Cook pasta according to package directions, omitting salt and fat. Drain and keep warm.
2. Combine pasta, Roasted Vegetables, and peas in a large bowl. Top with parsley and cheese. Yield: 4 servings (serving size: 1½ cups pasta and 1 tablespoon cheese).

CALORIES 338 (17% from fat); FAT 6g (sat 1.8g, mono 2.5g, poly 0.7g); PROTEIN 14.3g; CARB 54.9g; FIBER 5.5g; CHOL 5mg; IRON 3mg; SODIUM 485mg; CALC 106mg

Roasted Vegetables
Prep: 5 minutes • Cook: 22 minutes

1 (8-ounce) package baby portobello mushrooms, halved
2 cups grape or cherry tomatoes
1 red onion, sliced
1 tablespoon olive oil
½ teaspoon salt
¼ teaspoon freshly ground black pepper
¼ cup dry white wine

1. Preheat oven to 475°.
2. Combine first 6 ingredients in a bowl; toss well to coat. Arrange mushroom mixture in a single layer on a jelly-roll pan.
3. Bake at 475° for 15 minutes; turn vegetables over. Drizzle wine evenly over vegetables; bake an additional 7 minutes or until vegetables are tender and lightly browned. Yield: 2 cups (serving size: ½ cup).

CALORIES 84 (42% from fat); FAT 3.9g (sat 0.6g, mono 2.5g, poly 0.7g); PROTEIN 2.4g; CARB 9.3g; FIBER 2.2g; CHOL 0mg; IRON 0.8mg; SODIUM 302mg; CALC 15mg

Navy beans bump up the protein in this satisfying and healthy one-dish supper that's brimming with the tastes of summer.

Sweet Grape Tomato and White Bean Pasta

Prep: 1 minute • Cook: 14 minutes

1¾ cups uncooked multigrain penne (tube-shaped pasta)
1 tablespoon extra-virgin olive oil
2 cups halved grape tomatoes
2 garlic cloves, minced
1 cup chopped bottled roasted red bell peppers
½ (15-ounce) can navy beans, rinsed and drained

3 cups fresh baby spinach
¼ cup torn basil leaves
2 teaspoons balsamic vinegar
½ teaspoon salt
¼ cup (1 ounce) grated fresh Parmesan cheese

1. Cook pasta according to package directions, omitting salt and fat.
2. While pasta cooks, heat oil in a large nonstick skillet over medium-high heat. Add tomatoes; cook 3 minutes or until skins begin to wrinkle and burst. Add garlic; cook 1 minute, stirring constantly. Add bell pepper, beans, and spinach; cook 3 minutes or until spinach is slightly wilted. Stir in basil, vinegar, salt, and pasta. Cook 2 minutes or until thoroughly heated. Sprinkle evenly with cheese. Yield: 4 servings (serving size: 1½ cups pasta and 1 tablespoon cheese).

CALORIES 269 (25% from fat); FAT 7g (sat 1.6g, mono 2.5g, poly 1.8g); PROTEIN 12.3g; CARB 45.5g; FIBER 8.3g; CHOL 5mg; IRON 2.9mg; SODIUM 647mg; CALC 161mg

Grape tomatoes These tiny tomatoes have an elliptical shape, similar to a grape. They have a more intense sweetness than cherry tomatoes, balanced by a subtle acidity. For the best flavor, look for grape tomatoes that are no larger than an inch in diameter. If they're larger, they'll have a higher water content and a diluted taste.

Use pasta that steams in the microwave to avoid the step of bringing a large pot of water to a boil before cooking.

Ravioli with Sun-Dried Tomato Cream Sauce
Prep: 4 minutes • Cook: 8 minutes

1 (18-ounce) package frozen steam-n-eat small cheese ravioli (such as Rosetto)
2 teaspoons olive oil
1 (8-ounce) package baby portobello mushrooms, quartered
½ cup coarsely chopped onion
½ teaspoon all-purpose flour

½ cup plus 2 tablespoons half-and-half
2 tablespoons sun-dried tomato pesto (such as Classico)
¼ teaspoon salt
¼ teaspoon black pepper
¼ cup (1 ounce) shaved fresh Asiago cheese
Basil leaves (optional)

1. Cook ravioli in microwave according to package directions.
2. While ravioli cooks, heat oil in a large nonstick skillet over medium-high heat. Add mushrooms and onion; sauté 3 to 4 minutes or until richly browned. Combine flour and next 4 ingredients in a small bowl, stirring until smooth. Add to pan, stirring well. Cook over medium-low heat 2 minutes or until mixture thickens slightly.
3. Divide cooked ravioli evenly among 4 shallow bowls or plates; spoon mushroom mixture evenly over ravioli. Sprinkle cheese evenly over each serving; garnish with basil, if desired. Yield: 4 servings (serving size: 13 ravioli, about ½ cup mushroom sauce, and 1 tablespoon cheese).

CALORIES 306 (26% from fat); FAT 9g (sat 3.8g, mono 2.3g, poly 0.5g); PROTEIN 13.8g; CARB 41.5g; FIBER 3.1g; CHOL 21mg; IRON 2.9mg; SODIUM 583mg; CALC 199mg

serve with
Sautéed Zucchini Spears
Prep: 3 minutes • Cook: 6 minutes

3 medium zucchini (about 1 pound)
1½ teaspoons olive oil
½ cup coarsely chopped onion

¼ teaspoon salt
⅛ teaspoon black pepper

1. Cut zucchini in half lengthwise; cut each half crosswise into 2 pieces. Cut each zucchini piece into 3 spears.
2. Heat oil in a large nonstick skillet over medium-high heat; add zucchini and onion. Sauté 5 to 6 minutes or until vegetables are lightly browned. Sprinkle with salt and pepper; toss well. Yield: 4 servings (serving size: about ¾ cup).

CALORIES 47 (38% from fat); FAT 2g (sat 0.3g, mono 1.3g, poly 0.4g); PROTEIN 2g; CARB 6.8g; FIBER 2g; CHOL 0mg; IRON 0.6mg; SODIUM 161mg; CALC 27mg

Rinse the canned beans and warm them in the process by draining the pasta over the beans. Start boiling the water for the pasta, and then prepare the rest of the ingredients for this menu.

Rosemary and White Bean Pasta
Prep: 10 minutes • Cook: 14 minutes

1¾ cups uncooked multigrain rotini
   (corkscrew pasta)
1 cup halved grape tomatoes
12 pimiento-stuffed olives, chopped
3 tablespoons pine nuts, toasted
1 teaspoon chopped fresh rosemary
1 garlic clove, minced

¼ teaspoon salt, divided
1 (15.5-ounce) can navy beans, undrained
1 cup packed baby spinach, coarsely
   chopped
⅓ cup (1.3 ounces) reduced-fat feta cheese
2 teaspoons extra-virgin olive oil

1. Cook pasta according to package directions, omitting salt and fat.
2. While pasta cooks, combine tomatoes, next 4 ingredients, and ⅛ teaspoon salt in a small bowl; set aside.
3. Place beans in a colander; add cooked pasta. Drain. Combine pasta, beans, tomato mixture, spinach, cheese, oil, and remaining ⅛ teaspoon salt in a large bowl; toss well. Yield: 4 servings (serving size: about 1¼ cups).

CALORIES 306 (39% from fat); FAT 13g (sat 2g, mono 5.2g, poly 3.4g); PROTEIN 13.4g; CARB 36.5g; FIBER 8.5g; CHOL 3mg; IRON 3.6mg; SODIUM 829mg; CALC 94mg

serve with
Lemon-Balsamic Broccoli
Prep: 3 minutes • Cook: 3 minutes

1 (12-ounce) package fresh broccoli florets
1 tablespoon butter
1 teaspoon grated lemon rind

1 teaspoon fresh lemon juice
1 teaspoon balsamic vinegar
¼ teaspoon salt

1. Cook broccoli according to package directions; keep warm.
2. Combine butter and remaining ingredients in a small microwave-safe bowl. Microwave at HIGH 30 seconds or until butter melts. Pour butter mixture over broccoli; toss gently to coat. Yield: 4 servings (serving size: 1 cup).

CALORIES 51 (53% from fat); FAT 3g (sat 1.8g, mono 0.8g, poly 0.3g); PROTEIN 2.6g; CARB 4.9g; FIBER 2.5g; CHOL 8mg; IRON 0.8mg; SODIUM 189mg; CALC 43mg

Vietnamese cuisine is truly light Asian food. Rice noodles make this a hearty dish without leaving you feeling overly full.

Vietnamese Noodle-Vegetable Toss
Prep: 7 minutes • Cook: 5 minutes • Other: 3 minutes

6 cups water
6 ounces uncooked linguine-style rice noodles (such as Thai Kitchen)
1 tablespoon sugar
2 tablespoons water
1 tablespoon fish sauce
1 tablespoon fresh lime juice

2 cups packaged tricolor slaw mix
1 cup grated English cucumber
1 cup fresh bean sprouts
1 cup fresh cilantro leaves
½ cup chopped unsalted, dry-roasted peanuts

1. Bring 6 cups water to a boil in a large saucepan. Remove from heat; add rice noodles. Let soak 3 minutes or until tender. Drain.
2. While noodles soak, combine sugar and next 3 ingredients in a small bowl, stirring well with a whisk.
3. Combine noodles, slaw mix, and next 3 ingredients in a large bowl. Toss with sugar mixture. Sprinkle with peanuts. Serve immediately. Yield: 3 servings (serving size: 1⅓ cups).

CALORIES 388 (28% from fat); FAT 12g (sat 1.7g, mono 6g, poly 3.9g); PROTEIN 10.7g; CARB 61g; FIBER 3.8g; CHOL 0mg; IRON 2mg; SODIUM 397mg; CALC 49mg

English cucumbers English, or seedless, cucumbers are usually twice the size of regular cucumbers and contain fewer seeds and less water. They're also usually milder in flavor than regular cucumbers.

fish & shellfish

Catfish with Cilantro-Chipotle Rice
Baked Flounder with Dill and Caper Cream
Pistachio-Crusted Grouper with Lavender Honey Sauce
Lemon-Artichoke Halibut en Papillote
Grilled Halibut with Onion, Spicy Tomatoes, and Avocado
Halibut with Quick Lemon Pesto
Sunflower Seed–Crusted Orange Roughy
Chili-Garlic Glazed Salmon
Seared Salmon Fillets with Edamame Succotash
Peach-Glazed Salmon with Fresh Raspberries
Pan-Seared Snapper with Fennel-Olive Topping
Lemon Red Snapper with Herbed Butter
Spicy Louisiana Tilapia Fillets with Sautéed Vegetable Relish
Almond-Crusted Tilapia
Tilapia with Warm Olive Salsa
Pan-Seared Tarragon Trout
Seared Sesame Tuna with Orange-Ginger Sauce
Grilled Tuna Steaks with Cucumber–Pickled Ginger Relish
Spicy Thai Tuna Cakes with Cucumber Aïoli
Fresh Garlic Linguine with Clams
Seared Scallops with Warm Fruit Salsa
Scallops in Buttery Wine Sauce
Scallops with Capers and Tomatoes
Chili-Lime Shrimp
Greek-Style Shrimp Sauté
Spicy Grilled Shrimp Kebabs with Avocado and Papaya Salad
Broiled Shrimp Kebabs with Horseradish-Herb Sour Cream Sauce
Skillet Barbecue Shrimp
Szechuan Shrimp
Shrimp with Creamy Orange-Chipotle Sauce
Spicy Green Curry–Cilantro Shrimp
Deep South Shrimp and Sausage
Pesto Shrimp Pasta
Creamy Garlic Shrimp and Pasta
Quick Paella

The mild flavor and buttery texture of the catfish go well with the spicy heat of the chipotle salsa. The fillets are delicate, but a good sear on the underside keeps them from falling apart when turned over in the skillet.

Catfish with Cilantro-Chipotle Rice
Prep: 5 minutes • Cook: 14 minutes

4 (6-ounce) farm-raised catfish fillets
Cooking spray
¼ teaspoon salt
¼ teaspoon freshly ground black pepper
¼ cup bottled chipotle salsa, divided
Lime wedges
Cilantro-Chipotle Rice

1. Heat a large nonstick skillet over medium-high heat. Coat pan and fillets with cooking spray. Sprinkle fillets evenly with salt and pepper. Add 2 fillets to pan, flat sides up; cook 4 minutes on 1 side or until browned. Turn fillets over; spoon 1 tablespoon salsa over each fillet. Cook 3 minutes or until fish flakes easily when tested with a fork or until desired degree of doneness. Repeat procedure with remaining 2 fillets. Serve with lime wedges and Cilantro-Chipotle Rice. Yield: 4 servings (serving size: 1 fillet and ½ cup rice).

CALORIES 322 (37% from fat); FAT 13g (sat 3.1g, mono 6.3g, poly 2.8g); PROTEIN 28.6g; CARB 19.1g; FIBER 2.1g; CHOL 80mg; IRON 0.9mg; SODIUM 507mg; CALC 28mg

Cilantro-Chipotle Rice
Prep: 2 minutes • Cook: 4 minutes

1 (10-ounce) package frozen brown rice
   (such as Birds Eye)
⅓ cup bottled chipotle salsa
¼ cup chopped fresh cilantro

1. Heat rice according to package directions. Transfer rice to a medium bowl. Stir in salsa and cilantro. Serve immediately. Yield: 4 servings (serving size: ½ cup).

CALORIES 85 (5% from fat); FAT 1g (sat 0.1g, mono 0.2g, poly 0.2g); PROTEIN 2.1g; CARB 17.5g; FIBER 1.6g; CHOL 0mg; IRON 0mg; SODIUM 156mg; CALC 11mg

Fresh dill contributes sharp flavor and feathery elegance to this simple flounder recipe. Since heat diminishes the potency of fresh dill, it's best to add it to the dish near the end of the suggested cooking time.

Baked Flounder with Dill and Caper Cream

Prep: 8 minutes • Cook: 12 minutes

¼ teaspoon black pepper	1 tablespoon chopped fresh dill
⅛ teaspoon salt	½ cup reduced-fat sour cream
4 (6-ounce) flounder fillets	2 tablespoons capers, drained
Cooking spray	4 lemon wedges

1. Preheat oven to 425°.

2. Sprinkle pepper and salt evenly over fillets. Place fish on a foil-lined baking sheet coated with cooking spray. Bake at 425° for 10 minutes; sprinkle evenly with dill. Bake an additional 2 minutes or until fish flakes easily when tested with a fork or until desired degree of doneness.

3. While fish bakes, combine sour cream and capers in a small bowl. Place fish on a serving plate. Squeeze 1 lemon wedge over each serving. Serve with Caper Cream. Yield: 4 servings (serving size: 1 fillet and about 2 tablespoons cream).

CALORIES 205 (25% from fat); FAT 6g (sat 2.9g, mono 0.4g, poly 0.6g); PROTEIN 33.6g; CARB 2.8g; FIBER 0.2g; CHOL 97mg; IRON 0.7mg; SODIUM 356mg; CALC 83mg

Dill Since ancient Roman times, dill has served as a symbol of vitality. Its fernlike deep green leaves enhance all kinds of foods—especially fish. Avoid leaves that look wet or wilted. Store fresh dill in a plastic bag in the refrigerator.

The delicate, subtle flavors of roasted pistachios and lavender honey transform this baked grouper into an easy, yet refined meal that family and friends will remember. Serve with sautéed spinach.

Pistachio-Crusted Grouper with Lavender Honey Sauce
Prep: 12 minutes • Cook: 12 minutes

5 tablespoons dry breadcrumbs
5 tablespoons finely chopped unsalted shelled dry-roasted pistachios
4 (6-ounce) grouper fillets
¼ teaspoon salt

¼ teaspoon freshly ground black pepper
2 large egg whites, lightly beaten
Lavender Honey Sauce
Lemon wedges (optional)
Lavender sprigs (optional)

1. Preheat oven to 450°.
2. Combine breadcrumbs and pistachios in a shallow dish. Sprinkle fillets evenly with salt and pepper. Dip fillets in egg whites; dredge in breadcrumb mixture.
3. Place fish on a jelly-roll pan lined with parchment paper; bake at 450° for 12 minutes or until fish flakes easily when tested with a fork or until desired degree of doneness. Drizzle fillets evenly with Lavender Honey Sauce. Garnish with lemon wedges and lavender sprigs, if desired. Yield: 4 servings (serving size: 1 fillet and about 1 tablespoon sauce).

CALORIES 337 (33% from fat); FAT 12g (sat 4.7g, mono 4.3g, poly 2.3g); PROTEIN 37.7g; CARB 18.1g; FIBER 1.5g; CHOL 78mg; IRON 2.4mg; SODIUM 360mg; CALC 76mg

Lavender Honey Sauce
Prep: 2 minutes • Cook: 2 minutes

2 tablespoons butter
2 tablespoons lavender honey

1 tablespoon fresh lemon juice

1. Melt butter in a small saucepan over medium heat. Add honey and lemon juice, stirring to combine. Yield: about ¼ cup (serving size: about 1 tablespoon).

CALORIES 83 (62% from fat); FAT 6g (sat 3.6g, mono 1.5g, poly 0.2g); PROTEIN 0.1g; CARB 9.1g; FIBER 0g; CHOL 15mg; IRON 0.1mg; SODIUM 41mg; CALC 3mg

En papillote is the French term for food baked in a parchment paper packet. Steam trapped inside the packet gently cooks the fish as the other ingredients meld into an intensely flavorful, chunky vegetable sauce. Serve the dish with crusty French bread.

Lemon-Artichoke Halibut en Papillote

Prep: 15 minutes • Cook: 15 minutes

4 (6-ounce) halibut fillets (about 1 inch thick)
¼ teaspoon salt
¼ teaspoon freshly ground black pepper
1 shallot, thinly sliced
¼ cup fresh salsa, divided
1 (9-ounce) package frozen artichoke hearts, thawed
1 lemon, thinly sliced

1. Preheat oven to 400°.
2. Pat fillets dry with a paper towel; sprinkle evenly with salt and pepper.
3. Cut 4 (15-inch) squares of parchment paper. Fold each square in half; open each. Divide shallot evenly among squares, placing near fold; top each with 1 fillet and 1 tablespoon salsa. Divide artichoke hearts and lemon slices evenly over fillets. Fold paper; seal edges well with narrow folds. Place packets on a baking sheet. Bake at 400° for 15 minutes or until a thermometer registers 140° to 145° when inserted through the paper into the fish. Place 1 packet on each of 4 plates; cut open. Serve immediately. Yield: 4 servings (serving size: 1 fillet and about 1 cup vegetables).

CALORIES 232 (18% from fat); FAT 5g (sat 0.6g, mono 1.3g, poly 1.3g); PROTEIN 37.3g; CARB 8.4g; FIBER 4.2g; CHOL 54mg; IRON 1.9mg; SODIUM 317mg; CALC 115mg

serve with
Zabaglione with Fresh Berries

Prep: 3 minutes • Cook: 7 minutes

2 large eggs
2 large egg yolks
½ cup sugar
½ cup sweet Marsala wine
3 cups whole mixed berries
1½ cups light canned refrigerated whipped topping (such as Reddi-wip)

1. Combine first 4 ingredients in top of a double boiler, stirring with a whisk. Cook over simmering water, whisking constantly, about 7 minutes or until a thermometer registers 160°. Serve over berries. Top each serving with whipped topping. Yield: 6 servings (serving size: about ½ cup zabaglione, ½ cup berries, and ¼ cup whipped topping).

CALORIES 200 (23% from fat); FAT 5g (sat 2.8g, mono 1.3g, poly 0.6g); PROTEIN 3.6g; CARB 32g; FIBER 1.8g; CHOL 139mg; IRON 0.9mg; SODIUM 29mg; CALC 32mg

The pungent green onions mellow as they grill. Be sure to place the onions crosswise on the grill rack. Use kitchen shears to easily cut the cooked onions into 1-inch pieces. For a quick accompaniment, grill slices of bread alongside the fish and onions.

Grilled Halibut with Onion, Spicy Tomatoes, and Avocado

Prep: 7 minutes • Cook: 8 minutes

4 (6-ounce) halibut fillets
1 bunch green onions (about 10 onions), trimmed
Cooking spray
¼ teaspoon black pepper

⅛ teaspoon salt
1 (10-ounce) can mild diced tomatoes and green chiles, undrained
1 avocado, peeled and diced
4 lime wedges

1. Prepare grill.
2. Coat fillets and onions with cooking spray. Sprinkle fish evenly with pepper and salt. Place fish and onions on grill rack coated with cooking spray; cover and grill fish 4 minutes on each side or until fish flakes easily when tested with a fork or until desired degree of doneness. Grill onions 3 minutes on each side or until charred and tender.
3. While fish and onions grill, combine tomatoes and avocado in a small bowl.
4. Cut grilled onions into 1-inch pieces. Place grilled fish on a serving plate. Top with tomato mixture; sprinkle with grilled onions. Squeeze 1 lime wedge over each serving. Yield: 4 servings (serving size: 1 fillet, ½ cup tomato topping, and about ¼ cup onions).

CALORIES 292 (36% from fat); FAT 12g (sat 1.8g, mono 6.1g, poly 2.3g); PROTEIN 37.6g; CARB 9.5g; FIBER 4.3g; CHOL 54mg; IRON 2.7mg; SODIUM 460mg; CALC 128mg

Grated lemon rind and juice lend tartness to the pesto that enhances the natural flavors of this simple grilled fish.

Halibut with Quick Lemon Pesto
Prep: 3 minutes • Cook: 8 minutes

4   (6-ounce) halibut or other firm white fish fillets
Cooking spray
¼   teaspoon salt, divided
⅛   teaspoon freshly ground black pepper
⅔   cup firmly packed basil leaves

¼   cup (1 ounce) grated fresh Parmesan cheese
2   tablespoons extra-virgin olive oil
2   garlic cloves, peeled
1   tablespoon grated lemon rind
1   tablespoon fresh lemon juice

1. Prepare grill.
2. Place fillets on grill rack coated with cooking spray. Sprinkle fish evenly with ⅛ teaspoon salt and pepper. Cover and grill 4 minutes on each side or until fish flakes easily when tested with a fork or until desired degree of doneness.
3. While fish grills, combine ⅛ teaspoon salt, basil, and remaining 5 ingredients in a blender or food processor. Process until finely minced. Serve grilled fish over pesto. Yield: 4 servings (serving size: 1 fillet and about 1 tablespoon pesto).

CALORIES 283 (41% from fat); FAT 13g (sat 2.6g, mono 6.3g, poly 2.3g); PROTEIN 38.7g; CARB 1.4g; FIBER 0.5g; CHOL 59mg; IRON 1.7mg; SODIUM 363mg; CALC 195mg

serve with
Grilled Zucchini and Red Bell Pepper with Corn
Prep: 5 minutes • Cook: 10 minutes

1   medium zucchini, halved lengthwise
1   red bell pepper, halved lengthwise and seeded
Cooking spray
1   cup frozen whole-kernel corn, thawed and drained

1½ tablespoons Parmesan and roasted garlic salad dressing (such as Newman's Own)
¼   teaspoon salt
⅛   teaspoon crushed red pepper

1. Prepare grill.
2. Coat zucchini and bell pepper halves with cooking spray; place on grill rack. Cover and grill 5 minutes on each side or until bell pepper is charred and zucchini is tender.
3. Remove vegetables from grill; cut into 1-inch pieces. Place in a medium bowl. Stir in corn and remaining 3 ingredients, tossing gently to combine. Yield: 4 servings (serving size: about ½ cup).

CALORIES 74 (32% from fat); FAT 3g (sat 0.5g, mono 0.1g, poly 0.2g); PROTEIN 2.3g; CARB 12.9g; FIBER 2.3g; CHOL 0mg; IRON 0.6mg; SODIUM 217mg; CALC 11mg

When breading the fish, use one hand for the dry mixture and the other hand for the wet, so you don't lose any panko crumbs. Serve with steamed asparagus tossed with grated lemon rind.

Sunflower Seed–Crusted Orange Roughy

Prep: 8 minutes • Cook: 10 minutes • Other: 10 minutes

2 large egg whites
½ teaspoon freshly ground black pepper
½ teaspoon grated lemon rind
½ cup Italian-seasoned panko (Japanese breadcrumbs)
3 tablespoons unsalted sunflower seed kernels

4 (6-ounce) orange roughy fillets (about ½ inch thick)
Cooking spray
Lemon slices (optional)

1. Preheat oven to 475°. Place a jelly-roll pan in oven while preheating.
2. Combine first 3 ingredients in a medium bowl; stir with a whisk until foamy. Combine panko and sunflower seed kernels in a shallow dish. Dip fillets in egg white mixture; dredge in panko mixture. Place fish on a wire rack; let stand 10 minutes.
3. Remove jelly-roll pan from oven; coat pan with cooking spray. Coat fish with cooking spray; place on pan. Bake at 475° for 10 minutes or until fish flakes easily when tested with a fork or until desired degree of doneness. Serve with lemon slices, if desired. Yield: 4 servings (serving size: 1 fillet).

CALORIES 206 (20% from fat); FAT 4g (sat 0.3g, mono 1g, poly 2.2g); PROTEIN 31.5g; CARB 9.1g; FIBER 1.7g; CHOL 102mg; IRON 2.4mg; SODIUM 212mg; CALC 21mg

Asparagus When selecting asparagus, reach for green instead of white. The green variety is higher in vitamins A and C and in folate. Choose asparagus spears with tight, compact tips and a similar diameter so they'll all cook at the same rate.

The sweet, salty, and spicy flavors of this colorful glaze permeate the salmon as it cooks, creating a succulent dish that tantalizes the taste buds.

Chili-Garlic Glazed Salmon

Prep: 4 minutes • Cook: 7 minutes

3 tablespoons chili sauce with garlic (such as Hokan)
3 tablespoons minced green onions (about 3 green onions)
1½ tablespoons low-sugar orange marmalade
¾ teaspoon low-sodium soy sauce
4 (6-ounce) salmon fillets
Cooking spray

1. Preheat broiler.
2. Combine first 4 ingredients in a small bowl; brush half of chili sauce mixture over fillets. Place fillets, skin sides down, on a baking sheet coated with cooking spray. Broil fish 5 minutes; brush with remaining chili sauce mixture. Broil 2 more minutes or until fish flakes easily when tested with a fork or until desired degree of doneness. Yield: 4 servings (serving size: 1 fillet).

CALORIES 298 (40% from fat); FAT 13g (sat 3.1g, mono 5.7g, poly 3.2g); PROTEIN 36.3g; CARB 5.6g; FIBER 0.5g; CHOL 87mg; IRON 0.6mg; SODIUM 171mg; CALC 23mg

serve with
Minted Sugar Snap Peas

Prep: 2 minutes • Cook: 3 minutes

1 teaspoon canola oil
1 (8-ounce) package fresh sugar snap peas
1 tablespoon chopped fresh mint
1 teaspoon grated orange rind
¼ teaspoon salt

1. Heat oil in a large nonstick skillet over medium-high heat; add peas. Sauté 2 minutes or just until peas are crisp-tender. Stir in mint, orange rind, and salt. Yield: 4 servings (serving size: ½ cup).

CALORIES 38 (28% from fat); FAT 1g (sat 0.1g, mono 0.7g, poly 0.4g); PROTEIN 1.4g; CARB 4.9g; FIBER 1.4g; CHOL 0mg; IRON 0.8mg; SODIUM 152mg; CALC 42mg

Applewood-smoked bacon imbues this upscale version of succotash with its sweet, smoky essence. Green soybeans replace the traditional limas.

Seared Salmon Fillets with Edamame Succotash

Prep: 1 minute • Cook: 14 minutes

3 applewood-smoked bacon slices
4 (6-ounce) salmon fillets (about 1 inch thick)
¼ teaspoon salt
¼ teaspoon freshly ground black pepper
¼ cup water
1 (8-ounce) container refrigerated prechopped tomato, onion, and bell pepper mix

1 cup frozen yellow and white whole-kernel corn
1 cup frozen shelled edamame (green soybeans)
½ teaspoon dried thyme
⅛ teaspoon salt

1. Cook bacon in a large nonstick skillet over medium heat 7 minutes or until crisp.
2. While bacon cooks, sprinkle fillets evenly with ¼ teaspoon salt and black pepper. When bacon is done, transfer it to paper towels to drain; crumble bacon.
3. Add fillets, skin sides up, to drippings in pan. Cook 4 minutes over medium-high heat or until browned. Turn fish over; add crumbled bacon, ¼ cup water, and remaining ingredients to pan. Cover and steam 3 minutes or until fish flakes easily when tested with a fork or until desired degree of doneness. Serve fillets over succotash. Yield: 4 servings (serving size: 1 fillet and about ¾ cup succotash).

CALORIES 397 (42% from fat); FAT 19g (sat 4.7g, mono 6g, poly 3.4g); PROTEIN 43.3g; CARB 13.7g; FIBER 3.2g; CHOL 95mg; IRON 1.6mg; SODIUM 468mg; CALC 49mg

Edamame Fresh soybeans (edamame) are packed with potential health benefits. Each ½-cup serving contains 4 grams of fiber and only 3 grams of fat, all of which are the heart-healthy mono- and polyunsaturated kind. The beans are also high in soy protein, which may help reduce cholesterol when part of a low-fat diet.

The addition of Balsamic Grilled Peaches makes this menu exceptional. Simply grill the peach halves alongside the fish to quickly caramelize their natural sugars. The mahogany-hued balsamic glaze pools in the center of the peaches, and a sprinkle of blue cheese provides a sharp flavor contrast.

Peach-Glazed Salmon with Raspberries

Prep: 5 minutes • Cook: 11 minutes

½ cup peach spread (such as Polaner
  All Fruit)
1½ tablespoons dark brown sugar
2 tablespoons balsamic vinegar
⅛ teaspoon crushed red pepper

1 cup fresh raspberries
4 (6-ounce) salmon fillets
¼ teaspoon salt
Cooking spray

1. Prepare grill.
2. Combine peach spread and next 3 ingredients in a medium saucepan over medium-high heat; cook 2 minutes, stirring frequently. Reserve 2 tablespoons sauce. Add raspberries to pan; cook over medium heat 1 minute, stirring gently.
3. Sprinkle fish evenly with salt. Place fish, skin sides up, on grill rack coated with cooking spray; grill 4 minutes. Turn fish over; grill 4 minutes or until fish flakes easily when tested with a fork, basting with reserved 2 tablespoons sauce. Spoon raspberry sauce evenly over fillets. Yield: 4 servings (serving size: 1 fillet and ¼ cup sauce).

CALORIES 391 (30% from fat); FAT 13g (sat 3.1g, mono 5.7g, poly 3.2g); PROTEIN 36.5g; CARB 30.7g; FIBER 0g; CHOL 87mg; IRON 0.8mg; SODIUM 229mg; CALC 32mg

serve with
Balsamic Grilled Peaches

Prep: 2 minutes • Cook: 6 minutes

2 large firm ripe peaches, halved and pitted
Cooking spray
3 tablespoons balsamic glaze, divided

4 tablespoons crumbled blue cheese
¼ teaspoon freshly ground black pepper

1. Prepare grill.
2. Place peaches, cut sides down, on grill rack coated with cooking spray, and grill 3 minutes. Turn peaches; brush tops and sides with 2 tablespoons glaze. Grill 3 minutes or until tender. Sprinkle with cheese and pepper; drizzle with 1 table-spoon glaze. Yield: 4 servings (serving size: 1 peach half and 1 tablespoon cheese).

CALORIES 86 (30% from fat); FAT 3g (sat 1.8g, mono 0.1g, poly 0.1g); PROTEIN 2.8g; CARB 13.4g; FIBER 1.5g; CHOL 9mg; IRON 0.2mg; SODIUM 134mg; CALC 49mg

Peaches To get the best, freshest peaches, scout local orchards and farmers' markets. Look for golden peaches without traces of green near the stem.

Fennel bulb, when eaten raw in salads, has a subtle licorice flavor and crisp texture. When cooked, it mellows and softens. In this recipe the sautéed fennel combines with the piquant tapenade to create a saucy and savory vegetable topping for the fish. Serve over rice.

Pan-Seared Snapper with Fennel-Olive Topping
Prep: 6 minutes • Cook: 13 minutes

4 (6-ounce) red snapper or other firm white fish fillets
½ teaspoon salt
¼ teaspoon freshly ground black pepper
Cooking spray

1 fennel bulb, thinly sliced (about 3½ cups)
½ cup thinly sliced onion
1 large tomato, chopped
3 tablespoons refrigerated olive tapenade
2 tablespoons fresh lemon juice

1. Sprinkle fillets evenly with salt and pepper. Heat a large nonstick skillet over medium-high heat; coat pan and fillets with cooking spray. Add fish to pan, skin sides up. Cook 3 minutes or until lightly browned. Remove from pan.
2. Coat pan with cooking spray. Add fennel and onion; sauté 3 minutes. Add tomato, tapenade, and lemon juice; stir well. Return fillets to pan, nestling them into fennel mixture. Cover and cook 7 minutes or until fish flakes easily when tested with a fork or until desired degree of doneness. Spoon fennel mixture over fillets to serve. Yield: 4 servings (serving size: 1 fillet and ¾ cup fennel topping).

CALORIES 238 (22% from fat); FAT 6g (sat 1.3g, mono 0.4g, poly 0.8g); PROTEIN 37g; CARB 8.9g; FIBER 3.4g; CHOL 63mg; IRON 1.4mg; SODIUM 545mg; CALC 107mg

Fennel Look for small, heavy, white fennel bulbs that are firm and free of cracks, browning, or moist areas. The stalks should be crisp, with feathery, bright green fronds. Store fennel bulbs in a perforated plastic bag in the refrigerator for up to five days. After five days, the bulbs begin to toughen and lose flavor.

A fragrant herbed butter and roasted lemon slices complement the sweet, nutty flavor of red snapper for a super-fresh dish. Complete the meal with colorful Sautéed Zucchini and Bell Peppers.

Lemon Red Snapper with Herbed Butter
Prep: 9 minutes • Cook: 13 minutes

2 lemons
Cooking spray
4 (6-ounce) red snapper or other firm white fish fillets
¼ teaspoon salt
¼ teaspoon paprika
¼ teaspoon black pepper
2 tablespoons butter, softened
1½ teaspoons chopped fresh herbs (such as rosemary, thyme, basil, or parsley)
Fresh herb sprigs (optional)

1. Preheat oven to 425°.
2. Cut 1 lemon into 8 slices. Place slices, in pairs, on a rimmed baking sheet coated with cooking spray. Grate remaining lemon to get 1 teaspoon lemon rind; set aside. Reserve lemon for another use.
3. Place 1 fillet on top of each pair of lemon slices. Combine salt, paprika, and pepper; sprinkle evenly over fish. Bake at 425° for 13 minutes or until fish flakes easily when tested with a fork or until desired degree of doneness.
4. While fish bakes, combine reserved lemon rind, butter, and herbs in a small bowl.
5. Place fish and lemon slices on individual serving plates; top each fillet with herbed butter, spreading to melt, if desired. Garnish with herb sprigs, if desired. Yield: 4 servings (serving size: 1 fillet and about 1½ teaspoons herbed butter).

CALORIES 223 (32% from fat); FAT 8g (sat 4.1g, mono 1.9g, poly 1g); PROTEIN 34g; CARB 2.9g; FIBER 0.9g; CHOL 75mg; IRON 0.5mg; SODIUM 259mg; CALC 62mg

serve with
Sautéed Zucchini and Bell Peppers
Prep: 3 minutes • Cook: 7 minutes

1 teaspoon olive oil
1 medium zucchini, quartered lengthwise and cut into 2-inch pieces
1 cup refrigerated prechopped tricolor bell pepper
1 garlic clove, minced
¼ teaspoon salt

1. Heat oil in a large nonstick skillet over medium-high heat. Add zucchini and remaining ingredients; sauté 7 minutes. Yield: 4 servings (serving size: ½ cup).

CALORIES 28 (42% from fat); FAT 1g (sat 0.2g, mono 0.8g, poly 0.2g); PROTEIN 1.1g; CARB 3.9g; FIBER 0.8g; CHOL 0mg; IRON 0.4mg; SODIUM 148mg; CALC 14mg

Louisiana hot sauce is not as spicy as other hot sauces. Use a hotter sauce if you prefer more heat.

Spicy Louisiana Tilapia Fillets with Sautéed Vegetable Relish
Prep: 5 minutes • Cook: 10 minutes

Cooking spray
1 (8-ounce) container refrigerated prechopped tomato, onion, and bell pepper mix
4 (6-ounce) tilapia fillets

2 tablespoons water
2 teaspoons Louisiana hot sauce
1½ teaspoons chopped fresh thyme
½ teaspoon salt
1 tablespoon butter

1. Heat a large nonstick skillet over medium-high heat; coat pan with cooking spray. Add tomato mixture; sauté 2 minutes. Remove from pan.
2. Coat pan and fillets with cooking spray; add fish to pan. Cook 2 minutes or until lightly browned. Turn fillets over; add tomato mixture to pan, spooning mixture over and around fillets. Cover and cook 5 minutes or until fish flakes easily when tested with a fork or until desired degree of doneness.
3. While fish cooks, combine 2 tablespoons water, hot sauce, thyme, and salt in a small bowl.
4. Carefully remove fish and tomato mixture from pan; place on a serving platter. Reduce heat to medium; add hot sauce mixture and butter to pan. Cook until butter melts. Spoon butter mixture evenly over fish and tomato mixture. Yield: 4 servings (serving size: 1 fillet and about ¼ cup tomato mixture).

CALORIES 210 (25% from fat); FAT 6g (sat 2.8g, mono 1.6g, poly 0.8g); PROTEIN 35g; CARB 4.8g; FIBER 1.4g; CHOL 93mg; IRON 1.4mg; SODIUM 465mg; CALC 34mg

serve with
Hoppin' John–Style Rice
Prep: 4 minutes • Cook: 4 minutes

2 teaspoons olive oil
¼ cup finely chopped green onions
1 garlic clove, minced
1 (15.8-ounce) can black-eyed peas, rinsed and drained

1 (8.8-ounce) pouch microwaveable cooked brown rice (such as Uncle Ben's Ready Rice)

1. Heat oil in a large nonstick skillet over medium-high heat; add onions and garlic. Sauté 30 seconds or until lightly browned. Add peas; cook 2 minutes or until thoroughly heated.
2. While peas cook, microwave rice according to package directions.
3. Add rice to pea mixture; toss well. Yield: 4 servings (serving size: ¾ cup).

CALORIES 176 (23% from fat); FAT 5g (sat 0.7g, mono 1.7g, poly 0.5g); PROTEIN 5.8g; CARB 28.6g; FIBER 3.4g; CHOL 0mg; IRON 1.1mg; SODIUM 131mg; CALC 20mg

Reminiscent of a restaurant-style fish amandine, this recipe easily doubles to serve a small dinner party. Almonds add such a rich, nutty flavor to the tilapia that even the pickiest eater will think it is delicious. Serve with green beans and Mashed Red Potatoes with Chives.

Almond-Crusted Tilapia

Prep: 5 minutes • Cook: 6 minutes

¼ cup whole natural almonds
2 tablespoons dry breadcrumbs
1 teaspoon salt-free garlic and herb seasoning blend (such as Mrs. Dash)
⅛ teaspoon freshly ground black pepper
1 tablespoon canola oil
1 tablespoon Dijon mustard
2 (6-ounce) tilapia fillets
Chopped fresh parsley (optional)

1. Place first 4 ingredients in a blender or food processor; process 45 seconds or until finely ground. Transfer crumb mixture to a shallow dish.
2. Heat oil in a large nonstick skillet over medium heat. Brush mustard over both sides of fillets; dredge in crumb mixture. Add fish to pan; cook 3 minutes on each side or until fish flakes easily when tested with a fork or until desired degree of doneness. Sprinkle with parsley, if desired. Yield: 2 servings (serving size: 1 fillet).

CALORIES 367 (47% from fat); FAT 19g (sat 2.1g, mono 10.6g, poly 4.8g); PROTEIN 38.9g; CARB 9.9g; FIBER 2.5g; CHOL 85mg; IRON 1.3mg; SODIUM 321mg; CALC 28mg

serve with
Mashed Red Potatoes with Chives

Prep: 1 minute • Cook: 8 minutes

1 red potato (about ½ pound)
1 garlic clove, minced
2 tablespoons reduced-fat sour cream
1½ tablespoons fat-free milk
1 tablespoon yogurt-based spread (such as Brummel and Brown)
⅛ teaspoon salt
⅛ teaspoon freshly ground black pepper
½ tablespoon minced fresh chives

1. Scrub potato; place in a medium-sized microwave-safe bowl (do not pierce potato with a fork). Cover bowl with plastic wrap (do not allow plastic wrap to touch food); vent. Microwave at HIGH 8 minutes or until tender.
2. Add garlic and next 5 ingredients to potatoes. Mash to desired consistency. Stir in chives. Yield: 2 servings (serving size: about ½ cup).

CALORIES 120 (27% from fat); FAT 4g (sat 1.1g, mono 0g, poly 0.1g); PROTEIN 3.0g; CARB 20g; FIBER 2g; CHOL 4mg; IRON 1mg; SODIUM 208mg; CALC 41mg

Squeeze a lemon wedge over the fish before drizzling with olive oil to tie together the components of this dish. Any thin white fillets, such as sole or flounder, can be substituted for tilapia.

Tilapia with Warm Olive Salsa

Prep: 3 minutes • Cook: 9 minutes

Cooking spray
1 cup chopped plum tomato (about ⅓ pound)
12 small pimiento-stuffed olives, chopped
2 tablespoons chopped fresh parsley
1½ teaspoons chopped fresh oregano, divided

4 (6-ounce) tilapia fillets, rinsed and patted dry
¼ teaspoon salt
¼ teaspoon freshly ground black pepper
4 lemon wedges
1 tablespoon extra-virgin olive oil

1. Heat a large nonstick skillet over medium-high heat. Coat pan with cooking spray. Add tomato; cook 1 minute or until thoroughly heated. Combine cooked tomato, olives, parsley, and ¾ teaspoon oregano in a small bowl; keep warm.
2. Wipe pan dry with a paper towel; return pan to medium-high heat. Recoat pan with cooking spray. Sprinkle fillets evenly with ¾ teaspoon oregano, salt, and pepper. Add fillets to pan; cook 3 minutes on each side or until fish flakes easily when tested with a fork or until desired degree of doneness. Squeeze 1 lemon wedge over each fillet; drizzle each evenly with oil. Top evenly with olive salsa. Yield: 4 servings (serving size: 1 fillet and ¼ cup olive salsa).

CALORIES 218 (32% from fat); FAT 8g (sat 1.7g, mono 4.5g, poly 1.1g); PROTEIN 34.8g; CARB 3.1g; FIBER 1g; CHOL 85mg; IRON 1.4mg; SODIUM 485mg; CALC 36mg

serve with
Lemon Couscous with Toasted Pine Nuts

Prep: 3 minutes • Cook: 5 minutes • Other: 5 minutes

1 cup water
⅔ cup uncooked whole wheat couscous
1 teaspoon grated lemon rind

¼ cup pine nuts, toasted
2 teaspoons extra-virgin olive oil
¼ teaspoon salt

1. Bring 1 cup water to a boil in a small saucepan. Stir in couscous and lemon rind. Remove from heat; cover and let stand 5 minutes. Add pine nuts and remaining ingredients; fluff with a fork. Yield: 4 servings (serving size: about ½ cup).

CALORIES 148 (52% from fat); FAT 8g (sat 0.7g, mono 3.4g, poly 3.1g); PROTEIN 3.8g; CARB 16.2g; FIBER 2.7g; CHOL 0mg; IRON 1.1mg; SODIUM 146mg; CALC 9mg

Steelhead, also known as ocean trout, is a fine choice for its bright pink color and rich flavor, but any trout can be used.

Pan-Seared Tarragon Trout
Prep: 7 minutes • Cook: 8 minutes

1 lemon
2 tablespoons all-purpose flour
2 (6-ounce) trout fillets
¼ teaspoon salt
¼ teaspoon freshly ground black pepper

1 tablespoon butter
1 garlic clove, minced
¼ cup dry white wine
1 teaspoon dried tarragon

1. Zest and juice lemon, reserving ¼ teaspoon zest and 1 teaspoon juice.
2. Place flour in a shallow dish. Sprinkle fish evenly with salt and pepper; dredge fish in flour.
3. Melt butter in a large nonstick skillet over medium-high heat. Add fish; cook 2 to 3 minutes on each side or until fish flakes easily when tested with a fork or until desired degree of doneness. Remove fish from pan; keep warm.
4. Add garlic to pan; sauté 1 minute or until browned. Add wine; cook until liquid almost evaporates, scraping pan to loosen browned bits. Stir in tarragon and reserved lemon zest and juice. Pour garlic sauce over fish. Yield: 2 servings (serving size: 1 fillet and about 1 tablespoon sauce).

CALORIES 293 (36% from fat); FAT 12g (sat 4.8g, mono 3.4g, poly 2.4g); PROTEIN 36g; CARB 6.2g; FIBER 0.4g; CHOL 115mg; IRON 1.8mg; SODIUM 385mg; CALC 133mg

serve with
Fig, Carrot, and Ginger Rice Pilaf
Prep: 4 minutes • Cook: 5 minutes

1 (8.8-ounce) pouch microwaveable cooked brown rice (such as Uncle Ben's Ready Rice)
1 tablespoon olive oil

1 cup matchstick-cut carrots
1 tablespoon minced peeled fresh ginger
2 garlic cloves, minced
½ cup small dried figs, quartered

1. Heat rice according to package directions; keep warm.
2. While rice cooks, heat oil in a large nonstick skillet over medium-high heat; add carrots, ginger, and garlic. Sauté 3 minutes or until browned. Add figs; sauté 2 minutes or until hot. Remove from heat; stir in rice. Serve immediately. Yield: 4 servings (serving size: about ½ cup).

CALORIES 217 (24% from fat); FAT 6g (sat 0.8g, mono 2.6g, poly 0.6g); PROTEIN 3.7g; CARB 39.8g; FIBER 4.3g; CHOL 0mg; IRON 1mg; SODIUM 24mg; CALC 52mg

The sesame seeds tend to pop out of the skillet as the tuna cooks, so use caution and wear an oven mitt when you turn over the fish.

Seared Sesame Tuna with Orange-Ginger Sauce

Prep: 7 minutes • Cook: 7 minutes

1 garlic clove, minced
3 tablespoons orange-ginger sauce and glaze (such as Iron Chef)
1 tablespoon seasoned rice vinegar
1 teaspoon low-sodium soy sauce
½ teaspoon dark sesame oil
2 teaspoons canola oil

4 (6-ounce) tuna steaks (about 1 inch thick)
⅛ teaspoon salt
3 tablespoons sesame seeds
3 tablespoons black sesame seeds
Cooking spray
¼ cup sliced green onions

1. Combine first 5 ingredients, stirring well with a whisk; set aside.
2. Heat canola oil in a large nonstick skillet over medium-high heat. Sprinkle steaks evenly with salt. Combine sesame seeds and black sesame seeds in a shallow dish. Dredge steaks in sesame seeds. Lightly coat both sides of fish with cooking spray. Add fish to pan; cook 3 minutes on each side or until desired degree of doneness. Sprinkle evenly with onions; serve with orange-ginger sauce. Yield: 4 servings (serving size: 1 steak and 1½ tablespoons sauce).

CALORIES 317 (32% from fat); FAT 11g (sat 1.6g, mono 4.2g, poly 4.1g); PROTEIN 42.3g; CARB 10.4g; FIBER 1.9g; CHOL 77mg; IRON 3.3mg; SODIUM 302mg; CALC 165mg

serve with
Edamame and Corn Salad

Prep: 7 minutes

¼ cup seasoned rice vinegar
2 tablespoons water
1 tablespoon olive oil
1 teaspoon brown sugar
1 teaspoon minced peeled fresh ginger
⅛ teaspoon salt

1 (10-ounce) package refrigerated shelled edamame (green soybeans)
1 cup frozen whole-kernel corn, thawed and drained
1 tablespoon chopped fresh cilantro

1. Combine first 6 ingredients in a medium bowl, stirring well with a whisk. Add edamame, corn, and cilantro; toss gently to coat. Yield: 4 servings (serving size: ⅔ cup).

CALORIES 156 (41% from fat); FAT 7g (sat 0.5g, mono 2.6g, poly 0.6g); PROTEIN 8.4g; CARB 17.7g; FIBER 4.3g; CHOL 0mg; IRON 1.7mg; SODIUM 376mg; CALC 45mg

The pickled ginger adds a sweet, spicy bite to the cucumber relish. Prepare the relish while the tuna grills. Make a quick side by steaming snow peas in the microwave. Serve with Wasabi Ice Cream with Honey (page 267) for a delightful end to this Asian-inspired meal.

Grilled Tuna Steaks with Cucumber–Pickled Ginger Relish

Prep: 9 minutes • Cook: 6 minutes

4 (6-ounce) tuna steaks (about 1 inch thick)
1 tablespoon canola oil
½ teaspoon black pepper
¼ teaspoon salt
Cooking spray
1 cup diced seeded peeled cucumber

6 tablespoons finely chopped red onion
6 tablespoons pickled ginger, coarsely chopped
3 tablespoons chopped fresh cilantro
1½ tablespoons fresh lime juice

1. Prepare grill.
2. Brush steaks with oil; sprinkle evenly with pepper and salt. Place fish on grill rack coated with cooking spray; grill 3 minutes on each side or until medium-rare or until desired degree of doneness.
3. While fish cooks, combine cucumber and remaining 4 ingredients in a medium bowl, tossing well. Serve relish over fish. Yield: 4 servings (serving size: 1 steak and about ⅓ cup relish).

CALORIES 257 (18% from fat); FAT 5g (sat 0.7g, mono 2.3g, poly 1.5g); PROTEIN 40.2g; CARB 8.8g; FIBER 1g; CHOL 77mg; IRON 1.6mg; SODIUM 360mg; CALC 49mg

Cool cucumber aïoli puts out the fire of the Thai spices in these tuna cakes. Although the cakes are portioned as a main dish, you can also form eight smaller appetizer cakes when entertaining guests.

Spicy Thai Tuna Cakes with Cucumber Aïoli
Prep: 10 minutes • Cook: 2 minutes

3 (5-ounce) cans Thai chili-flavored tuna (such as Bumble Bee), drained
1 large egg white, lightly beaten
½ cup panko (Japanese breadcrumbs)
2 tablespoons chopped fresh cilantro
Cooking spray
½ cup shredded cucumber
¼ cup light mayonnaise

1. Combine first 4 ingredients in a medium bowl. Divide tuna mixture into 4 equal portions, shaping each into a ¾-inch-thick patty.
2. Heat a large nonstick skillet over medium heat. Coat pan and patties with cooking spray. Add patties; cook 1 to 2 minutes on each side or until lightly browned.
3. While patties cook, combine cucumber and mayonnaise in a small bowl. Serve with tuna cakes. Yield: 4 servings (serving size: 1 cake and 2 tablespoons aïoli).

CALORIES 173 (47% from fat); FAT 9g (sat 1.2g, mono 3.8g, poly 3.6g); PROTEIN 10.1g; CARB 11.9g; FIBER 0.9g; CHOL 26mg; IRON 0.8mg; SODIUM 413mg; CALC 4mg

serve with
Orange and Radish Cabbage Slaw
Prep: 6 minutes

4 cups shredded napa (Chinese) cabbage
½ cup sliced radishes (about 3 radishes)
⅓ cup orange sections (about 1 small orange)
2 tablespoons rice vinegar
1 tablespoon canola oil
2 teaspoons sugar
1 teaspoon dark sesame oil

1. Combine first 3 ingredients in a large bowl.
2. Combine vinegar and remaining 3 ingredients in a small bowl, stirring well with a whisk. Pour vinegar mixture over cabbage mixture; toss gently to coat. Yield: 4 servings (serving size: 1¼ cups).

CALORIES 76 (56% from fat); FAT 5g (sat 0.4g, mono 2.1g, poly 1g); PROTEIN 1.2g; CARB 8g; FIBER 1.6g; CHOL 0mg; IRON 0mg; SODIUM 11mg; CALC 70mg

Pay close attention to the clams when scrubbing them. If some are opened slightly, give them a gentle tap. If they close, they're fine; if they don't, discard them. If any clams remain closed after they have cooked, discard them as well.

Fresh Garlic Linguine with Clams

Prep: 3 minutes • Cook: 8 minutes

1 (9-ounce) package refrigerated linguine or angel hair pasta
2 teaspoons olive oil
4 garlic cloves, minced
½ cup chopped bottled roasted red bell peppers

24 littleneck clams, scrubbed
¼ cup dry white wine
⅓ cup finely chopped fresh parsley, divided
¾ cup (3 ounces) grated Asiago cheese, divided

1. Cook pasta according to package directions, omitting salt and fat. Drain, reserving ¼ cup pasta water.

2. While pasta cooks, heat oil in a large nonstick skillet over medium-high heat. Add garlic and bell peppers. Cook 1 minute, stirring constantly. Add clams and wine. Cover and cook 3 to 4 minutes or until shells open.

3. Add pasta and half of parsley to clams in pan, tossing well to blend. Add reserved ¼ cup pasta water and half of cheese, tossing well to blend. Sprinkle remaining parsley and cheese evenly over each serving. Yield: 4 servings (serving size: 6 clams and 1 cup pasta).

CALORIES 339 (28% from fat); FAT 11g (sat 4.9g, mono 3.3g, poly 0.7g); PROTEIN 20.8g; CARB 38.1g; FIBER 1.7g; CHOL 75mg; IRON 9.3mg; SODIUM 155mg; CALC 258mg

Garlic The most pungent of all alliums, garlic becomes stronger in taste the more it is chopped or minced. Be careful when you sauté garlic. If burned, garlic will add an acrid, bitter flavor to the finished dish.

A hot skillet is key to a deep golden sear on the scallops. Prepare the Warm Fruit Salsa in the same skillet as the scallops for an easy one-pan cleanup. Jasmine rice rounds out the meal.

Seared Scallops with Warm Fruit Salsa
Prep: 2 minutes • Cook: 8 minutes

12 large sea scallops (about 1¼ pounds)
Cooking spray
¼ teaspoon freshly ground black pepper
⅛ teaspoon salt
Warm Fruit Salsa
4 teaspoons sliced green onions

1. Pat scallops dry with paper towels. Heat a large nonstick skillet over medium-high heat. Coat pan with cooking spray. Sprinkle scallops evenly with pepper and salt. Add scallops to pan; cook 3 minutes on each side or until done. Remove scallops from pan; keep warm.
2. Prepare Warm Fruit Salsa.
3. Discard any accumulated juices from scallops; top evenly with Warm Fruit Salsa and onions. Serve immediately. Yield: 4 servings (serving size: 3 scallops and about ⅔ cup salsa).

CALORIES 202 (16% from fat); FAT 4g (sat 0.5g, mono 1.7g, poly 0.8g); PROTEIN 24.9g; CARB 17.7g; FIBER 2.2g; CHOL 47mg; IRON 1mg; SODIUM 394mg; CALC 52mg

Warm Fruit Salsa
Prep: 8 minutes • Cook: 4 minutes

2 teaspoons olive oil
1 garlic clove, minced
2 cups diced pineapple
1¼ cups chopped red bell pepper
¼ cup green tea with mango (such as Snapple)
2 teaspoons low-sodium soy sauce
1 tablespoon chopped fresh mint

1. Heat oil in a large nonstick skillet over medium-high heat. Add garlic; sauté 1 minute. Stir in pineapple and next 3 ingredients, scraping pan to loosen browned bits; cook 3 minutes. Stir in mint. Yield: 2¾ cups (serving size: about ⅔ cup).

CALORIES 77 (30% from fat); FAT 3g (sat 0.4g, mono 1.7g, poly 0.4g); PROTEIN 1.1g; CARB 14.3g; FIBER 2.2g; CHOL 0mg; IRON 1mg; SODIUM 166mg; CALC 18mg

Pat the scallops dry with a paper towel to remove any excess moisture before searing. This step ensures a nicely browned exterior.

Scallops in Buttery Wine Sauce
Prep: 1 minute • Cook: 12 minutes

1½ pounds large sea scallops	¼ teaspoon salt
1 tablespoon olive oil	1 tablespoon butter
½ cup dry white wine	Freshly ground black pepper (optional)
1½ teaspoons chopped fresh tarragon	

1. Pat scallops dry with paper towels. Heat oil in a large nonstick skillet over medium-high heat; add scallops. Cook 3 minutes on each side or until done. Transfer scallops to a serving platter; keep warm.

2. Add white wine, tarragon, and salt to pan, scraping pan to loosen browned bits. Boil 1 minute. Remove from heat; add butter, stirring until butter melts. Pour sauce over scallops. Sprinkle with pepper, if desired; serve immediately. Yield: 4 servings (serving size: about 3 scallops and about 1 tablespoon sauce).

CALORIES 225 (30% from fat); FAT 8g (sat 2.4g, mono 3.3g, poly 1.1g); PROTEIN 28.6g; CARB 4.7g; FIBER 0g; CHOL 64mg; IRON 0.6mg; SODIUM 441mg; CALC 45mg

serve with
Asparagus with Feta and Oregano
Prep: 2 minutes • Cook: 4 minutes

1 cup water	1½ teaspoons chopped fresh oregano
1 pound asparagus spears, trimmed	¼ teaspoon salt
1 teaspoon extra-virgin olive oil	3 tablespoons crumbled feta cheese

1. Bring 1 cup water to a boil in a large nonstick skillet; add asparagus. Cover, reduce heat, and simmer 4 to 5 minutes or until asparagus is crisp-tender. Drain well; place on a serving platter. Drizzle oil over asparagus. Sprinkle with oregano and salt; toss well. Sprinkle with cheese. Yield: 4 servings (serving size: ¼ of asparagus spears).

CALORIES 40 (45% from fat); FAT 2g (sat 0.7g, mono 0.8g, poly 0.2g); PROTEIN 2.7g; CARB 3.1g; FIBER 1.6g; CHOL 2mg; IRON 1.5mg; SODIUM 222mg; CALC 35mg

Always request dry-packed sea scallops. They tend to be fresher and haven't been soaked in water to increase their weight. Serve these scallops over hot cooked angel hair pasta.

Scallops with Capers and Tomatoes
Prep: 5 minutes • Cook: 7 minutes

12 large sea scallops (about 1½ pounds)
Cooking spray
 1 garlic clove, minced
 ½ cup dry white wine
 1 tomato, seeded and diced (about 1 cup)

3 tablespoons capers, drained
2 tablespoons chopped fresh basil
¼ teaspoon salt
1 tablespoon extra-virgin olive oil

1. Pat scallops dry with paper towels. Heat a large nonstick skillet over medium-high heat. Coat pan with cooking spray. Add scallops to pan; cook 3 minutes on each side or until done. Remove scallops from pan; keep warm.
2. Add garlic to pan; cook 15 seconds. Add wine and next 4 ingredients to pan. Spoon mixture over scallops; drizzle evenly with oil just before serving. Yield: 4 servings (serving size: 3 scallops and ⅓ cup sauce).

CALORIES 212 (21% from fat); FAT 5g (sat 0.7g, mono 2.8g, poly 0.8g); PROTEIN 29.1g; CARB 6.8g; FIBER 0.7g; CHOL 56mg; IRON 0.8mg; SODIUM 614mg; CALC 53mg

Capers Capers add a bold, distinctly briny flavor to food—and a little can go a long way. You'll find capers in the condiment section of your supermarket.

The bright, tart flavor of freshly squeezed lime juice balances the heat of the chili powder in the rich sauce that coats these shrimp. Serve with crusty whole wheat French bread to soak up the sauce.

Chili-Lime Shrimp

Prep: 4 minutes • Cook: 6 minutes

Cooking spray
¾ cup chopped green onions, divided
1½ pounds peeled and deveined large shrimp
1 teaspoon chili powder

2 tablespoons fresh lime juice (about 1 lime)
2 tablespoons butter
½ teaspoon salt

1. Heat a large nonstick skillet over medium-high heat. Coat pan with cooking spray. Add ½ cup onions; coat onions with cooking spray. Cook 1 minute, stirring occasionally. Add shrimp and chili powder; cook 4 minutes or until desired degree of doneness, stirring occasionally. Remove from heat. Add lime juice, butter, and salt, and stir until butter melts. Sprinkle with ¼ cup onions. Yield: 4 servings (serving size: 1 cup).

CALORIES 186 (34% from fat); FAT 7g (sat 4g, mono 1.7g, poly 0.8g); PROTEIN 27.5g; CARB 2g; FIBER 0.5g; CHOL 267mg; IRON 4.3mg; SODIUM 644mg; CALC 67mg

Limes Persian limes, which have dark green skins, are the variety of limes you see most often at the supermarket. In addition to being smaller and slightly more delicate than lemons, limes are also more perishable. The best way to store them is in a plastic bag in the refrigerator up to 1½ weeks. Exposure to light and air decreases the tartness of the juice.

An authentic Greek trio of tomatoes, olives, and feta cheese accompanies this shrimp dish. Serve over orzo, and garnish with lemon wedges, if desired.

Greek-Style Shrimp Sauté
Prep: 2 minutes • Cook: 6 minutes

Cooking spray
4 tablespoons light olive oil vinaigrette, divided (such as Ken's Steak House Lite)
1½ pounds peeled and deveined large shrimp
1 cup grape tomatoes, halved

12 chopped pitted kalamata olives
¼ cup chopped fresh basil
1½ ounces crumbled reduced-fat feta cheese
Chopped fresh basil (optional)
Lemon wedges (optional)

1. Heat a large nonstick skillet over medium-high heat. Coat pan with cooking spray. Add 1 tablespoon vinaigrette and shrimp. Cook shrimp 3 minutes or until done, stirring frequently.
2. Remove shrimp from pan; keep warm. Add tomatoes, 3 tablespoons vinaigrette, olives, and basil to pan. Cook 1 minute or until tomatoes are thoroughly heated. Remove pan from heat. Add shrimp to pan; toss gently. Sprinkle with cheese and additional basil, if desired; toss well. Serve with lemon wedges, if desired. Yield: 4 servings (serving size: 1 cup).

CALORIES 220 (37% from fat); FAT 9g (sat 1.9g, mono 3.5g, poly 2.5g); PROTEIN 29.8g; CARB 4.8g; FIBER 0.8g; CHOL 256mg; IRON 4.3mg; SODIUM 743mg; CALC 90mg

Kalamata Olives One of the more popular olive varieties, kalamatas are Greek black olives that are plump and juicy with a powerful flavor, bright acidity, and high salt content. Olives are available either pitted or unpitted and may be packed in brine or oil, dried in salt, or stuffed.

We loved the way the spicy kick from the shrimp mellowed with each bite of sweet papaya and cool, creamy avocado—so much, in fact, that we gave this dish our highest rating. To cut down on prep time, we recommend using metal skewers. If you prefer to use wooden ones, be sure to soak them in water 30 minutes before grilling.

Spicy Grilled Shrimp Kebabs with Avocado and Papaya Salad
Prep: 5 minutes • Cook: 4 minutes

24 jumbo shrimp, peeled and deveined with tails intact (about 1½ pounds)	¼ teaspoon crushed red pepper Cooking spray
1 tablespoon olive oil	Avocado and Papaya Salad
¼ teaspoon salt	Lime wedges (optional)

1. Prepare grill or grill pan.

2. Thread 3 shrimp onto each of 8 skewers. Brush with olive oil; sprinkle evenly with salt and red pepper. Place kebabs on grill rack or grill pan coated with cooking spray; grill over medium-high heat 2 minutes on each side or until shrimp are done. Keep warm.

3. Serve kebabs with Avocado and Papaya Salad. Garnish with lime wedges, if desired. Yield: 4 servings (serving size: 2 skewers and about ⅔ cup salad).

CALORIES 353 (52% from fat); FAT 20g (sat 3.3g, mono 12.4g, poly 3.1g); PROTEIN 29.3g; CARB 16.3g; FIBER 5.7g; CHOL 252mg; IRON 5.1mg; SODIUM 592mg; CALC 72mg

Avocado and Papaya Salad
Prep: 5 minutes

3 tablespoons fresh lime juice (about 2 limes)	1 cup diced peeled papaya (about 1 medium)
1 tablespoon honey	2 avocados, peeled and diced
¼ teaspoon salt	

1. Combine first 3 ingredients in a bowl, stirring well with a whisk. Add papaya and avocado; toss gently to coat. Yield: 2⅔ cups (serving size: about ⅔ cup).

CALORIES 194 (72% from fat); FAT 15g (sat 2.5g, mono 9.7g, poly 2g); PROTEIN 2.3g; CARB 16.2g; FIBER 5.7g; CHOL 0mg; IRON 1.2mg; SODIUM 157mg; CALC 21mg

The warm, juicy cherry tomatoes offer a hint of acidity and a pleasing contrast to the shrimp. Soak the wooden skewers in water at least 30 minutes prior to broiling so they don't burn.

Broiled Shrimp Kebabs with Horseradish-Herb Sour Cream Sauce
Prep: 9 minutes • Cook: 4 minutes

40 large shrimp, peeled and deveined with tails intact (about 1½ pounds)	¼ teaspoon salt
16 cherry tomatoes	Lemon wedges
Olive oil-flavored cooking spray	Horseradish-Herb Sour Cream Sauce
2 teaspoons salt-free steak seasoning (such as Mrs. Dash)	

1. Preheat broiler.

2. Place shrimp and tomatoes in a large bowl; coat with cooking spray. Sprinkle evenly with steak seasoning and salt, tossing to coat. Thread 5 shrimp and 2 tomatoes onto each of 8 (10-inch) wooden skewers.

3. Place kebabs on a foil-lined baking sheet coated with cooking spray. Broil 4 to 5 minutes or until shrimp are done, turning once. Serve with lemon wedges and Horseradish-Herb Sour Cream Sauce. Yield: 4 servings (serving size: 2 skewers and 2 tablespoons sauce).

CALORIES 205 (35% from fat); FAT 8g (sat 2.2g, mono 1.9g, poly 0.9g); PROTEIN 26.2g; CARB 6.8g; FIBER 0.9g; CHOL 241mg; IRON 3.9mg; SODIUM 675mg; CALC 55mg

Horseradish-Herb Sour Cream Sauce
Prep: 3 minutes

⅓ cup light sour cream	1 teaspoon prepared horseradish
2 tablespoons light mayonnaise	1 teaspoon Dijon mustard
1 teaspoon chopped fresh rosemary	¼ teaspoon salt
2 teaspoons extra-virgin olive oil	

1. Combine all ingredients in a small bowl, stirring until well blended. Yield: ½ cup (serving size: 1 tablespoon).

CALORIES 36 (78% from fat); FAT 3g (sat 0.9g, mono 0.9g, poly 0.1g); PROTEIN 0.3g; CARB 1.8g; FIBER 0g; CHOL 5mg; IRON 0mg; SODIUM 130mg; CALC 1mg

Traditionally prepared in the oven, barbecue shrimp can be ready in far less time on the stove top, making it a fast, fabulous ending to a day at the beach or pool. Pair with mixed salad greens lightly dressed with extra-virgin olive oil and fresh lemon juice.

Skillet Barbecue Shrimp

Prep: 2 minutes • Cook: 6 minutes

¾ cup fat-free Italian dressing (such as Wish-Bone)
2 tablespoons butter
1 tablespoon Worcestershire ground black pepper blend (such as McCormick)

1 teaspoon dried rosemary, crushed
2 pounds large shrimp with tails intact
5 lemon wedges

1. Combine first 4 ingredients in a large skillet; bring to a boil. Add shrimp; cook 6 minutes or until shrimp are done, stirring occasionally. Serve with lemon wedges. Yield: 5 servings (serving size: 5 ounces shrimp and about 1 tablespoon sauce).

CALORIES 161 (34% from fat); FAT 6g (sat 3.3g, mono 1.5g, poly 0.7g); PROTEIN 22.1g; CARB 3.8g; FIBER 0.5g; CHOL 214mg; IRON 3.4mg; SODIUM 644mg; CALC 57mg

serve with
Bananas in Warm Rum Sauce

Prep: 1 minute • Cook: 9 minutes

1 tablespoon butter
⅓ cup dark rum
¼ cup water

¼ cup turbinado sugar or granulated sugar
3 bananas
2½ cups vanilla light ice cream (such as Edy's)

1. Melt butter in a large nonstick skillet over medium-high heat. While butter melts, stir together rum and water. Add sugar to melted butter in skillet. Stir in rum mixture. Bring to a boil; cook 4 minutes or until bubbly and slightly reduced.
2. While sauce reduces, slice bananas diagonally to create oval-shaped slices; add to sauce. Cook 3 minutes, turning until coated and thoroughly heated. Remove from heat. Serve bananas with ice cream. Yield: 5 servings (serving size: about ⅓ cup bananas with sauce and ½ cup ice cream).

CALORIES 257 (19% from fat); FAT 6g (sat 3.4g, mono 1.4g, poly 0.2g); PROTEIN 3.8g; CARB 44.6g; FIBER 2g; CHOL 24mg; IRON 0.3mg; SODIUM 65mg; CALC 107mg

Similar in texture and flavor to peanuts, soy nuts add a nutty crunch to this Chinese classic. If you can't find soy nuts, substitute lightly salted or unsalted dry-roasted peanuts. Serve with rice and steamed broccoli.

Szechuan Shrimp
Prep: 2 minutes • Cook: 7 minutes

Cooking spray
1½ pounds peeled and deveined large shrimp
¾ teaspoon crushed red pepper
½ cup light sesame-ginger dressing (such as Newman's Own)

4 green onions, cut into 1-inch pieces
2 tablespoons lightly salted toasted soy nuts, coarsely chopped

1. Heat a large nonstick skillet over medium-high heat; coat with cooking spray. Coat shrimp with cooking spray; add shrimp and red pepper to pan. Stir-fry 2 minutes. Add dressing and onions. Cook 3 minutes or until shrimp are done, stirring constantly. Sprinkle evenly with soy nuts; serve immediately. Yield: 4 servings (serving size: 1 cup).

CALORIES 190 (18% from fat); FAT 4g (sat 0.6g, mono 0.3g, poly 0.6g); PROTEIN 29.5g; CARB 7.9g; FIBER 1.4g; CHOL 252mg; IRON 4.4mg; SODIUM 708mg; CALC 72mg

The half-and-half and grated orange rind create a citrusy cream sauce that tames the spiciness of the chipotle chile.

Shrimp with Creamy Orange-Chipotle Sauce

Prep: 3 minutes • Cook: 6 minutes

⅔ cup half-and-half
1 large chipotle chile, canned in adobo sauce
1 teaspoon grated orange rind
Cooking spray
1½ pounds peeled and deveined large shrimp

¾ teaspoon ground cumin
¼ teaspoon salt
2 tablespoons chopped fresh cilantro
Hot cooked linguine (optional)

1. Place first 3 ingredients in a blender; process until smooth.

2. Heat a large nonstick skillet over medium-high heat. Coat pan with cooking spray; add shrimp. Coat shrimp with cooking spray; sprinkle with cumin and salt. Sauté 4 minutes or until shrimp are done, stirring frequently. Transfer shrimp to a serving platter. Reduce heat to medium, add half-and-half mixture to pan, and cook 1 minute, stirring constantly. Pour sauce over shrimp; sprinkle with cilantro. Serve over linguine, if desired. Yield: 4 servings (serving size: ½ cup shrimp and 2 tablespoons sauce).

CALORIES 186 (30% from fat); FAT 6g (sat 3.3g, mono 0.3g, poly 0.6g); PROTEIN 28.3g; CARB 2.6g; FIBER 0.5g; CHOL 267mg; IRON 4.3mg; SODIUM 494mg; CALC 97mg

Serve this fiery, Thai-inspired dish over boil-in-bag jasmine rice and with Honey-Spiced Pineapple.

Spicy Green Curry–Cilantro Shrimp

Prep: 2 minutes • Cook: 12 minutes

Cooking spray
1½ pounds peeled and deveined medium shrimp
1 cup light coconut milk
2 tablespoons sugar
2 tablespoons fresh lime juice (about 1 lime)

1 tablespoon green curry paste
1 teaspoon cornstarch
¼ teaspoon salt
⅓ cup chopped fresh cilantro
Lime wedges

1. Heat a large nonstick skillet over medium-high heat. Coat pan with cooking spray. Add shrimp; cook 3 minutes, stirring occasionally.
2. While shrimp cook, combine coconut milk and next 5 ingredients, stirring with a whisk until smooth. Add to shrimp in pan; bring to a boil. Reduce heat; simmer 5 minutes or until slightly thickened. Sprinkle with cilantro; serve with lime wedges. Yield: 4 servings (serving size: 1 cup).

CALORIES 189 (20% from fat); FAT 4g (sat 2.9g, mono 0.3g, poly 0.6g); PROTEIN 27.8g; CARB 10.1g; FIBER 0.1g; CHOL 252mg; IRON 4.3mg; SODIUM 517mg; CALC 53mg

serve with
Honey-Spiced Pineapple

Prep: 2 minutes • Cook: 6 minutes

1 tablespoon butter
3 cups fresh pineapple chunks

1 tablespoon honey
½ teaspoon curry powder

1. Melt butter in a large nonstick skillet over medium-high heat. Add pineapple, honey, and curry powder; cook 3 minutes or until thoroughly heated, stirring frequently. Yield: 4 servings (serving size: ¾ cup).

CALORIES 120 (23% from fat); FAT 3g (sat 1.8g, mono 0.8g, poly 0.2g); PROTEIN 1g; CARB 25.1g; FIBER 2.4g; CHOL 8mg; IRON 0.6mg; SODIUM 22mg; CALC 24mg

Our lightened version of low-country shrimp and grits is high on flavor and low in fat and calories.

Deep South Shrimp and Sausage

Prep: 4 minutes • Cook: 9 minutes • Other: 2 minutes

Cooking spray
¾ pound peeled and deveined medium shrimp
1 teaspoon Old Bay seasoning
¼ teaspoon freshly ground black pepper
1 cup refrigerated prechopped tricolor bell pepper

1 (6.5-ounce) link smoked turkey sausage, cut into ⅛-inch-thick slices
2 garlic cloves, minced
¼ cup water

1. Heat a large nonstick skillet over medium-high heat. Coat pan with cooking spray. Add shrimp, seasoning, and black pepper, tossing to coat. Cook 3 minutes or until shrimp are done, stirring frequently. Remove from pan; keep warm.

2. Return pan to medium-high heat. Coat pan with cooking spray. Add bell pepper; cook 2 minutes, stirring frequently. Add sausage; cook 2 minutes or until lightly browned, stirring frequently. Add reserved shrimp mixture and garlic. Cook 1 minute, stirring constantly. Add ¼ cup water; cook 30 seconds, scraping pan to loosen browned bits. Remove from heat; let stand 2 minutes. Yield: 4 servings (serving size: ¾ cup).

CALORIES 142 (18% from fat); FAT 3g (sat 1g, mono 0.1g, poly 0.3g); PROTEIN 19.7g; CARB 7.6g; FIBER 0.6g; CHOL 147mg; IRON 2.8mg; SODIUM 701mg; CALC 48mg

serve with
Spicy Cheese Grits

Prep: 3 minutes • Cook: 7 minutes

1½ cups water
½ cup uncooked quick-cooking grits
½ cup fat-free milk
¼ teaspoon salt

¼ teaspoon Worcestershire sauce
¾ teaspoon hot sauce
¼ cup (1 ounce) grated fresh Parmesan cheese

1. Bring 1½ cups water to a boil in a medium saucepan. Gradually stir in grits. Cover, reduce heat, and simmer 5 minutes. Stir in milk. Remove from heat; add remaining ingredients, stirring until cheese melts. Yield: 4 servings (serving size: ½ cup).

CALORIES 111 (18% from fat); FAT 2g (sat 1.2g, mono 0.1g, poly 0.1g); PROTEIN 5.1g; CARB 17.5g; FIBER 0.3g; CHOL 7mg; IRON 0.8mg; SODIUM 275mg; CALC 113mg

This delectable pasta dish features swirls of tender angel hair, plump shrimp, and grape tomatoes tossed with pesto. Garnish with sprigs of basil just before serving for extra color and a burst of freshness.

Pesto Shrimp Pasta

Prep: 8 minutes • Cook: 15 minutes

4 ounces uncooked angel hair pasta	1 cup halved grape tomatoes
6 cups water	¼ cup (1 ounce) shaved fresh Parmesan
1¼ pounds peeled and deveined large shrimp	cheese
¼ cup commercial pesto, divided	Basil sprigs (optional)

1. Cook pasta according to package directions, omitting salt and fat; drain.

2. While pasta cooks, bring 6 cups water to a boil in a large saucepan. Add shrimp; cook 2 to 3 minutes or until done. Drain shrimp; toss with 2 tablespoons pesto and tomatoes. Stir in pasta and 2 tablespoons pesto. Top with cheese. Garnish with basil, if desired. Yield: 4 servings (serving size: 1 cup shrimp pasta and 1 tablespoon cheese).

CALORIES 320 (31% from fat); FAT 11g (sat 2.7g, mono 6.3g, poly 1.7g); PROTEIN 31.4g; CARB 23.6g; FIBER 1.9g; CHOL 220mg; IRON 4.7mg; SODIUM 505mg; CALC 189mg

Basil Basil is one of the most important culinary herbs. Sweet basil, the most common type, is redolent of licorice and cloves. Basil is used in the south of France to make *pistou;* its Italian cousin, pesto, is made just over the border. Used in sauces, sandwiches, soups, and salads, basil is in top form when married with tomatoes.

To save prep time, have your fishmonger peel and devein the shrimp. Or if you'd like to do it yourself, be sure to start with 1¼ pounds of unpeeled shrimp.

Creamy Garlic Shrimp and Pasta
Prep: 2 minutes • Cook: 9 minutes

    3   quarts water
    1   (9-ounce) package fresh linguine
    1   pound peeled and deveined large shrimp
    ¼   cup dry white wine
    ⅓   cup plus 1½ tablespoons (3 ounces) light
        garlic-and-herbs spreadable cheese
        (such as Alouette Light)

    ½   cup fat-free milk
    3   garlic cloves, pressed
    ½   teaspoon salt
    1½ tablespoons chopped fresh oregano
    Oregano sprigs (optional)

1. Bring 3 quarts water to a boil in a large Dutch oven; add pasta and shrimp. Cook 3 to 4 minutes or until pasta is tender and shrimp are done. Drain and keep warm.
2. While pasta and shrimp cook, combine wine and next 4 ingredients in a large non-stick skillet over medium-high heat. Bring to a boil. Reduce heat; simmer 2 minutes or until slightly thickened, stirring constantly.
3. Add pasta and shrimp to sauce in pan, tossing to coat. Stir in chopped oregano just before serving. Garnish with oregano sprigs, if desired. Yield: 4 servings (serving size: 1¼ cups).

CALORIES 337 (18% from fat); FAT 7g (sat 3.3g, mono 0.2g, poly 0.4g); PROTEIN 28.7g; CARB 38.4g; FIBER 1.6g; CHOL 220mg; IRON 4.1mg; SODIUM 571mg; CALC 116mg

serve with
Skillet Asparagus and Roasted Bell Peppers
Prep: 2 minutes • Cook: 7 minutes

    Cooking spray
    3   tablespoons light balsamic vinaigrette
        (such as Ken's Steak House Lite), divided
    1   tablespoon water

    12 ounces asparagus spears, trimmed
    1   cup chopped bottled roasted red bell
        peppers
    2   tablespoons finely chopped fresh parsley

1. Heat a large nonstick skillet over medium-high heat. Coat pan with cooking spray. Add 1 tablespoon vinaigrette and 1 tablespoon water to pan. Place asparagus in pan. Cook, covered, 5 minutes or until asparagus is crisp-tender, stirring frequently. Remove from pan onto a serving platter.
2. Add 1 tablespoon vinaigrette to pan. Add bell pepper; cook 1 minute. Spoon over asparagus. Drizzle 1 tablespoon vinaigrette over asparagus and bell pepper; sprinkle with parsley. Yield: 4 servings (serving size: about 7 asparagus spears and ¼ cup bell pepper).

CALORIES 37 (39% from fat); FAT 2g (sat 0.2g, mono 0g, poly 0g); PROTEIN 1.2g; CARB 4.1g; FIBER 1.2g; CHOL 0mg; IRON 1.3mg; SODIUM 279mg; CALC 16mg

Spicy chipotle seasoning, precooked vegetable rice, and shrimp transform traditional paella into a fast weeknight fiesta.

Quick Paella
Prep: 4 minutes • Cook: 9 minutes

¼ teaspoon saffron threads
⅓ cup hot water
2 teaspoons salt-free Southwest chipotle seasoning (such as Mrs. Dash)
12 ounces peeled and deveined medium shrimp
½ pound chicken tenders, cut crosswise into bite-sized pieces

Butter-flavored cooking spray
2 (8.8-ounce) pouches microwaveable cooked garden vegetable rice (such as Uncle Ben's Ready Rice)
½ cup frozen petite green peas

1. Combine saffron and ⅓ cup hot water in a small bowl.
2. Sprinkle chipotle seasoning over shrimp and chicken in a large bowl; toss well to coat. Heat a large nonstick skillet over medium-high heat; coat pan with cooking spray. Add shrimp mixture to pan; coat mixture with cooking spray. Cook 5 minutes, stirring frequently.
3. Stir in saffron mixture, rice, and peas, breaking up rice with a wooden spoon. Steam, covered, 3 minutes or until rice is thoroughly heated, shrimp and chicken are done, and peas are hot. Fluff with a fork. Yield: 4 servings (serving size: 1½ cups).

CALORIES 322 (12% from fat); FAT 4g (sat 0.2g, mono 0.1g, poly 0.3g); PROTEIN 30.6g; CARB 39.3g; FIBER 1.2g; CHOL 159mg; IRON 4.9mg; SODIUM 868mg; CALC 60mg

serve with
Sangría
Prep: 5 minutes

1 navel orange, halved
1 large lime, halved
1⅓ cups merlot, chilled
1⅓ cups pomegranate juice, chilled
¼ cup sugar
1 (8.4-ounce) bottle sparkling apple cider (such as Martinelli's), chilled

1. Squeeze juice from half of orange and half of lime to measure 2 tablespoons and 1 tablespoon, respectively. Cut remaining orange and lime halves into thin slices.
2. Combine citrus juices, wine, pomegranate juice, and sugar in a pitcher, stirring until sugar dissolves. Slowly add sparkling cider, stirring gently. Add citrus slices; serve immediately. Yield: 4 servings (serving size: 1 cup).

CALORIES 221 (0% from fat); FAT 0g (sat 0g, mono 0g, poly 0g); PROTEIN 0.9g; CARB 42g; FIBER 1.5g; CHOL 0mg; IRON 0.5mg; SODIUM 13mg; CALC 35mg

meats

Individual Salsa Meat Loaves
Smothered Pepper Steak
Ginger-Lime Beef Stir-Fry
Orange Beef and Broccoli
Mongolian Beef
Mustard-Molasses Flank Steak
Beer-Braised Beef
Beef Tenderloin Steaks with Red Wine–Mushroom Sauce
Seared Beef Tenderloin Steaks with Dark Beer Reduction and Blue Cheese
Slow-Cooker Beef Pot Roast
Seared Pork Chops with Spicy Roasted Pepper Sauce
Spiced Pork Chops with Butternut Squash
Lemon-Herb Skillet Pork Chops
Curried Pork and Chai Rice
Asiago-Crusted Pork Chops
Hoisin Pork and Boston Lettuce Wraps
Spiced Pork Tenderloin
Pork Tenderloin with Balsamic Onion-Fig Relish
Sherried Pineapple Pork Tenderloin
Spinach, Pesto, and Feta–Stuffed Pork Tenderloin with Chunky Tomato Sauce
Pork Medallions with Spicy Pomegranate-Blueberry Reduction
Skillet-Grilled Ham with Glazed Pineapple
Sweet-Spiced Grilled Lamb Chops
Broiled Lamb Chops with Lemon-Arugula Pesto

Making meat loaf in single-serving portions reduces the cooking time by half and keeps the meat juicy.

Individual Salsa Meat Loaves
Prep: 10 minutes • Cook: 30 minutes

2 large egg whites	¼ cup ketchup, divided
⅓ cup quick-cooking oats	1 pound ground beef, extra lean
½ cup plus 2 tablespoons chipotle salsa, divided	Cooking spray

1. Preheat oven to 350°.
2. Combine egg whites in a large bowl, stirring well with a whisk. Stir in oats, ½ cup salsa, and 2 tablespoons ketchup. Add beef; mix well. Divide beef mixture into 4 equal portions, shaping each into an oval-shaped loaf. Coat a foil-lined rimmed baking sheet with cooking spray. Place loaves on prepared pan.
3. Bake at 350° for 30 minutes or until done.
4. Combine remaining 2 tablespoons salsa and remaining 2 tablespoons ketchup in a small bowl; spread mixture evenly over loaves. Yield: 4 servings (serving size: 1 meat loaf).

CALORIES 190 (26% from fat); FAT 6g (sat 2.1g, mono 2.1g, poly 0.7g); PROTEIN 25g; CARB 10.9g; FIBER 1.7g; CHOL 60mg; IRON 2.2mg; SODIUM 548mg; CALC 7mg

serve with
Green Beans with Country Mustard and Herbs
Prep: 2 minutes • Cook: 5 minutes

1 (12-ounce) package trimmed green beans	1½ teaspoons minced fresh oregano
1 tablespoon butter	2 teaspoons whole-grain Dijon mustard
2 tablespoons chopped fresh parsley	¼ teaspoon salt

1. Microwave green beans according to package directions.
2. While beans cook, place butter and remaining ingredients in a serving bowl. Add beans; toss gently until butter melts. Yield: 4 servings (serving size: ½ cup).

CALORIES 55 (49% from fat); FAT 3g (sat 1.8g, mono 0.8g, poly 0.2g); PROTEIN 1.7g; CARB 6.8g; FIBER 3g; CHOL 8mg; IRON 1mg; SODIUM 232mg; CALC 37mg

To capture all of its saucy flavor, plate this quick weeknight family favorite over hot cooked rice.

Smothered Pepper Steak

Prep: 4 minutes • Cook: 25 minutes

3 tablespoons all-purpose flour
4 (4-ounce) ground sirloin patties
¼ teaspoon salt
¼ teaspoon black pepper
Cooking spray
1 (16-ounce) package frozen bell pepper stir-fry (such as Birds Eye)

1 (14.5-ounce) can diced tomatoes with balsamic vinegar, basil, and olive oil (such as Hunt's), undrained
1 tablespoon low-sodium soy sauce

1. Place flour in a shallow dish. Dredge sirloin patties in flour; sprinkle patties evenly with salt and pepper. Heat a large nonstick skillet over medium-high heat; coat pan with cooking spray. Coat patties with cooking spray. Add patties to pan; cook 3 minutes on each side or until lightly browned.

2. Add stir-fry, tomatoes, and soy sauce to meat in pan; bring to a boil. Reduce heat; simmer 15 minutes or until meat is done and pepper mixture is slightly thick. Yield: 4 servings (serving size: 1 sirloin patty and about ¾ cup sauce).

CALORIES 246 (28% from fat); FAT 8g (sat 2g, mono 2g, poly 0.5g); PROTEIN 25.1g; CARB 18.2g; FIBER 2g; CHOL 60mg; IRON 2.7mg; SODIUM 785mg; CALC 52mg

serve with
Chocolate-Peppermint Parfaits

Prep: 8 minutes

1 cup coarsely chopped vanilla meringue cookies (such as Miss Meringue; about 4 cookies)
2 cups chocolate low-fat ice cream (such as Edy's)
1 cup refrigerated canned light whipped topping (such as Reddi-wip)
½ cup finely crushed soft peppermint candies

1. Spoon ¼ cup cookies into each of 4 parfait glasses; top each serving with ¼ cup ice cream, 2 tablespoons whipped topping, and 1 tablespoon peppermint candies. Repeat layers with remaining ice cream, whipped topping, and peppermint candies. Yield: 4 servings (serving size: 1 parfait).

CALORIES 222 (16% from fat); FAT 4g (sat 2g, mono 0g, poly 0g); PROTEIN 2.1g; CARB 39.3g; FIBER 0g; CHOL 11mg; IRON 0.4mg; SODIUM 57mg; CALC 80mg

Peppery ginger adds a lively herbal note to this stir-fry. Serve over cellophane noodles.

Ginger-Lime Beef Stir-Fry
Prep: 4 minutes • Cook: 5 minutes

1 tablespoon sugar
1 tablespoon grated peeled fresh ginger
2 tablespoons fresh lime juice (about 1 lime)
1½ teaspoons low-sodium soy sauce
¼ teaspoon crushed red pepper

1 tablespoon canola oil
12 ounces boneless sirloin steak, cut into thin strips
½ cup diagonally cut green onions (optional)
4 lime wedges (optional)

1. Combine first 5 ingredients in a small bowl; stir well with a whisk.
2. Heat canola oil in a large nonstick skillet over medium-high heat. Add steak; cook 4 minutes or until browned, stirring frequently. Remove from heat; drizzle evenly with ginger-lime mixture. Garnish with onions and lime wedges, if desired. Yield: 3 servings (serving size: ⅔ cup).

CALORIES 197 (42% from fat); FAT 9g (sat 2g, mono 4.5g, poly 2g); PROTEIN 22.4g; CARB 5.5g; FIBER 0.1g; CHOL 42mg; IRON 2.8mg; SODIUM 197mg; CALC 16mg

Ginger Look for fresh ginger in the produce section of your supermarket. Choose the freshest, youngest-looking roots you can find because they are more flavorful and tender and less fibrous than old rhizomes.

For convenience, ask the butcher to cut the steak into thin slices. Round out this restaurant-inspired meal with a side of hot cooked rice and, for dessert, Wasabi Ice Cream with Honey.

Orange Beef and Broccoli
Prep: 7 minutes • Cook: 7 minutes

- 1 (12-ounce) package refrigerated broccoli florets
- ⅓ cup fat-free, less-sodium beef broth
- ⅓ cup low-sugar orange marmalade
- 2 tablespoons low-sodium soy sauce
- ¼ teaspoon salt
- 2 tablespoons cornstarch
- 1 (1-pound) flank steak, trimmed and cut into thin slices

Cooking spray

1. Microwave broccoli according to package directions.
2. While broccoli cooks, combine broth and next 3 ingredients in a small bowl, stirring with a whisk; set aside.
3. Place cornstarch in a shallow dish. Dredge steak in cornstarch.
4. Heat a large nonstick skillet over medium-high heat. Coat pan with cooking spray. Add steak; sauté 5 minutes or until browned on all sides. Add broth mixture; cook 1 minute or until thick. Stir in broccoli. Serve immediately. Yield: 4 servings (serving size: 1 cup).

CALORIES 238 (25% from fat); FAT 7g (sat 2.4g, mono 2.2g, poly 0.4g); PROTEIN 27.7g; CARB 16.6g; FIBER 2.5g; CHOL 37mg; IRON 2.6mg; SODIUM 570mg; CALC 68mg

serve with
Wasabi Ice Cream with Honey
Prep: 4 minutes • Cook: 4 minutes • Other: 2 hours and 46 minutes

- 1½ cups water
- ¾ cup sugar
- 1 tablespoon wasabi paste
- 4 teaspoons lemon juice
- 1¼ cups whole milk
- 3 tablespoons honey

1. Combine 1½ cups water and sugar in a saucepan; bring to a boil, stirring until sugar dissolves. Remove pan from heat; add wasabi paste and lemon juice, stirring with a whisk. Cover and chill completely.
2. Stir in milk. Pour mixture into the freezer can of an ice-cream freezer; freeze according to manufacturer's instructions. Spoon ice cream into a freezer-safe container; cover and freeze 1 hour or until firm. Drizzle each serving with honey. Yield: 6 servings (serving size: about ½ cup ice cream and 1½ teaspoons honey).

CALORIES 178 (10% from fat); FAT 2g (sat 1g, mono 0.4g, poly 0.1g); PROTEIN 1.7g; CARB 37.7g; FIBER 0g; CHOL 5mg; IRON 0.1mg; SODIUM 71mg; CALC 59mg

This spicy Asian favorite gets its flavor from hoisin sauce and dark sesame oil. Hoisin sauce is a versatile, sweet-and-spicy condiment that is used in Chinese cooking and dining much the same way Westerners use ketchup. The dark sesame oil imparts a distinctive nutty taste and aroma to the dish. Serve with boil-in-bag jasmine rice and steamed snow peas.

Mongolian Beef
Prep: 4 minutes • Cook: 6 minutes

1 (1-pound) flank steak, trimmed and cut into thin slices
Butter-flavored cooking spray
⅓ cup hoisin sauce
2 tablespoons water

2 teaspoons minced peeled fresh ginger
1 teaspoon bottled minced roasted garlic
2 teaspoons dark sesame oil
½ teaspoon crushed red pepper
4 green onions

1. Heat a large nonstick skillet over medium-high heat. Coat steak with cooking spray. Cook steak in pan over medium-high heat 3 minutes or until browned and liquid has almost evaporated, stirring occasionally.

2. While steak cooks, combine hoisin sauce and next 5 ingredients in a small bowl. Cut onions crosswise into 1-inch pieces. Add sauce mixture and onions to meat in pan; cook 1 to 2 minutes or until sauce is slightly reduced (do not overcook meat). Serve immediately. Yield: 4 servings (serving size: about ½ cup).

CALORIES 240 (37% from fat); FAT 10g (sat 2.8g, mono 3.4g, poly 2.6g); PROTEIN 25.5g; CARB 11.1g; FIBER 1.1g; CHOL 38mg; IRON 2.2mg; SODIUM 410mg; CALC 45mg

Snow Peas Snow peas are at their best when steamed. To steam them, cook, covered, in a steamer basket or on a rack above boiling water 2 to 3 minutes. Or sauté them in 1 teaspoon oil or cooking spray over medium-high heat 3 to 4 minutes or until crisp-tender.

Reducing the tangy-sweet marinade for this recipe on the stove top deepens its rich flavor. Use leftovers to top a green salad for lunch the next day.

Mustard-Molasses Flank Steak
Prep: 4 minutes • Cook: 10 minutes • Other: 30 minutes

⅓ cup balsamic vinegar
¼ cup fat-free, less-sodium beef broth
2 tablespoons molasses
2 tablespoons whole-grain Dijon mustard
¼ teaspoon salt

¼ teaspoon freshly ground black pepper
1 (1-pound) flank steak, trimmed
Cooking spray
Chopped green onions (optional)

1. Combine first 7 ingredients in a large zip-top plastic bag; seal. Marinate in refrigerator 30 minutes.
2. Preheat broiler.
3. Remove steak from bag, reserving marinade. Place steak on a broiler pan coated with cooking spray; broil 5 minutes on each side or until desired degree of doneness. Remove steak from oven; loosely cover with foil.
4. While steak broils, place reserved marinade in a small nonstick skillet. Bring to a boil; cook until reduced to ⅓ cup (about 6 minutes), stirring occasionally.
5. Cut steak diagonally across the grain into ¼-inch-thick slices. Drizzle mustard-molasses sauce over steak. Top with onions, if desired. Yield: 4 servings (serving size: 3 ounces steak and about 1½ tablespoons sauce).

CALORIES 219 (28% from fat); FAT 7g (sat 2.3g, mono 2.2g, poly 0.2g); PROTEIN 25.2g; CARB 12.4g; FIBER 0.3g; CHOL 37mg; IRON 2.6mg; SODIUM 397mg; CALC 60mg

serve with
Sweet Potatoes with Orange-Thyme Butter
Prep: 3 minutes • Cook: 8 minutes

4 (6-ounce) sweet potatoes
2 tablespoons butter, softened
2 teaspoons grated orange rind

1 teaspoon chopped fresh thyme
¼ teaspoon freshly ground black pepper
⅛ teaspoon salt

1. Scrub potatoes and place in a medium bowl (do not pierce potatoes with a fork). Cover bowl with plastic wrap (do not allow plastic wrap to touch food); vent. Microwave at HIGH 8 minutes or until done.
2. While potatoes cook, combine butter and remaining 4 ingredients in a small bowl.
3. Cut each potato lengthwise; fluff with a fork. Top each potato evenly with butter mixture. Yield: 4 servings (serving size: 1 sweet potato and 2¼ teaspoons butter).

CALORIES 145 (36% from fat); FAT 6g (sat 3.6g, mono 1.5g, poly 0.3g); PROTEIN 2.2g; CARB 21.8g; FIBER 3.6g; CHOL 15mg; IRON 0.8mg; SODIUM 150mg; CALC 44mg

An oval 3- to 3½-quart slow cooker works best for this recipe because of the shape of the meat. If you don't own an oval slow cooker, cut the meat in half to fit the one you have. Spoon this fork-tender, saucy beef over mashed potatoes.

Beer-Braised Beef

Prep: 4 minutes • Cook: 8 hours and 7 minutes • Other: 10 minutes

1 cup refrigerated prechopped onion	½ cup light beer
Cooking spray	2 tablespoons molasses
1 pound boneless top round steak, trimmed	¼ teaspoon salt
1 (14.5-ounce) can diced tomatoes with basil, garlic, and oregano, undrained	

1. Place onion in a 3- to 3½-quart electric slow cooker coated with cooking spray.

2. Heat a large nonstick skillet over medium-high heat; coat pan with cooking spray. Add steak; cook 3 minutes on each side or until browned. Place steak over onion in cooker; pour tomatoes and beer over steak. Cover and cook on LOW for 8 hours or until steak is very tender.

3. Shred steak with 2 forks in slow cooker; stir in molasses and salt. Let steak stand 10 minutes before serving. Yield: 4 servings (serving size: 1 cup).

CALORIES 265 (28% from fat); FAT 8g (sat 3.1g, mono 3.4g, poly 0.3g); PROTEIN 25.5g; CARB 20.4g; FIBER 1.5g; CHOL 64mg; IRON 3.7mg; SODIUM 514mg; CALC 64mg

serve with
Raspberry-Lemon Parfaits

Prep: 5 minutes • Other: 5 minutes

2 (6-ounce) packages fresh raspberries (about 2¾ cups)	1½ cups (4 ounces) frozen fat-free whipped topping, thawed
2 tablespoons sugar	3 cups (1-inch) cubed angel food cake
2 (6-ounce) cartons lemon meringue light yogurt (such as Yoplait Light Thick and Creamy)	Raspberries (optional)

1. Combine raspberries and sugar in a medium bowl. Let stand 5 minutes, stirring occasionally.

2. Place yogurt in another bowl; gently fold in whipped topping until combined.

3. Layer about ⅓ cup each angel food cake, raspberry mixture, and yogurt mixture in each of 4 stemmed glasses. Repeat procedure once. Garnish with additional raspberries, if desired. Serve immediately, or chill until ready to serve. Yield: 4 servings (serving size: 1 parfait).

CALORIES 257 (3% from fat); FAT 1g (sat 0.1g, mono 0.1g, poly 0.5g); PROTEIN 5.6g; CARB 56g; FIBER 6g; CHOL 2mg; IRON 0.8mg; SODIUM 327mg; CALC 171mg

Stirring the mushrooms constantly helps release their juices, allowing them to caramelize quickly. Complete the meal with Wedge Salad with Sour Cream–Mustard Seed Dressing or roasted potatoes.

Beef Tenderloin Steaks with Red Wine–Mushroom Sauce
Prep: 1 minute • Cook: 10 minutes

4 (4-ounce) beef tenderloin steaks, trimmed (about ½ inch thick)
¼ teaspoon salt
¼ teaspoon freshly ground black pepper
Butter-flavored cooking spray
1 (8-ounce) package presliced baby portobello mushrooms
1 cup dry red wine
2 tablespoons butter
1 teaspoon minced fresh rosemary

1. Heat a large nonstick skillet over medium-high heat. Sprinkle steaks with salt and pepper; coat with cooking spray. Add steaks to pan; cook 3 minutes on each side or until desired degree of doneness. Transfer steaks to a serving platter; keep warm.
2. Add mushrooms to pan. Coat mushrooms with cooking spray; sauté 3 minutes or until browned. Stir in wine, scraping pan to loosen browned bits. Cook until liquid almost evaporates. Remove pan from heat; add butter and rosemary, stirring until butter melts. Pour sauce over steaks. Yield: 4 servings (serving size: 1 steak and ¼ cup sauce).

CALORIES 244 (46% from fat); FAT 13g (sat 6g, mono 4g, poly 0.9g); PROTEIN 23.3g; CARB 3.8g; FIBER 0.9g; CHOL 74mg; IRON 1.9mg; SODIUM 235mg; CALC 24mg

serve with
Wedge Salad with Sour Cream–Mustard Seed Dressing
Prep: 6 minutes

⅓ cup reduced-fat sour cream
3 tablespoons water
2 tablespoons light mayonnaise
2 teaspoons whole-grain Dijon mustard
1 garlic clove, minced
⅛ teaspoon salt
½ head iceberg lettuce, cut into 4 wedges
½ cup diced plum tomato (about 1 tomato)
Freshly ground black pepper

1. Combine first 6 ingredients in a medium bowl, stirring well with a whisk.
2. Place 1 lettuce wedge on each of 4 plates. Drizzle with dressing. Top with tomato and pepper. Yield: 4 servings (serving size: 1 lettuce wedge, about 3 tablespoons dressing, and 2 tablespoons tomato).

CALORIES 73 (63% from fat); FAT 5g (sat 2g, mono 0.7g, poly 2.4g); PROTEIN 1.8g; CARB 5.5g; FIBER 1g; CHOL 13mg; IRON 0.4mg; SODIUM 212mg; CALC 49mg

Dark beer sauce and piquant blue cheese elevate this dish to steak-house quality. Finish cooking the steaks in the oven after searing; place them on the same pan as the Garlic-Herb Steak Fries to save cleanup time.

Seared Beef Tenderloin Steaks with Dark Beer Reduction and Blue Cheese

Prep: 2 minutes • Cook: 13 minutes

2 teaspoons steak rub (such as McCormick Grill Mates)
4 (4-ounce) beef tenderloin steaks, trimmed (about 1 inch thick)
1 teaspoon olive oil

1 (12-ounce) bottle dark lager (such as Michelob AmberBock)
2 tablespoons light brown sugar
2 tablespoons crumbled blue cheese

1. Preheat oven to 450°.
2. Rub steak seasoning over both sides of steaks.
3. Heat olive oil in a large nonstick skillet over medium-high heat. Add steaks; cook 2 minutes on each side or until browned. Remove steaks from pan; place on a baking sheet. Bake at 450° for 4 to 5 minutes or until desired degree of doneness.
4. While steaks bake, combine beer and brown sugar in a medium bowl; add to skillet, scraping pan to loosen browned bits. Cook 6 minutes or until mixture is slightly syrupy and reduced to about ¼ cup. Serve steaks with reduced sauce; sprinkle evenly with cheese. Yield: 4 servings (serving size: 1 steak, about 1½ tablespoons sauce, and 1½ teaspoons cheese).

CALORIES 209 (37% from fat); FAT 8g (sat 3.2g, mono 3.4g, poly 0.4g); PROTEIN 22.7g; CARB 6.2g; FIBER 0g; CHOL 62mg; IRON 1.5mg; SODIUM 362mg; CALC 37mg

serve with
Garlic-Herb Steak Fries

Prep: 4 minutes • Cook: 17 minutes

3 cups (15 ounces) frozen steak fries
1 tablespoon chopped fresh rosemary
1 tablespoon olive oil

1 teaspoon garlic–sea salt blend (such as McCormick)

1. Preheat oven to 450°.
2. Combine all ingredients in a large bowl. Arrange fries in a single layer on a large baking sheet. Bake at 450° for 17 minutes or until lightly browned, stirring once. Yield: 4 servings (serving size: about ¾ cup).

CALORIES 170 (38% from fat); FAT 7g (sat 2.4g, mono 2.5g, poly 0.5g); PROTEIN 2.6g; CARB 24.2g; FIBER 2.6g; CHOL 0mg; IRON 0.5mg; SODIUM 489mg; CALC 2mg

Pair this home-style favorite with mashed potatoes to soak up the sauce. Leftover meat makes great hot roast beef sandwiches the next day.

Slow-Cooker Beef Pot Roast
Prep: 4 minutes • Cook: 7 hours and 7 minutes

1 (8-ounce) package presliced mushrooms
1 (8-ounce) container refrigerated
   prechopped green bell pepper
Cooking spray
¼ cup plus 2 tablespoons ketchup

¼ cup water
1 tablespoon Worcestershire sauce
½ teaspoon black pepper
¼ teaspoon salt
2 pounds boneless shoulder pot roast

1. Place mushrooms and bell pepper in a 3½- to 4-quart electric slow cooker coated with cooking spray.
2. Combine ketchup and next 4 ingredients in a small bowl, stirring until blended.
3. Heat a large nonstick skillet over medium-high heat. Coat pan and roast with cooking spray. Cook 3 minutes on each side or until browned. Place roast over vegetables in cooker; pour ketchup mixture over roast. Cover and cook on HIGH for 1 hour. Reduce heat to LOW; cook 6 to 7 hours or until roast is very tender. Serve vegetables and sauce over roast. Yield: 6 servings (serving size: 3 ounces beef and ½ cup vegetables and sauce).

CALORIES 228 (31% from fat); FAT 8g (sat 2g, mono 3.1g, poly 0.1g); PROTEIN 31.3g; CARB 7.4g; FIBER 1.1g; CHOL 89mg; IRON 4.2mg; SODIUM 397mg; CALC 21mg

Rather than searing the chops in oil, extra-virgin olive oil is drizzled over the cooked chops just before serving for a boost of flavor. Though not ideal as a cooking fat due to its low smoke point, extra-virgin olive oil has a richer, more complex character than refined varieties. Serve this dish with steamed green beans.

Seared Pork Chops with Spicy Roasted Pepper Sauce
Prep: 2 minutes • Cook: 10 minutes

4 (4-ounce) boneless center-cut loin pork chops (about ½ inch thick)
2 teaspoons 25%-less-sodium Montreal steak seasoning (such as McCormick Grill Mates)
Olive oil-flavored cooking spray

1 cup bottled roasted red bell peppers, drained
1 chipotle chile, canned in adobo sauce
2 tablespoons water
½ teaspoon ground cumin
2 teaspoons extra-virgin olive oil

1. Sprinkle pork evenly with steak seasoning. Heat a large nonstick skillet over medium-high heat. Coat pork with cooking spray. Add pork to pan; cook 4 minutes. Turn pork over; cook 3 minutes.
2. While pork cooks, place bell peppers and next 3 ingredients in a blender; process until smooth. When pork is done, remove pan from heat. Remove pork from pan; cover and keep warm.
3. Add bell pepper mixture to pan; return pan to medium heat. Cook 1 to 2 minutes, stirring often. Spoon 2 tablespoons sauce onto each of 4 serving plates. Top each with a pork chop; drizzle with ½ teaspoon oil. Yield: 4 servings (serving size: 1 pork chop and 2 tablespoons sauce).

CALORIES 194 (41% from fat); FAT 9g (sat 2.7g, mono 4.7g, poly 0.7g); PROTEIN 23.9g; CARB 1.7g; FIBER 0.3g; CHOL 65mg; IRON 0.8mg; SODIUM 443mg; CALC 27mg

Don't reserve pumpkin pie spice for desserts alone; sprinkle this blend of cinnamon, ginger, nutmeg, and allspice on pork chops for a fragrant, home-style dish.

Spiced Pork Chops with Butternut Squash
Prep: 4 minutes • Cook: 21 minutes

Cooking spray
4 (4-ounce) boneless center-cut loin pork chops (about ¾ inch thick)
1 teaspoon pumpkin pie spice
½ teaspoon freshly ground black pepper

¼ teaspoon salt, divided
1 butternut squash (about 1¼ pound)
1 cup refrigerated prechopped onion
¼ cup water
1 tablespoon chopped fresh mint

1. Heat a large nonstick skillet over medium-high heat. Coat pan with cooking spray. Sprinkle pork evenly with spice, pepper, and ⅛ teaspoon salt. Add pork to pan; sauté 3 to 4 minutes on each side or until done. Remove pork from pan; keep warm.
2. While pork cooks, pierce squash several times with a fork; place on paper towels in microwave oven. Microwave at HIGH 1 minute. Peel squash; cut in half lengthwise. Discard seeds and membrane. Coarsely chop squash.
3. Coat pan with cooking spray. Add squash; cover and cook 7 minutes, stirring occasionally. Add onion; cook, uncovered, 5 minutes, stirring frequently. Add ¼ cup water; cook until liquid evaporates, scraping pan to loosen browned bits. Remove from heat; stir in ⅛ teaspoon salt and mint. Spoon squash mixture evenly over pork. Yield: 4 servings (serving size: 1 pork chop and ¾ cup squash).

CALORIES 232 (26% from fat); FAT 7g (sat 2.4g, mono 2.9g, poly 0.5g); PROTEIN 25.6g; CARB 18.2g; FIBER 3.2g; CHOL 65mg; IRON 1.7mg; SODIUM 200mg; CALC 96mg

serve with
Ginger Couscous with Jalapeños and Cilantro
Prep: 2 minutes • Cook: 2 minutes • Other: 5 minutes

⅔ cup uncooked whole wheat couscous
1 jalapeño pepper, seeded and minced
2 tablespoons chopped fresh cilantro

1½ teaspoons grated peeled fresh ginger
2 teaspoons canola oil
¼ teaspoon salt

1. Prepare couscous according to package directions for 2 servings, omitting salt and fat. Fluff with a fork; stir in jalapeño pepper and remaining ingredients. Yield: 4 servings (serving size: about ½ cup).

CALORIES 92 (26% from fat); FAT 3g (sat 0.2g, mono 1.4g, poly 0.7g); PROTEIN 2.7g; CARB 15.4g; FIBER 2.5g; CHOL 0mg; IRON 0.6mg; SODIUM 146mg; CALC 8mg

Jalapeño Peppers These smooth, dark green chiles become bright red when ripe and can be very hot. As a general rule, the larger the chile, the milder the flavor.

A squeeze of fresh lemon completes the dish and provides a hint of tartness that enhances the natural mild sweetness of the chops.

Lemon-Herb Skillet Pork Chops

Prep: 2 minutes • Cook: 11 minutes

4 (4-ounce) boneless center-cut loin pork chops (about ½ inch thick)
½ teaspoon salt
½ teaspoon black pepper
3 tablespoons all-purpose flour
¾ teaspoon dried thyme
¾ teaspoon paprika
¼ teaspoon dried rubbed sage
1 tablespoon olive oil
4 lemon wedges

1. Sprinkle both sides of pork evenly with salt and pepper. Combine flour and next 3 ingredients in a shallow dish. Dredge pork in flour mixture.
2. Heat oil in a large nonstick skillet over medium-high heat. Add pork; cook 4 minutes on each side or until pork is done. Serve with lemon wedges. Yield: 4 servings (serving size: 1 pork chop and 1 lemon wedge).

CALORIES 218 (42% from fat); FAT 10g (sat 2.9g, mono 5.4g, poly 1g); PROTEIN 24.7g; CARB 5.9g; FIBER 0.7g; CHOL 65mg; IRON 1.1mg; SODIUM 340mg; CALC 41mg

serve with
Sweet Pea and Bell Pepper Toss

Prep: 1 minute • Cook: 7 minutes

Cooking spray
1 cup refrigerated prechopped onion
1 cup refrigerated prechopped tricolor bell pepper
1 cup frozen petite green peas
¼ teaspoon salt

1. Heat a large nonstick skillet over medium-high heat. Coat pan with cooking spray. Add onion to pan; coat with cooking spray. Cook 2 minutes. Add bell pepper; coat with cooking spray. Cook 3 minutes or until vegetables are tender and lightly browned, stirring frequently.
2. Stir in peas and salt; cook 1 to 2 minutes or until thoroughly heated, stirring frequently. Yield: 4 servings (serving size: ½ cup).

CALORIES 34 (5% from fat); FAT 0g (sat 0g, mono 0g, poly 0.1g); PROTEIN 1.4g; CARB 7.5g; FIBER 1.7g; CHOL 0mg; IRON 0.4mg; SODIUM 160mg; CALC 15mg

Delight your palate by cooking with chai tea. Chai is a fragrantly spiced, sweetened black tea served in India. It typically includes a combination of cinnamon, cloves, cardamom, and black peppercorns.

Curried Pork and Chai Rice
Prep: 3 minutes • Cook: 12 minutes • Other: 5 minutes

1 large navel orange	4 (4-ounce) boneless center-cut loin pork
¾ cup plus 2 tablespoons water	chops (about ½ inch thick)
2 spiced chai tea bags	1 teaspoon curry powder
1 cup uncooked instant brown rice	¼ teaspoon ground cumin (optional)
½ teaspoon salt, divided	Cooking spray

1. Grate rind from orange to measure 1 teaspoon. Squeeze juice from orange to measure 6 tablespoons. Combine 2 tablespoons orange juice, ¾ cup plus 2 tablespoons water, and tea bags in a medium saucepan; bring to a boil. Add rice; cover, reduce heat, and simmer 5 minutes. Remove from heat; let stand, covered, 5 minutes. Remove tea bags; stir in orange rind and ¼ teaspoon salt.

2. While rice cooks, sprinkle pork evenly with ¼ teaspoon salt, curry powder, and cumin, if desired. Heat a large nonstick skillet over medium-high heat. Coat pan with cooking spray. Add pork; cook 4 minutes on each side or until done. Transfer to a serving platter, and keep warm. Add remaining 4 tablespoons orange juice to pan; cook 1 minute, scraping pan to loosen browned bits or until reduced to 2 tablespoons. Drizzle sauce over pork; serve with rice. Yield: 4 servings (serving size: 1 pork chop and ½ cup rice).

CALORIES 254 (26% from fat); FAT 7g (sat 2.4g, mono 2.9g, poly 0.5g); PROTEIN 25.8g; CARB 22.2g; FIBER 2g; CHOL 65mg; IRON 1.1mg; SODIUM 344mg; CALC 43mg

Asiago cheese—a popular Italian cow's milk cheese—and crunchy breadcrumbs form a delicate crust on these fork-tender pork chops. Accompany with Broccoli with Sour Cream Sauce for a hearty meal that can be on the table in less than 15 minutes.

Asiago-Crusted Pork Chops

Prep: 5 minutes • Cook: 9 minutes

4 (4-ounce) boneless center-cut loin pork chops
1 egg white, lightly beaten
½ cup panko (Japanese breadcrumbs)
¼ cup (1 ounce) grated Asiago cheese
¼ teaspoon salt
¼ teaspoon black pepper
1 tablespoon extra-virgin olive oil
4 lemon wedges
2 teaspoons chopped fresh thyme

1. Place pork between 2 sheets of plastic wrap; pound to an even thickness (about ¼ inch) using a meat mallet or a small heavy skillet.
2. Place egg white in a shallow dish. Combine panko, cheese, salt, and pepper in a shallow dish. Dip pork in egg white; dredge in panko mixture, pressing gently with fingers to coat.
3. Heat oil in a large nonstick skillet over medium heat. Add pork; cook 3 to 4 minutes on each side or until lightly browned. Squeeze 1 lemon wedge over each pork chop; sprinkle each evenly with thyme. Yield: 4 servings (serving size: 1 pork chop).

CALORIES 253 (44% from fat); FAT 12g (sat 4.1g, mono 5.4g, poly 1g); PROTEIN 27.4g; CARB 6.2g; FIBER 0.6g; CHOL 71mg; IRON 0.7mg; SODIUM 297mg; CALC 83mg

serve with
Broccoli with Sour Cream Sauce

Prep: 2 minutes • Cook: 6 minutes

1 (12-ounce) package refrigerated broccoli florets
⅓ cup reduced-fat sour cream
2 tablespoons 1% low-fat milk
1 teaspoon Dijon mustard
¼ teaspoon salt

1. Microwave broccoli according to package directions.
2. While broccoli cooks, combine sour cream and remaining ingredients in a small saucepan. Cook over medium heat until thoroughly heated, stirring frequently (do not boil).
3. Arrange broccoli on a serving plate; drizzle with sauce. Yield: 4 servings (serving size: about 1 cup broccoli and about 1½ tablespoons sauce).

CALORIES 60 (43% from fat); FAT 3g (sat 1.7g, mono 0g, poly 0.2g); PROTEIN 3.7g; CARB 6.4g; FIBER 2.5g; CHOL 11mg; IRON 0.8mg; SODIUM 214mg; CALC 84mg

Tender strips of pork, coated with a lime-infused hoisin sauce, are nestled in the delicate folds of soft, buttery Boston lettuce leaves and topped with a crunchy coleslaw. Three wraps are perfect for a light summer meal; individual wraps make excellent appetizers.

Hoisin Pork and Boston Lettuce Wraps
Prep: 11 minutes • Cook: 4 minutes

⅓ cup hoisin sauce
1 tablespoon plus 1 teaspoon lime juice
1 tablespoon plus 1 teaspoon water
3 cups packaged cabbage-and-carrot coleslaw
½ cup chopped fresh cilantro

⅓ cup unsalted peanuts
Cooking spray
3 (4-ounce) boneless center-cut loin pork chops, cut into 24 thin strips
12 Boston lettuce leaves

1. Combine first 3 ingredients in a small bowl; set aside.
2. Combine coleslaw, cilantro, and peanuts; set aside.
3. Heat a large nonstick skillet over medium-high heat. Coat pan with cooking spray. Add pork; sauté 4 minutes or until lightly browned. Remove from pan.
4. Arrange 3 lettuce leaves on each of 4 plates. Top each lettuce leaf with 2 slices pork, hoisin-lime sauce, and coleslaw. Yield: 4 servings (serving size: 3 lettuce leaves, 6 slices pork, about 2 tablespoons hoisin-lime sauce, and about ¾ cup coleslaw).

CALORIES 252 (41% from fat); FAT 12g (sat 2.7g, mono 5.4g, poly 2.6g); PROTEIN 22.2g; CARB 14.9g; FIBER 2.6g; CHOL 49mg; IRON 1.4mg; SODIUM 389mg; CALC 57mg

serve with
Fresh Ginger, Mushroom, and Basil Soup
Prep: 3 minutes • Cook: 6 minutes

Cooking spray
½ cup enoki mushrooms
1 tablespoon grated peeled fresh ginger
2 (14-ounce) cans fat-free, less-sodium chicken broth

1 teaspoon low-sodium soy sauce
½ cup finely chopped green onions
2 tablespoons chopped fresh basil

1. Heat a large saucepan over medium-high heat. Coat pan with cooking spray. Add mushrooms and ginger; sauté 2 minutes or until mushrooms are browned. Add chicken broth and soy sauce. Bring to a boil.
2. Remove pan from heat; stir in onions and basil. Serve immediately. Yield: 4 servings (serving size: about ¾ cup).

CALORIES 76 (1% from fat); FAT 0g (sat 0g, mono 0g, poly 0g); PROTEIN 4.2g; CARB 14.6g; FIBER 0.7g; CHOL 0mg; IRON 0.6mg; SODIUM 651mg; CALC 13mg

A marinade of sugar, bourbon, Worcestershire sauce, and ground cinnamon infuses this succulent grilled pork tenderloin. Arrange the sliced pork over a bed of Sweet Pea and Fresh Mint Couscous for a beautiful restaurant-style presentation.

Spiced Pork Tenderloin
Prep: 2 minutes • Cook: 20 minutes • Other: 13 minutes

2 tablespoons sugar	1 (1-pound) pork tenderloin, trimmed
2 tablespoons bourbon	¼ teaspoon salt
2 tablespoons Worcestershire sauce	¼ teaspoon freshly ground black pepper
½ teaspoon ground cinnamon	Cooking spray

1. Prepare grill.
2. Combine first 4 ingredients in a large zip-top plastic bag. Add pork to bag; seal and shake well. Let stand 10 minutes, turning frequently.
3. Remove pork from bag, reserving marinade. Sprinkle pork evenly with salt and pepper. Place pork on a grill rack coated with cooking spray; grill 10 minutes on each side or until a thermometer registers 160° (slightly pink), basting with reserved marinade. Remove from grill; let stand 3 minutes before slicing. Yield: 4 servings (serving size: 3 ounces pork).

CALORIES 178 (20% from fat); FAT 4g (sat 1.3g, mono 1.5g, poly 0.3g); PROTEIN 22.5g; CARB 8.2g; FIBER 0.2g; CHOL 63mg; IRON 1.8mg; SODIUM 274mg; CALC 18mg

serve with
Sweet Pea and Fresh Mint Couscous
Prep: 2 minutes • Cook: 2 minutes • Other: 5 minutes

¾ cup water	½ cup uncooked whole wheat couscous
¼ teaspoon salt	½ cup frozen petite green peas
⅛ teaspoon ground turmeric	2 tablespoons chopped fresh mint

1. Combine first 3 ingredients in a medium saucepan. Bring to a boil. Remove from heat; stir in couscous. Cover and let stand 5 minutes.
2. Place peas in mesh strainer. Rinse under warm water; drain well. Add peas and mint to couscous. Toss well with a fork. Yield: 4 servings (serving size: about ½ cup).

CALORIES 64 (4% from fat); FAT 0g (sat 0g, mono 0g, poly 0g); PROTEIN 2.8g; CARB 13.4g; FIBER 2.4g; CHOL 0mg; IRON 0.7mg; SODIUM 161mg; CALC 10mg

Caramelized onion, balsamic vinegar, and figs combine to create a subtly sweet topping for savory roasted pork. A side of acorn squash, available in peak form throughout the winter, rounds out this hearty meal.

Pork Tenderloin with Balsamic Onion-Fig Relish

Prep: 4 minutes • Cook: 19 minutes • Other: 5 minutes

1 (1-pound) pork tenderloin, trimmed	2 tablespoons balsamic vinegar
¼ teaspoon salt	2 tablespoons water
¼ teaspoon black pepper	1 tablespoon low-sodium soy sauce
Cooking spray	1 (8-ounce) container refrigerated
8 dried Mission figs	prechopped onion

1. Preheat oven to 425°.

2. Sprinkle pork evenly with salt and pepper; coat with cooking spray. Heat a medium-sized cast-iron skillet or other ovenproof skillet over medium-high heat. Coat pan with cooking spray. Add pork; cook 4 minutes or until browned on all sides, turning occasionally.

3. While pork browns, coarsely chop figs. Combine vinegar, 2 tablespoons water, and soy sauce in a small bowl. When pork is browned, remove pan from heat. Add figs, onion, and vinegar mixture to pan, stirring to loosen browned bits.

4. Bake, uncovered, at 425° for 15 minutes or until a thermometer registers 160° (slightly pink). Stir onion mixture; cover pan loosely with foil. Let stand 5 minutes before slicing. Yield: 4 servings (serving size: 3 ounces pork and ¼ cup relish).

CALORIES 256 (15% from fat); FAT 4g (sat 1.4g, mono 1.6g, poly 0.5g); PROTEIN 24.6g; CARB 30.6g; FIBER 4.6g; CHOL 63mg; IRON 2.1mg; SODIUM 349mg; CALC 81mg

serve with

Acorn Squash with Butter Sauce

Prep: 2 minutes • Cook: 12 minutes

1 acorn squash (about 1½ pounds)	2 tablespoons maple syrup
⅓ cup water	¼ teaspoon ground nutmeg
1 tablespoon butter	⅛ teaspoon salt

1. Pierce squash several times with a sharp knife; place on paper towels in microwave oven. Microwave at HIGH 1 minute. Cut squash in half lengthwise. Discard seeds and membrane. Cut each squash half lengthwise into 4 wedges. Pour ⅓ cup water into an 11 x 7–inch baking dish. Place squash, cut sides up, in pan. Cover with plastic wrap, turning back 1 corner to vent (do not allow plastic wrap to touch food). Microwave at HIGH 10 minutes or until tender.

2. Place butter in a small microwave-safe bowl. Cover and microwave at HIGH 20 seconds or until butter melts. Stir in syrup, nutmeg, and salt. Spoon sauce over squash wedges. Yield: 4 servings (serving size: 2 squash wedges and about 2 teaspoons sauce).

CALORIES 120 (23% from fat); FAT 3g (sat 1.9g, mono 0.8g, poly 0.2g); PROTEIN 1.4g; CARB 24.5g; FIBER 2.6g; CHOL 8mg; IRON 1.3mg; SODIUM 99mg; CALC 64mg

Impress your guests with this company-worthy main dish served alongside a colorful slaw.

Sherried Pineapple Pork Tenderloin
Prep: 1 minute • Cook: 29 minutes • Other: 3 minutes

½ teaspoon black pepper
1 (1-pound) pork tenderloin, trimmed
Cooking spray
1 (6-ounce) can pineapple juice

2 tablespoons sugar
2 tablespoons dry sherry
1 tablespoon low-sodium soy sauce

1. Sprinkle pepper evenly over pork.
2. Heat a nonstick skillet over medium-high heat. Coat pan with cooking spray; add pork. Cook pork 3 to 4 minutes or until browned, turning occasionally. Reduce heat to medium-low; cover and cook 10 minutes. Turn pork over; cook 10 minutes or until a thermometer registers 160° (slightly pink).
3. Place pork on a cutting board; let stand 3 minutes. Cut into ¼-inch-thick slices.
4. While pork stands, combine pineapple juice and remaining 3 ingredients; add to pan drippings. Bring to a boil; boil 5 minutes or until liquid is reduced to ¼ cup. Spoon sauce over pork slices. Yield: 4 servings (serving size: 3 ounces pork and 1 tablespoon sauce).

CALORIES 190 (18% from fat); FAT 4g (sat 1.3g, mono 1.5g, poly 0.3g); PROTEIN 22.8g; CARB 13.5g; FIBER 0.1g; CHOL 63mg; IRON 1.3mg; SODIUM 243mg; CALC 6mg

serve with
Red Cabbage and Carrot Slaw
Prep: 6 minutes

2 cups matchstick-cut carrots
¾ cup very thinly sliced red cabbage
½ cup refrigerated prechopped tricolor bell pepper
3 tablespoons unsalted, dry-roasted peanuts

2 tablespoons cider vinegar
1 teaspoon grated peeled fresh ginger
⅛ teaspoon salt

1. Combine all ingredients in a medium bowl, tossing gently to coat. Yield: 4 servings (serving size: ¾ cup).

CALORIES 100 (32% from fat); FAT 3g (sat 0.5g, mono 1.7g, poly 1.1g); PROTEIN 2.4g; CARB 16.1g; FIBER 1.9g; CHOL 0mg; IRON 0.5mg; SODIUM 78mg; CALC 20mg

Canned tomatoes spiked with balsamic vinegar and basil roast with the pork to create an easy sauce. Hot cooked orzo soaks up the juices.

Spinach, Pesto, and Feta–Stuffed Pork Tenderloin with Chunky Tomato Sauce
Prep: 9 minutes • Cook: 22 minutes • Other: 5 minutes

1 (1-pound) pork tenderloin, trimmed
¼ cup sun-dried tomato pesto (such as Classico)
1 cup baby spinach
¼ cup (1 ounce) crumbled feta cheese with basil and sun-dried tomatoes

Olive oil-flavored cooking spray
¼ teaspoon black pepper
1 (14.5-ounce) can diced tomatoes with balsamic vinegar, basil, and olive oil (such as Hunt's), undrained

1. Preheat oven to 500°.
2. Cut pork lengthwise, cutting to, but not through, other side. Open halves, laying pork flat. Place pork halves between 2 sheets of heavy-duty plastic wrap; pound to an even thickness using a meat mallet or small heavy skillet. Spread pesto evenly down length of tenderloin; top with spinach and feta. Close tenderloin; secure at intervals with wooden picks (about 12). Place pork in a 13 x 9–inch baking pan coated with cooking spray. Coat pork with cooking spray; sprinkle evenly with pepper. Pour tomatoes around pork in pan.
3. Bake at 500° for 22 minutes or until a thermometer registers 160° (slightly pink). Let stand 5 minutes. Discard wooden picks; cut pork into 8 slices. Serve roasted tomatoes over pork. Yield: 4 servings (serving size: 3 ounces pork and about ⅓ cup tomato sauce).

CALORIES 240 (36% from fat); FAT 10g (sat 2.7g, mono 2.7g, poly 1.2g); PROTEIN 25.7g; CARB 9.7g; FIBER 1g; CHOL 69mg; IRON 2.3mg; SODIUM 702mg; CALC 83mg

The smokiness of chipotle chiles complements the concentrated sweetness of pomegranate and blueberry juices in this tender entrée.

Pork Medallions with Spicy Pomegranate-Blueberry Reduction
Prep: 2 minutes • Cook: 11 minutes

1   (1-pound) pork tenderloin, cut crosswise into ¾-inch round slices
¼   teaspoon garlic powder
¼   teaspoon salt
¼   teaspoon black pepper
    Butter-flavored cooking spray
¼   cup water
⅓   cup frozen pomegranate-blueberry juice concentrate (such as Old Orchard), undiluted
1½ teaspoons minced chipotle chiles, canned in adobo sauce

1. Heat a large nonstick skillet over medium-high heat. While pan heats, pound pork slices slightly with the heel of your hand or a meat mallet; sprinkle with garlic powder, salt, and pepper. Coat pork with cooking spray.
2. Cook pork 3 minutes on each side or until desired degree of doneness (do not overcook). Remove pork from pan; place on a serving platter. Add ¼ cup water to pan, scraping pan to loosen browned bits. Stir in juice concentrate and chipotle chiles. Reduce heat to medium; simmer 3 to 4 minutes or until slightly syrupy.
3. Return pork and juices to pan, turning pork to coat. Serve pork with sauce. Yield: 4 servings (serving size: 3 ounces pork and about 1 tablespoon sauce).

CALORIES 147 (25% from fat); FAT 4g (sat 1.3g, mono 1.5g, poly 0.3g); PROTEIN 22.5g; CARB 3.3g; FIBER 0.2g; CHOL 63mg; IRON 1.2mg; SODIUM 206mg; CALC 7mg

serve with
Balsamic and Blue Salad
Prep: 4 minutes

3   tablespoons fat-free balsamic vinaigrette (such as Girard's)
1   tablespoon honey
1   (5-ounce) package spring mix salad greens (such as Fresh Express)
1   cup halved grape tomatoes (about 5 ounces)
2   tablespoons thinly sliced green onions
⅛   teaspoon freshly ground black pepper
¼   cup (1 ounce) crumbled blue cheese (such as Maytag)

1. Combine vinaigrette and honey in a large bowl. Add spring mix, tomatoes, and onions; toss well to coat. Sprinkle with pepper and cheese; toss gently. Yield: 4 servings (serving size: about 1½ cups).

CALORIES 69 (34% from fat); FAT 3g (sat 1.6g, mono 0.7g, poly 0.1g); PROTEIN 2.8g; CARB 9.6g; FIBER 1.3g; CHOL 6mg; IRON 0.7mg; SODIUM 279mg; CALC 71mg

A dash of curry and a maple syrup glaze transform pineapple into an elegant topping for ham. Steam asparagus or green beans for a quick side.

Skillet-Grilled Ham with Glazed Pineapple

Prep: 1 minute • Cook: 12 minutes

Cooking spray
1 (1-pound) slice 25%-less-sodium ham (about ½ inch thick), cut into 4 pieces
2 cups refrigerated prechopped fresh pineapple, cut into bite-sized pieces

2 tablespoons maple syrup
½ teaspoon curry powder
1 tablespoon butter
1 tablespoon dark brown sugar

1. Heat a large nonstick skillet over medium-high heat. Coat pan with cooking spray. Add ham; cook 3 to 4 minutes on each side or until browned. Remove from pan; keep warm.

2. Combine pineapple, syrup, and curry powder; toss well.

3. Melt butter in pan over medium heat; add pineapple mixture. Cook 4 minutes or until pineapple is tender, stirring frequently. Add brown sugar; cook 1 minute or until sugar melts. Serve glazed pineapple over ham. Yield: 4 servings (serving size: 3 ounces ham and about ½ cup glazed pineapple).

CALORIES 278 (49% from fat); FAT 15g (sat 5.9g, mono 7.9g, poly 1.2g); PROTEIN 18g; CARB 24.1g; FIBER 1.2g; CHOL 62mg; IRON 1mg; SODIUM 1,130mg; CALC 22mg

Pineapple The flavor of pineapple is a delicate balance between sweet and tart. Purchase pineapple that is heavy for its size. To store, refrigerate fresh pineapple, tightly wrapped, for two to three days. Avoid fruit that has dark, mushy spots or a woody-looking or whitish appearance.

On cold days when you don't want to brave the outdoor grill, broil these lamb chops in the oven instead.

Sweet-Spiced Grilled Lamb Chops
Prep: 2 minutes • Cook: 8 minutes

¾ teaspoon ground cinnamon
½ teaspoon freshly ground black pepper
¼ teaspoon ground allspice
¼ teaspoon ground cumin
⅛ teaspoon salt

⅛ teaspoon ground red pepper
8 (4-ounce) lamb loin chops, trimmed (about 1 inch thick)
Cooking spray
Lime wedges (optional)

1. Prepare grill.
2. Combine first 6 ingredients in a small bowl. Rub mixture evenly over lamb. Place lamb on a grill rack coated with cooking spray. Grill 4 to 5 minutes on each side or until desired degree of doneness. Serve with lime wedges, if desired. Yield: 4 servings (serving size: 2 lamb chops).

CALORIES 209 (40% from fat); FAT 9g (sat 3.3g, mono 4.1g, poly 0.6g); PROTEIN 28.7g; CARB 0.7g; FIBER 0.4g; CHOL 90mg; IRON 2.1mg; SODIUM 153mg; CALC 26mg

serve with
Bulgur-Golden Raisin Pilaf
Prep: 3 minutes • Cook: 11 minutes • Other: 2 minutes

1 cup water
½ cup bulgur wheat with soy grits hot cereal (such as Hodgson Mill)
½ cup golden raisins

¼ teaspoon crushed red pepper
¼ cup slivered almonds, toasted
2 teaspoons butter
¼ teaspoon salt

1. Combine first 4 ingredients in a medium saucepan; bring to a boil. Cover, reduce heat, and simmer 8 minutes or until water is almost absorbed.
2. Remove from heat; stir in remaining ingredients. Let stand, uncovered, 2 minutes. Yield: 4 servings (serving size: ½ cup).

CALORIES 176 (31% from fat); FAT 6g (sat 1.5g, mono 2.7g, poly 0.9g); PROTEIN 7.2g; CARB 28.8g; FIBER 3.2g; CHOL 5mg; IRON 1.6mg; SODIUM 161mg; CALC 49mg

Arugula is used for the pesto instead of the traditional basil to give this bright green sauce a hint of peppery flavor. The chops and carrots can broil at the same time, allowing you to get dinner on the table even faster.

Broiled Lamb Chops with Lemon-Arugula Pesto

Prep: 3 minutes • Cook: 10 minutes

8 (4-ounce) lean lamb loin chops, trimmed
½ teaspoon salt, divided
½ teaspoon freshly ground black pepper, divided
Cooking spray
1 lemon
1 tablespoon pine nuts, toasted
2 garlic cloves
4 cups baby arugula leaves
2 teaspoons olive oil
2 tablespoons water

1. Preheat broiler.
2. Sprinkle lamb evenly with ¼ teaspoon salt and ¼ teaspoon pepper. Arrange lamb in a single layer on a broiler pan coated with cooking spray; broil 5 to 6 minutes on each side or until desired degree of doneness.
3. While lamb broils, grate 1 teaspoon lemon rind; squeeze juice from lemon to measure 2 teaspoons.
4. Place pine nuts and garlic in a blender or food processor; process until minced. Add lemon rind, lemon juice, arugula, oil, 2 tablespoons water, ¼ teaspoon salt, and ¼ teaspoon pepper; process until smooth. Serve with lamb. Yield: 4 servings (serving size: 2 lamb chops and 2 tablespoons pesto).

CALORIES 249 (48% from fat); FAT 13g (sat 3.8g, mono 6.1g, poly 1.7g); PROTEIN 29.5g; CARB 2g; FIBER 0.6g; CHOL 90mg; IRON 2.4mg; SODIUM 376mg; CALC 55mg

serve with
Honey-Roasted Carrots

Prep: 3 minutes • Cook: 16 minutes

1 (12-ounce) package carrot sticks (about 3 cups)
Cooking spray
¼ teaspoon salt
¼ teaspoon freshly ground black pepper
1 tablespoon butter, melted
1 tablespoon brown sugar
1 tablespoon honey
2 teaspoons chopped fresh parsley

1. Preheat broiler.
2. Arrange carrot sticks on a jelly-roll pan coated with cooking spray. Coat carrots with cooking spray. Sprinkle evenly with salt and pepper, tossing to coat.
3. Broil 14 minutes or until carrots begin to brown, stirring once.
4. While carrots broil, combine butter, brown sugar, and honey in a small bowl. Pour butter mixture over carrots, tossing to coat. Broil 2 minutes or until carrots are browned and tender. Sprinkle with parsley. Yield: 4 servings (serving size: ¾ cup).

CALORIES 85 (33% from fat); FAT 3g (sat 1.8g, mono 0.8g, poly 0.2g); PROTEIN 0.9g; CARB 14.9g; FIBER 2.5g; CHOL 8mg; IRON 0.4mg; SODIUM 226mg; CALC 33mg

poultry

Barbecue-Stuffed Potatoes
Chicken-Tortilla Pie
"Fried" Panko Chicken Tenders
Cumin-Spiced Chicken with Chunky Tomato Sauce
Apricot-Lemon Chicken
Tarragon Chicken
Kalamata-Balsamic Chicken with Feta
Balsamic Chicken with Roasted Tomatoes
Mushroom-Herb Chicken
Chicken and Shiitake Marsala
Rosemary-Fig Chicken with Port
South-of-the-Border Grilled Chicken and Green Tomatoes
Grilled Chicken with Rustic Mustard Cream
Cumin-Seared Chicken with Pineapple-Mint Salsa
Chicken with Pomegranate-Sake Poached Raisins
Grilled Asian Drumsticks
Five-Spice Grilled Chicken Thighs with Blackberry Glaze
Sweet Mustard Chicken Thighs
Smothered Green Chile Pepper Chicken
Chicken Tagine
Turkey-Basil Rolls
Smoked Sausage and Corn Frittata
Smoked Sausage-and-Vegetable Pile-Up

The home-style flavors of baked potatoes topped with tender barbecue chicken and all the fixin's go perfectly with old-fashioned banana pudding. Top the pudding with some beautiful strawberries, and you've got a fresh new angle on a classic dessert.

Barbecue-Stuffed Potatoes

Prep: 5 minutes • Cook: 12 minutes

4 (6-ounce) baking potatoes
½ cup reduced-fat sour cream
2 green onions, finely chopped and divided
1⅓ cups shredded barbecue chicken (such as Lloyd's)

½ cup (2 ounces) reduced-fat shredded extra-sharp cheddar cheese

1. Pierce potatoes with a fork; arrange in a circle on paper towels in microwave oven. Microwave at HIGH 10 minutes or until done, rearranging potatoes after 5 minutes.
2. While potatoes cook, combine sour cream and 2 tablespoons onions; set aside.
3. Place chicken in a microwave-safe bowl; cover with plastic wrap (do not allow plastic wrap to touch food). Remove potatoes from microwave; place chicken in microwave. Microwave at HIGH 2 minutes or until thoroughly heated.
4. Slice potatoes lengthwise, cutting to, but not through, other side; fluff with fork. Top each potato evenly with chicken, sour cream mixture, cheese, and remaining onions. Yield: 4 servings (serving size: 1 potato, about ⅓ cup chicken, about 2 tablespoons sour cream topping, and 2 tablespoons cheese).

CALORIES 367 (22% from fat); FAT 9g (sat 5.3g, mono 2.4g, poly 1.2g); PROTEIN 16.5g; CARB 57.6g; FIBER 4.2g; CHOL 43mg; IRON 3.2mg; SODIUM 619mg; CALC 117mg

serve with
Strawberry-Banana Pudding

Prep: 10 minutes

1 (3.4-ounce) package vanilla instant pudding mix
1 cup fat-free milk
1 (8-ounce) container frozen fat-free whipped topping, thawed

3 ripe bananas, diced
1½ cups miniature vanilla wafers, divided
2 cups strawberries, sliced

1. Combine pudding mix and milk in a small bowl; stir with a whisk until smooth. Fold whipped topping into pudding mixture. Fold in bananas. Layer ¾ cup cookies in bottom of an 8-inch square baking dish. Spread half of pudding mixture over cookies. Repeat procedure with remaining cookies and pudding mixture. Top with strawberries. Serve immediately, or cover and chill. Yield: 6 servings (serving size: about 1½ cups).

CALORIES 263 (15% from fat); FAT 4g (sat 0.9g, mono 0.6g, poly 1.8g); PROTEIN 3.4g; CARB 46.4g; FIBER 2.3g; CHOL 4mg; IRON 0.8mg; SODIUM 160mg; CALC 81mg

The fresh salsa called for here has a natural low-sodium advantage over bottled commercial salsa. A rotisserie chicken with the skin removed can be used for the shredded chicken breast, but keep in mind that this will increase the amount of sodium in the dish.

Chicken-Tortilla Pie
Prep: 13 minutes • Cook: 10 minutes

2 cups shredded cooked chicken breast
¼ cup Fresh Salsa
1 cup spicy black bean dip (such as Guiltless Gourmet)
4 (8-inch) multigrain flour tortillas (such as Tumaro's)
½ cup (2 ounces) reduced-fat shredded Monterey Jack cheese
Cooking spray

1. Preheat oven to 450°.
2. Combine chicken and salsa in a medium bowl.
3. Spread ¼ cup black bean dip over each tortilla. Top each evenly with chicken mixture and 2 tablespoons cheese. Stack tortillas in bottom of a 9-inch springform pan coated with cooking spray. Bake at 450° for 10 minutes or until thoroughly heated and cheese melts. Remove sides of pan. Cut pie into 4 wedges. Serve immediately. Yield: 4 servings (serving size: 1 wedge).

CALORIES 380 (26% from fat); FAT 11g (sat 4.3g, mono 4.4g, poly 1.4g); PROTEIN 39.9g; CARB 28.7g; FIBER 12.2g; CHOL 80mg; IRON 0.8mg; SODIUM 660mg; CALC 215mg

Fresh Salsa
Prep: 5 minutes

1½ cups refrigerated prechopped tomato, onion, and bell pepper mix
2 tablespoons chopped fresh cilantro
2 tablespoons fresh lime juice
¼ teaspoon ground cumin

1. Combine all ingredients in a medium bowl, stirring gently. Serve immediately, or refrigerate. Yield: 6 servings (serving size: ¼ cup).

CALORIES 12 (7% from fat); FAT 0g (sat 0g, mono 0g, poly 0g); PROTEIN 0.4g; CARB 2.9g; FIBER 0.7g; CHOL 0mg; IRON 0.2mg; SODIUM 2mg; CALC 7mg

This oven-frying method delivers a crispy coating without deep-frying. Don't be tempted to skip any steps if you want a golden, crunchy chicken tender.

"Fried" Panko Chicken Tenders

Prep: 9 minutes • Cook: 23 minutes • Other: 10 minutes

1½ cups panko (Japanese breadcrumbs)
¼ teaspoon freshly ground black pepper
⅛ teaspoon salt
¾ cup nonfat buttermilk

1½ pounds chicken breast tenders (about 12 tenders)
Cooking spray
Cajun-Creole Dipping Sauce

1. Preheat oven to 450°.
2. Combine panko, pepper, and salt in a shallow dish. Pour buttermilk into another shallow dish.
3. Dip chicken in buttermilk; dredge in panko mixture, pressing firmly to coat. Shake off excess panko mixture. Place chicken on a wire rack; let stand 10 minutes. While chicken stands, place a jelly-roll pan in oven to heat.
4. Coat chicken well with cooking spray. Remove hot pan from oven; coat with cooking spray. Arrange chicken in a single layer on pan. Bake at 450° for 23 minutes or until chicken is lightly browned. Serve with Cajun-Creole Dipping Sauce. Yield: 4 servings (serving size: about 3 chicken tenders and 2 tablespoons dipping sauce).

CALORIES 310 (8% from fat); FAT 3g (sat 0.6g, mono 0.5g, poly 0.5g); PROTEIN 44g; CARB 23.8g; FIBER 0.8g; CHOL 99mg; IRON 1.3mg; SODIUM 666mg; CALC 76mg

Cajun-Creole Dipping Sauce

Prep: 6 minutes

6 tablespoons fat-free mayonnaise
2 tablespoons Dijon mustard
1½ teaspoons chopped fresh parsley
1 teaspoon salt-free Cajun-Creole seasoning (such as The Spice Hunter)

⅛ teaspoon freshly ground black pepper
1/16 teaspoon salt

1. Combine all ingredients in a small bowl, stirring until blended. Yield: ½ cup (serving size: 2 tablespoons).

CALORIES 23 (0% from fat); FAT 0g (sat 0g, mono 0g, poly 0g); PROTEIN 0g; CARB 6.1g; FIBER 0g; CHOL 0mg; IRON 0mg; SODIUM 374mg; CALC 1mg

Bright green cilantro tops this cumin-spiced chicken with an extra dimension of flavor. Round out the meal with Chili-Lime Corn on the Cob.

Cumin-Spiced Chicken with Chunky Tomato Sauce

Prep: 2 minutes • Cook: 15 minutes

Cooking spray
4 (6-ounce) skinless, boneless chicken breast halves
¾ teaspoon ground cumin, divided
¼ teaspoon salt

1 (10-ounce) can mild diced tomatoes and green chiles, undrained
¾ cup (3 ounces) preshredded reduced-fat Mexican blend cheese
2 tablespoons chopped fresh cilantro

1. Preheat broiler.
2. Heat a large ovenproof skillet over medium-high heat; coat pan with cooking spray. Sprinkle both sides of chicken evenly with ½ teaspoon cumin and salt; cook 6 minutes on each side or until done. Remove chicken from pan; keep warm.
3. Add ¼ teaspoon cumin and tomatoes to pan; cook 1 minute. Return chicken to pan; spoon tomato mixture evenly over chicken. Sprinkle evenly with cheese; broil 2 minutes or until cheese melts. Top with cilantro. Yield: 4 servings (serving size: 1 chicken breast half and about ¼ cup tomato sauce).

CALORIES 253 (20% from fat); FAT 6g (sat 2.9g, mono 0.5g, poly 0.5g); PROTEIN 45.9g; CARB 2.7g; FIBER 0.9g; CHOL 106mg; IRON 1.6mg; SODIUM 693mg; CALC 188mg

serve with
Chili-Lime Corn on the Cob

Prep: 3 minutes • Cook: 8 minutes

4 ears shucked corn
2 tablespoons butter
½ teaspoon chili powder

½ teaspoon grated lime rind
¼ teaspoon salt
¼ teaspoon freshly ground black pepper

1. Place corn in a microwave-safe dish; cover dish with wax paper. Microwave at HIGH 7 minutes or until tender.
2. Place butter in a small microwave-safe bowl. Microwave at HIGH 15 seconds or until butter melts. Stir in chili powder, lime rind, salt, and pepper. Brush butter mixture evenly over cooked corn. Yield: 4 servings (serving size: 1 ear).

CALORIES 131 (47% from fat); FAT 7g (sat 3.8g, mono 1.8g, poly 0.7g); PROTEIN 3g; CARB 18.1g; FIBER 2.7g; CHOL 15mg; IRON 0.5mg; SODIUM 209mg; CALC 7mg

Start with an apricot fruit spread to concoct a sauce that transforms simply prepared chicken breasts into this elegant dish.

Apricot-Lemon Chicken

Prep: 4 minutes • Cook: 14 minutes

1 teaspoon curry powder
½ teaspoon salt
¼ teaspoon freshly ground black pepper
4 (6-ounce) skinless, boneless chicken breast halves
Cooking spray

⅓ cup apricot spread (such as Polaner All Fruit)
2 tablespoons fresh lemon juice
2 tablespoons water
2 teaspoons grated lemon rind

1. Combine first 3 ingredients in a small bowl; rub mixture over chicken.
2. Place a large nonstick skillet over medium-high heat. Coat pan with cooking spray. Cook chicken 6 minutes on each side or until done. Remove chicken from pan, and keep warm.
3. Add apricot spread, lemon juice, and 2 tablespoons water to pan, stirring until smooth. Cook over medium heat 1 minute. Spoon sauce over chicken; sprinkle with lemon rind. Yield: 4 servings (serving size: 1 chicken breast half and about 1½ tablespoons apricot-lemon sauce).

CALORIES 245 (8% from fat); FAT 2g (sat 0.6g, mono 0.5g, poly 0.5g); PROTEIN 39.4g; CARB 14.5g; FIBER 0.3g; CHOL 99mg; IRON 1.4mg; SODIUM 402mg; CALC 24mg

serve with

Sweet Lemon-Mint Pear Salad

Prep: 9 minutes

1 tablespoon sugar
3 tablespoons fresh lemon juice
2 teaspoons canola oil
4 cups packed baby spinach and spring greens mix

1 firm pear, thinly sliced
½ cup sliced red onion
¼ cup torn fresh mint leaves

1. Combine first 3 ingredients in a large bowl, stirring with a whisk. Add greens mix and remaining ingredients; toss well. Serve immediately. Yield: 4 servings (serving size: 1½ cups).

CALORIES 72 (30% from fat); FAT 2g (sat 0.2g, mono 1.4g, poly 0.7g); PROTEIN 1g; CARB 13g; FIBER 2.3g; CHOL 0mg; IRON 1mg; SODIUM 20mg; CALC 35mg

Pears Perfectly ripe pears are sweet with a subtle, intoxicating perfume. To ripen, place pears on the kitchen counter in a brown paper bag and check them daily. It may take three to five days for them to fully ripen. If the neck area yields to gentle thumb pressure, the pear is ready to eat or cook.

Add the remaining olive oil–tarragon mixture at the final stage of the cooking process to preserve its full-bodied taste and citrus essence. This fast and easy entrée is ideal for weeknight guests.

Tarragon Chicken
Prep: 4 minutes • Cook: 7 minutes

4 (6-ounce) skinless, boneless chicken breast halves
¼ teaspoon salt
2 tablespoons extra-virgin olive oil
1 teaspoon grated lemon rind

2 tablespoons fresh lemon juice
1 garlic clove, minced
2 teaspoons minced fresh tarragon
⅛ teaspoon salt

1. Place each chicken breast half between 2 sheets of heavy-duty plastic wrap; pound to ¼-inch thickness using a meat mallet or small heavy skillet. Sprinkle chicken evenly with ¼ teaspoon salt.
2. Combine olive oil and remaining 5 ingredients in a small bowl, stirring well with a whisk. Heat a large nonstick skillet over medium-high heat. Add 2 teaspoons oil mixture to pan, spreading evenly over bottom of pan with a wide spatula. Add chicken; cook 2 minutes. Drizzle chicken with 2 teaspoons oil mixture. Turn chicken over; cook 2 minutes. Drizzle remaining oil mixture over chicken; reduce heat to low. Cover and cook 2 minutes or until done. Transfer chicken to a serving platter. Pour pan drippings over chicken; serve immediately. Yield: 4 servings (serving size: 1 chicken breast half).

CALORIES 251 (33% from fat); FAT 9g (sat 1.6g, mono 5.5g, poly 1.5g); PROTEIN 39.4g; CARB 1.1g; FIBER 0.1g; CHOL 99mg; IRON 1.3mg; SODIUM 329mg; CALC 23mg

serve with
Kalamata Barley
Prep: 1 minute • Cook: 13 minutes • Other: 5 minutes

1⅓ cups water
⅔ cup uncooked quick-cooking barley (such as Quaker)
½ cup refrigerated prechopped tricolor bell pepper

10 pitted kalamata olives, chopped
2 tablespoons chopped fresh parsley
1 teaspoon extra-virgin olive oil
⅛ teaspoon salt

1. Bring 1⅓ cups water to a boil in a medium saucepan; add barley. Cover and cook 12 minutes. Remove pan from heat; stir in bell pepper and remaining ingredients. Let stand 5 minutes; fluff with a fork before serving. Yield: 4 servings (serving size: about ½ cup).

CALORIES 122 (29% from fat); FAT 4g (sat 0.5g, mono 2.8g, poly 0.4g); PROTEIN 2.9g; CARB 20.5g; FIBER 3g; CHOL 0mg; IRON 0.6mg; SODIUM 227mg; CALC 8mg

To keep the total time to 15 minutes, start cooking the chicken first. It will be done by the time the other ingredients are prepared.

Kalamata-Balsamic Chicken with Feta
Prep: 4 minutes • Cook: 14 minutes

4 (6-ounce) skinless, boneless chicken breast halves
½ teaspoon freshly ground black pepper
Cooking spray
1 cup grape tomatoes, halved

16 pitted kalamata olives, halved
3 tablespoons light balsamic vinaigrette
3 tablespoons crumbled feta cheese
2 tablespoons small basil leaves

1. Sprinkle chicken evenly with pepper.
2. Heat a large nonstick skillet over medium-high heat. Coat pan with cooking spray. Cook chicken 6 to 7 minutes on each side or until done. Transfer chicken to a serving platter; keep warm.
3. While chicken cooks, combine tomatoes, olives, and vinaigrette in a medium bowl.
4. Add tomato mixture to pan; cook 1 to 2 minutes or until tomatoes soften. Spoon over chicken. Top evenly with cheese and basil. Yield: 4 servings (serving size: 1 chicken breast half, ¼ cup tomato mixture, and ¾ tablespoon cheese).

CALORIES 273 (30% from fat); FAT 9g (sat 2.3g, mono 3.9g, poly 1g); PROTEIN 40.9g; CARB 4.1g; FIBER 0.7g; CHOL 105mg; IRON 1.5mg; SODIUM 612mg; CALC 65mg

serve with
Orzo with Spring Greens and Rosemary
Prep: 1 minute • Cook: 10 minutes

¾ cup uncooked orzo (rice-shaped pasta)
1 cup spring greens mix, coarsely chopped
4 teaspoons pine nuts, toasted

1 tablespoon extra-virgin olive oil
½ teaspoon minced fresh rosemary
¼ teaspoon salt

1. Cook orzo according to package directions, omitting salt and fat. Drain pasta; place in a medium bowl.
2. Add greens mix and remaining ingredients, tossing well. Yield: 4 servings (serving size: about ⅔ cup).

CALORIES 171 (32% from fat); FAT 6g (sat 0.6g, mono 3g, poly 1.5g); PROTEIN 4.6g; CARB 24.7g; FIBER 1.5g; CHOL 0mg; IRON 0.4mg; SODIUM 149mg; CALC 9mg

The juices escaping from the roasting tomatoes combine with the honey and olive oil to make a syrupy glaze to coat the tomatoes and the chicken.

Balsamic Chicken with Roasted Tomatoes

Prep: 5 minutes • Cook: 12 minutes

1 pint grape tomatoes
1 tablespoon honey
1½ teaspoons olive oil
½ teaspoon salt, divided
4 (6-ounce) skinless, boneless chicken breast halves
½ teaspoon freshly ground black pepper
Cooking spray
Balsamic vinaigrette salad spritzer (such as Wish-Bone)

1. Preheat oven to 450°.

2. Combine first 3 ingredients in a small bowl; place tomato mixture on a foil-lined jelly-roll pan. Bake at 450° for 12 minutes or until tomato skins burst and begin to wrinkle, stirring once. Transfer tomatoes to a bowl, scraping juices into bowl. Stir ¼ teaspoon salt into tomato mixture.

3. Place each chicken breast half between 2 sheets of heavy-duty plastic wrap; pound to ¼-inch thickness using a meat mallet or small heavy skillet. Sprinkle chicken evenly with ¼ teaspoon salt and pepper.

4. Heat a large nonstick skillet over medium-high heat. Coat pan with cooking spray. Add chicken; cook 3 to 4 minutes on each side. Place chicken on individual plates; coat each breast half with 2 to 3 sprays of balsamic spritzer. Spoon tomatoes evenly over chicken. Yield: 4 servings (serving size: 1 chicken breast half and about ¼ cup tomatoes).

CALORIES 238 (16% from fat); FAT 4g (sat 0.8g, mono 1.8g, poly 0.8g); PROTEIN 40g; CARB 7.7g; FIBER 1g; CHOL 99mg; IRON 1.5mg; SODIUM 431mg; CALC 28mg

serve with
Mushroom and Zucchini Orzo

Prep: 6 minutes • Cook: 12 minutes

1 cup uncooked orzo (rice-shaped pasta)
Cooking spray
1 cup sliced mushrooms
1 cup diced zucchini
1 tablespoon butter
½ teaspoon dried oregano
¼ teaspoon salt
¼ teaspoon freshly ground black pepper

1. Cook orzo according to package directions, omitting salt and fat. Drain and keep warm.

2. While orzo cooks, heat a large nonstick skillet over medium-high heat. Coat pan with cooking spray. Add mushrooms and zucchini; sauté 6 minutes or until tender and browned.

3. Combine orzo, mushroom mixture, and remaining ingredients in a large bowl, tossing gently. Yield: 4 servings (serving size: ¾ cup).

CALORIES 197 (17% from fat); FAT 4g (sat 1.8g, mono 0.7g, poly 0.1g); PROTEIN 6.3g; CARB 34.2g; FIBER 2.1g; CHOL 8mg; IRON 0.3mg; SODIUM 171mg; CALC 11mg

Marjoram is oregano's mild cousin. Crush the dried leaves to release their delicate flavor. For this recipe, use the largest shallots you can find; three large shallots should yield 1 cup of slices. Refrigerated mashed potatoes and broccoli complete the meal.

Mushroom-Herb Chicken

Prep: 5 minutes • Cook: 14 minutes

4 (6-ounce) skinless, boneless chicken breast halves	3 large shallots, peeled
¼ teaspoon salt	1 (8-ounce) package presliced mushrooms
¼ teaspoon black pepper	⅓ cup dry sherry
Cooking spray	1 teaspoon dried marjoram, crushed
	Freshly ground black pepper (optional)

1. Place each chicken breast half between 2 sheets of heavy-duty plastic wrap; pound to ⅓-inch thickness using a meat mallet or small heavy skillet. Sprinkle chicken evenly with salt and ¼ teaspoon pepper; coat with cooking spray. Heat a large nonstick skillet over medium-high heat. Add chicken to pan; cook 5 to 6 minutes on each side or until browned.

2. While chicken cooks, cut shallots vertically into thin slices. Remove chicken from pan. Coat pan with cooking spray. Add mushrooms and shallots to pan; coat vegetables with cooking spray. Cook 1 minute, stirring constantly. Stir in sherry and marjoram. Return chicken to pan; cover and cook 3 to 4 minutes or until mushrooms are tender and chicken is done. Transfer chicken to a platter. Pour mushroom mixture over chicken; sprinkle with freshly ground pepper, if desired. Serve immediately. Yield: 4 servings (serving size: 1 chicken breast half and ⅓ cup mushroom sauce).

CALORIES 226 (10% from fat); FAT 3g (sat 0.6g, mono 0.5g, poly 0.6g); PROTEIN 41.6g; CARB 5g; FIBER 1g; CHOL 99mg; IRON 1.9mg; SODIUM 262mg; CALC 33mg

serve with
Chocolate Pretzel Bark

Prep: 6 minutes • Cook: 1 minute • Other: 20 minutes

12 ounces semisweet chocolate chips (such as Ghirardelli)	¾ cup chopped dried sweet cherries
	½ cup chopped pistachios
2 cups thin salted pretzel sticks	¼ cup chopped crystallized ginger

1. Place chocolate in a microwave-safe bowl. Microwave at HIGH 1 to 2 minutes or until melted, stirring after 30 seconds. Stir in pretzel sticks, coarsely chopping with a wooden spoon. Pour mixture into a 13 x 9–inch baking dish lined with wax paper, spreading to coat bottom of dish. Sprinkle remaining ingredients evenly on top, pressing into chocolate mixture. Refrigerate until hardened (about 20 minutes). Invert chocolate bark onto plate; carefully peel off wax paper. Cut into 16 pieces. Yield: about 1½ pounds (serving size: 1 piece).

CALORIES 175 (43% from fat); FAT 8g (sat 4g, mono 3.1g, poly 0.8g); PROTEIN 2.3g; CARB 25.8g; FIBER 2.4g; CHOL 0mg; IRON 1.4mg; SODIUM 130mg; CALC 21mg

Marsala, a fortified Italian wine recognized for its golden brown color and sweet, nutty flavor, is used in both sweet and savory dishes. Along with the smoky mushrooms in this recipe, the wine creates a rich, aromatic sauce. Dry sherry is a good substitute for Marsala.

Chicken and Shiitake Marsala
Prep: 1 minute • Cook: 14 minutes

4 (6-ounce) skinless, boneless chicken breast halves
Cooking spray
¼ teaspoon salt
¼ teaspoon black pepper
2 (3½-ounce) packages shiitake mushrooms, sliced
½ cup Marsala wine
2 green onions, finely chopped (about ⅓ cup) and divided
2 tablespoons butter

1. Place each chicken breast half between 2 sheets of heavy-duty plastic wrap; pound to ½-inch thickness using a meat mallet or small heavy skillet.
2. Heat a large nonstick skillet over medium-high heat. Coat pan with cooking spray. Sprinkle chicken evenly with salt and pepper. Add chicken to pan. Cook 5 to 6 minutes on each side or until done. Remove chicken and drippings from pan; set aside, and keep warm.
3. Heat pan over medium-high heat; coat pan with cooking spray. Add mushrooms. Coat mushrooms with cooking spray; cook 2 minutes or until tender, stirring frequently. Add wine and 3 tablespoons onions. Cook 30 seconds over high heat. Reduce heat; add butter, stirring until butter melts.
4. Add chicken and drippings to pan, stirring gently. Place chicken on platter. Spoon mushroom sauce over chicken; sprinkle with remaining onions. Yield: 4 servings (serving size: 1 chicken breast half and about ¼ cup mushroom sauce).

CALORIES 291 (24% from fat); FAT 8g (sat 4.2g, mono 2g, poly 0.7g); PROTEIN 40.9g; CARB 6.2g; FIBER 0.6g; CHOL 114mg; IRON 1.6mg; SODIUM 303mg; CALC 40mg

Shiitake Mushrooms The soft, brown, open cap of the shiitake mushroom lends itself to several cooking styles. Sautéing brings out the shiitake's strong smoky flavor, softens the texture to a velvety smoothness, and allows the mushroom to easily mingle with other ingredients.

This company-worthy dish received top reviews in our Test Kitchens because it's quick, easy, and simply unbeatable in terms of taste. Use garlic powder instead of fresh garlic; it won't burn when you sear the chicken.

Rosemary-Fig Chicken with Port
Prep: 4 minutes • Cook: 15 minutes

½ teaspoon salt
½ teaspoon garlic powder
½ teaspoon freshly ground black pepper
4 (6-ounce) skinless, boneless chicken breast halves

Butter-flavored cooking spray
⅔ cup fig preserves
1 tablespoon minced fresh rosemary
6 tablespoons port or other sweet red wine

1. Sprinkle first 3 ingredients evenly over chicken. Coat chicken with cooking spray.
2. Heat a large nonstick skillet over medium-high heat. Add chicken; cook 3 minutes on each side or until browned. Combine fig preserves, rosemary, and wine in a bowl; add to chicken, stirring gently. Cover, reduce heat to medium, and cook 6 minutes or until chicken is done. Uncover and cook 1 minute over medium-high heat or until sauce is slightly thick. Serve sauce over chicken. Yield: 4 servings (serving size: 1 chicken breast half and about 3 tablespoons sauce).

CALORIES 329 (7% from fat); FAT 2g (sat 0.6g, mono 0.5g, poly 0.5g); PROTEIN 39.4g; CARB 31.4g; FIBER 0.2g; CHOL 99mg; IRON 1.3mg; SODIUM 403mg; CALC 23mg

serve with
Lemon-Scented Broccoli Rabe
Prep: 1 minute • Cook: 14 minutes

4 quarts hot water
1½ pounds broccoli rabe (rapini)
½ teaspoon garlic powder
¼ teaspoon salt

¼ teaspoon crushed red pepper
1 tablespoon olive oil
2 teaspoons grated lemon rind

1. Bring 4 quarts hot water to a boil in a large, covered Dutch oven. Trim coarse ends from broccoli rabe. Combine garlic powder, salt, and red pepper; set aside.
2. Place broccoli rabe in boiling water; cook, uncovered, 5 to 6 minutes or until crisp-tender. Drain and plunge broccoli rabe into ice water; drain.
3. Heat oil in a large nonstick skillet over medium-high heat. Stir in garlic powder mixture. Add broccoli rabe, tossing to coat. Cook, turning every 1 to 2 minutes, until thoroughly heated. Sprinkle with lemon rind; toss well. Serve immediately. Yield: 4 servings (serving size: 1 cup).

CALORIES 69 (46% from fat); FAT 4g (sat 0.5g, mono 2.5g, poly 0.5g); PROTEIN 4.6g; CARB 6.5g; FIBER 0.2g; CHOL 0mg; IRON 1.1mg; SODIUM 183mg; CALC 62mg

The shortcut marinade begins with the flavorful drained liquid from the salsa. Choose a fresh juicy salsa with chunks of tomatoes and onions, which you can find in the deli or produce section of your supermarket, rather than a thick, tomato sauce–based product. Serve with tortillas.

South-of-the-Border Grilled Chicken and Green Tomatoes
Prep: 6 minutes • Cook: 12 minutes • Other: 30 minutes

1 (16-ounce) container fresh salsa	2 green tomatoes, each cut into 4 (½-inch-thick) slices
1 tablespoon olive oil	Cooking spray
¼ teaspoon salt	½ cup (2 ounces) crumbled queso fresco
¼ teaspoon black pepper	
4 (6-ounce) skinless, boneless chicken breast halves	

1. Drain salsa in a colander over a bowl, reserving liquid. Set salsa aside.
2. Combine reserved liquid, oil, salt, and pepper in a large zip-top plastic bag. Add chicken and tomato to bag; seal and shake gently to coat. Chill 30 minutes.
3. Prepare grill.
4. Remove chicken and tomato from bag, reserving marinade. Place chicken on grill rack coated with cooking spray; pour reserved marinade over chicken. Place tomato slices on grill rack. Grill chicken 6 minutes on each side or until done. Grill tomatoes 5 minutes on each side or until lightly browned. Serve chicken with tomatoes; top with reserved salsa and queso fresco. Yield: 4 servings (serving size: 2 tomato slices, 1 chicken breast half, about ½ cup salsa, and 2 tablespoons queso fresco).

CALORIES 314 (24% from fat); FAT 8g (sat 2.7g, mono 3.8g, poly 1.1g); PROTEIN 43.7g; CARB 8.7g; FIBER 0.7g; CHOL 109mg; IRON 1.7mg; SODIUM 588mg; CALC 115mg

Green Tomatoes There are two types of green tomatoes. The most common type is an immature tomato that's picked before it ripens. These green tomatoes have a sharp, tart taste and firm flesh. You wouldn't want to eat them raw, but cooking green tomatoes softens the flesh and balances the acidity. Green zebra tomatoes are yellowish green with dark green striations and remain green at full maturity. The flavor is mildly spicy and slightly tart.

The pronounced lemon-pine character of rosemary goes well with olive oil and Dijon mustard, giving this grilled chicken a rustic Mediterranean flair.

Grilled Chicken with Rustic Mustard Cream
Prep: 6 minutes • Cook: 12 minutes

1 tablespoon plus 1 teaspoon whole-grain Dijon mustard, divided	4 (6-ounce) skinless, boneless chicken breast halves
1 tablespoon olive oil	Cooking spray
1 teaspoon chopped fresh rosemary	3 tablespoons light mayonnaise
¼ teaspoon salt	1 tablespoon water
¼ teaspoon black pepper	Rosemary sprigs (optional)

1. Prepare grill.
2. Combine 1 teaspoon mustard, oil, and next 3 ingredients in a small bowl; brush evenly over chicken. Place chicken on grill rack coated with cooking spray; grill 6 minutes on each side or until done.
3. While chicken grills, combine 1 tablespoon mustard, mayonnaise, and 1 tablespoon water in a bowl. Serve mustard cream with grilled chicken. Garnish with rosemary sprigs, if desired. Yield: 4 servings (serving size: 1 chicken breast half and 1 tablespoon mustard cream).

CALORIES 262 (34% from fat); FAT 10g (sat 1.8g, mono 4g, poly 3g); PROTEIN 39.6g; CARB 1.7g; FIBER 0.2g; CHOL 102mg; IRON 1.4mg; SODIUM 448mg; CALC 25mg

serve with
Pan-Roasted Tomatoes with Herbs
Prep: 2 minutes • Cook: 4 minutes • Other: 5 minutes

2 teaspoons olive oil, divided	½ teaspoon chopped fresh rosemary
1 pint multicolored grape tomatoes	¼ teaspoon salt
1 teaspoon chopped fresh oregano	¼ teaspoon crushed red pepper

1. Heat 1 teaspoon oil in a medium nonstick skillet over medium-high heat. Add tomatoes; cook 3 to 4 minutes or until tomatoes begin to blister. Remove from heat; stir in 1 teaspoon oil and remaining ingredients, tossing gently to combine. Let stand 5 minutes. Yield: 4 servings (serving size: ½ cup).

CALORIES 34 (66% from fat); FAT 3g (sat 0.4g, mono 1.7g, poly 0.4g); PROTEIN 0.7g; CARB 3.1g; FIBER 0.9g; CHOL 0mg; IRON 0.2mg; SODIUM 149mg; CALC 10mg

Buying refrigerated precubed pineapple makes it a breeze to put together this colorful salsa.

Cumin-Seared Chicken with Pineapple-Mint Salsa
Prep: 1 minute • Cook: 14 minutes

1 teaspoon ground cumin
½ teaspoon salt
⅛ teaspoon ground red pepper
4 (6-ounce) skinless, boneless chicken breast halves
Cooking spray

1½ cups cubed pineapple, finely chopped
½ cup chopped fresh mint
¼ cup finely chopped red onion
2 tablespoons rice vinegar
2 teaspoons grated peeled fresh ginger

1. Combine cumin, salt, and red pepper; sprinkle evenly over chicken.
2. Heat a large nonstick skillet over medium-high heat. Coat pan with cooking spray. Add chicken; cook 7 to 8 minutes on each side or until done.
3. While chicken cooks, combine pineapple and remaining ingredients; toss gently to blend. Serve with chicken. Yield: 4 servings (serving size: 1 chicken breast half and ½ cup salsa).

CALORIES 224 (10% from fat); FAT 2g (sat 0.6g, mono 0.5g, poly 0.5g); PROTEIN 39.9g; CARB 9.2g; FIBER 1.5g; CHOL 99mg; IRON 1.8mg; SODIUM 405mg; CALC 41mg

serve with
Almond-Coconut Rice
Prep: 2 minutes • Cook: 6 minutes

1 (10-ounce) package frozen whole-grain brown rice
⅓ cup slivered almonds

3 tablespoons flaked sweetened coconut
½ teaspoon ground cumin
⅛ teaspoon salt

1. Microwave rice according to package directions.
2. While rice cooks, heat a medium nonstick skillet over medium-high heat. Add almonds and coconut; cook 2 minutes or until lightly browned, stirring constantly. Remove from heat; add rice, cumin, and salt, stirring to blend. Yield: 4 servings (serving size: ¾ cup).

CALORIES 147 (36% from fat); FAT 6g (sat 1.4g, mono 3.1g, poly 1.3g); PROTEIN 4.2g; CARB 19.8g; FIBER 2.5g; CHOL 0mg; IRON 0.5mg; SODIUM 86mg; CALC 35mg

Most of the sake's alcohol content will evaporate during cooking, but stirring an extra tablespoon of sake into the finished sauce enhances the dish without overpowering it.

Chicken with Pomegranate-Sake Poached Raisins
Prep: 4 minutes • Cook: 17 minutes

4   (6-ounce) skinless, boneless chicken
    breast halves
¼   teaspoon salt
¼   teaspoon ground red pepper
Cooking spray

½   cup plus 1 tablespoon sake (rice wine),
    divided
½   cup pomegranate-cherry juice
½   cup raisins or dried sweet cherries

1. Sprinkle both sides of chicken with salt and red pepper, rubbing to evenly distribute spices. Coat chicken with cooking spray.

2. Heat a large nonstick skillet over medium-high heat. Coat pan with cooking spray; add chicken. Cook 4 minutes on each side or until browned; add ½ cup sake, juice, and raisins. Cover and cook 6 minutes or until chicken is done. Uncover and transfer chicken to individual plates. Cook raisin mixture, stirring constantly, 2 to 3 minutes or until liquid almost evaporates.

3. Remove pan from heat; stir in 1 tablespoon sake. Spoon raisin sauce evenly over chicken. Yield: 4 servings (serving size: 1 chicken breast half and 2 tablespoons raisin sauce).

CALORIES 280 (7% from fat); FAT 2g (sat 0.6g, mono 0.5g, poly 0.5g); PROTEIN 39.9g; CARB 19.2g; FIBER 0.7g; CHOL 99mg; IRON 1.6mg; SODIUM 265mg; CALC 28mg

serve with
Roasted Green Beans with Onions
Prep: 3 minutes • Cook: 13 minutes

1   (12-ounce) package fresh green beans,
    trimmed
1   cup sliced onion (about ½ medium onion)

1   teaspoon dark sesame oil
¼   teaspoon salt
Sesame seeds, toasted (optional)

1. Preheat oven to 500°.

2. Combine first 4 ingredients in a large bowl; toss to coat. Arrange bean mixture in a single layer on a jelly-roll pan. Bake at 500° for 10 minutes; stir beans. Bake an additional 3 minutes or until beans are tender. Sprinkle with sesame seeds, if desired. Yield: 4 servings (serving size: ¾ cup).

CALORIES 39 (30% from fat); FAT 1g (sat 0.2g, mono 0g, poly 0.1g); PROTEIN 1.5g; CARB 6.6g; FIBER 2.8g; CHOL 0mg; IRON 0.8mg; SODIUM 150mg; CALC 31mg

These drumsticks are a perfect balance of smoky, sweet, and spicy.

Grilled Asian Drumsticks
Prep: 4 minutes • Cook: 20 minutes

8 chicken drumsticks (about 2 pounds), skinned
Cooking spray
3 tablespoons balsamic vinegar

3 tablespoons low-sodium soy sauce
3 tablespoons honey
2 teaspoons sambal oelek (ground fresh chile paste)

1. Preheat grill.
2. Coat chicken and grill rack with cooking spray. Grill chicken 20 minutes or until done, turning once.
3. While chicken grills, combine vinegar and remaining ingredients in a medium saucepan, stirring with a whisk. Bring to a boil; cook 4 minutes or until reduced to ⅓ cup.
4. Transfer chicken to a large bowl or pan. Pour sauce over chicken, turning to coat. Yield: 4 servings (serving size: 2 drumsticks and about 3 tablespoons sauce).

CALORIES 210 (18% from fat); FAT 4g (sat 1.1g, mono 1.4g, poly 1.1g); PROTEIN 26.3g; CARB 15.6g; FIBER 0g; CHOL 98mg; IRON 1.5mg; SODIUM 855mg; CALC 18mg

serve with
Spicy-Sweet Broccoli
Prep: 3 minutes • Cook: 4 minutes

1 (12-ounce) package refrigerated broccoli florets
2 tablespoons low-sodium soy sauce
2 tablespoons rice vinegar

1 tablespoon dark sesame oil
2 teaspoons sugar
¼ teaspoon crushed red pepper

1. Microwave broccoli according to package directions. Drain. Combine soy sauce and remaining ingredients in a small bowl. Drizzle over cooked broccoli. Yield: 4 servings (serving size: ¾ cup).

CALORIES 62 (55% from fat); FAT 4g (sat 0.6g, mono 1.4g, poly 1.7g); PROTEIN 2.6g; CARB 6.6g; FIBER 2.5g; CHOL 0mg; IRON 0.8mg; SODIUM 473mg; CALC 41mg

Broccoli It's available year-round, but the peak season for buying broccoli is October through April. Broccoli florets have more vitamin C than the stalks; florets that are bluish green or purplish green have more vitamin C than their paler counterparts.

Rev up simple grilled chicken thighs with aromatic Chinese five-spice powder—a blend of cinnamon, cloves, fennel seed, star anise, and Szechuan peppercorns. The glaze thickens as it cools; simply reheat it in the microwave for 10 seconds for the right consistency.

Five-Spice Grilled Chicken Thighs with Blackberry Glaze

Prep: 7 minutes • Cook: 12 minutes

1 tablespoon five-spice powder
½ teaspoon salt
¼ teaspoon freshly ground black pepper
8 (3-ounce) skinless, boneless chicken thighs
Cooking spray

¾ cup sugar-free seedless blackberry jam (such as Smucker's)
3 tablespoons cider vinegar
1 tablespoon water
¾ teaspoon grated peeled fresh ginger
Fresh blackberries (optional)

1. Prepare grill.
2. Combine first 3 ingredients in a small bowl. Sprinkle spice mixture evenly over chicken. Place chicken on grill rack coated with cooking spray; cook chicken 6 minutes on each side or until done.
3. While chicken grills, combine jam and next 3 ingredients in a nonstick skillet. Simmer over medium-low heat 8 minutes or until glaze is reduced to ½ cup. Drizzle glaze evenly over chicken; garnish with blackberries, if desired. Serve immediately. Yield: 4 servings (serving size: 2 chicken thighs and 2 tablespoons glaze).

CALORIES 285 (41% from fat); FAT 13g (sat 3.6g, mono 4.9g, poly 2.9g); PROTEIN 30.6g; CARB 17.3g; FIBER 0g; CHOL 112mg; IRON 2.7mg; SODIUM 395mg; CALC 32mg

serve with
Yellow Rice with Spring Peas

Prep: 3 minutes • Cook: 18 minutes

Cooking spray
½ cup chopped onion
1 (3½-ounce) bag boil-in-bag long-grain rice
½ teaspoon ground turmeric

¾ cup fat-free, less-sodium chicken broth
½ cup water
⅛ teaspoon salt
½ cup frozen petite green peas

1. Heat a large nonstick skillet over medium-high heat. Coat pan with cooking spray. Add onion to pan; sauté 4 minutes or until tender. Cut open rice bag; pour rice into pan. Add turmeric; sauté 2 minutes. Add broth, ½ cup water, and salt; bring to a boil. Cover, reduce heat, and simmer 12 minutes or until rice is tender and liquid is absorbed. Stir in peas. Yield: 4 servings (serving size: ½ cup).

CALORIES 54 (1% from fat); FAT 0g (sat 0g, mono 0g, poly 0g); PROTEIN 2.2g; CARB 10.9g; FIBER 1.3g; CHOL 0mg; IRON 0.6mg; SODIUM 219mg; CALC 5mg

These Carolina-style barbecue chicken thighs are smothered with a tangy-sweet sauce that will please the whole family.

Sweet Mustard Chicken Thighs
Prep: 3 minutes • Cook: 6 minutes

½ cup prepared mustard
⅓ cup packed dark brown sugar
1 teaspoon ground allspice
¼ teaspoon crushed red pepper

8 (3-ounce) skinless, boneless chicken thighs
Cooking spray

1. Prepare grill.
2. Combine first 4 ingredients in a small bowl, stirring well. Reserve and set aside ¼ cup sauce mixture.
3. Place chicken on grill rack coated with cooking spray. Brush half of remaining ½ cup sauce mixture over one side of chicken. Grill chicken 3 to 4 minutes. Turn chicken over; brush with remaining half of sauce mixture. Cook 3 to 4 minutes or until done. Place chicken on a serving platter; drizzle with reserved ¼ cup sauce mixture. Yield: 4 servings (serving size: 2 chicken thighs and 1 tablespoon sauce).

CALORIES 317 (36% from fat); FAT 13g (sat 3.6g, mono 4.9g, poly 2.9g); PROTEIN 30.5g; CARB 18.3g; FIBER 0.3g; CHOL 112mg; IRON 1.9mg; SODIUM 471mg; CALC 34mg

serve with
Warm Balsamic Potato Salad
Prep: 5 minutes • Cook: 7 minutes

1 pound mixed baby potatoes (such as fingerling, purple, and red), cut into wedges
1 tablespoon water
¼ cup light balsamic vinaigrette

½ cup chopped bottled roasted red bell peppers
2 tablespoons chopped fresh basil
¼ cup (1 ounce) crumbled goat cheese

1. Place potato wedges in a large microwave-safe bowl; add 1 tablespoon water. Cover with plastic wrap; vent (do not allow plastic wrap to touch food). Microwave at HIGH 7 minutes or until tender; drain.
2. Stir in vinaigrette, bell pepper, and basil. Top each serving with cheese. Yield: 4 servings (serving size: about ¾ cup potatoes and 1 tablespoon cheese).

CALORIES 131 (30% from fat); FAT 4g (sat 1.8g, mono 0.5g, poly 0.1g); PROTEIN 3.7g; CARB 19.9g; FIBER 2g; CHOL 6mg; IRON 1mg; SODIUM 329mg; CALC 35mg

Whole green chiles hug the chicken thighs and impart a mild, roasted flavor to both the meat and broth. The chiles used in this recipe come 3 per 4-ounce can.

Smothered Green Chile Pepper Chicken
Prep: 4 minutes • Cook: 35 minutes

8 (3-ounce) skinless, boneless chicken thighs
1 tablespoon fresh lime juice (about ½ lime)
3 tablespoons reduced-sodium taco seasoning

8 canned whole green chiles, drained
½ cup (2 ounces) shredded part-skim mozzarella cheese

1. Preheat oven to 400°.
2. Arrange chicken in an 8-inch square baking dish; squeeze lime juice evenly over chicken. Sprinkle evenly with taco seasoning.
3. Slice chiles lengthwise, cutting to, but not through, other side; open flat. Place 1 chile over each chicken thigh. Cover dish with foil; bake at 400° for 30 minutes. Sprinkle cheese evenly over chiles and chicken; bake, uncovered, an additional 5 minutes or until cheese melts. Yield: 4 servings (serving size: 2 chicken thighs and 3 tablespoons broth).

CALORIES 301 (45% from fat); FAT 15g (sat 5g, mono 5.5g, poly 3g); PROTEIN 34.1g; CARB 4.7g; FIBER 0.5g; CHOL 120mg; IRON 2mg; SODIUM 574mg; CALC 116mg

serve with
Corn-Filled Mini-Muffins
Prep: 7 minutes • Cook: 13 minutes • Other: 2 minutes

1 (6.5-ounce) package corn muffin mix (such as Betty Crocker)
⅓ cup fat-free milk
2 tablespoons canola oil

2 egg whites
1 cup frozen shoepeg white corn
Butter-flavored cooking spray

1. Preheat oven to 400°.
2. Combine all ingredients except cooking spray in a medium bowl; stir just until combined. Spoon batter evenly into 24 miniature muffin cups coated with cooking spray. Bake at 400° for 11 minutes. Spray tops of muffins with cooking spray; bake an additional 2 minutes. Remove from oven; let stand in pan 2 minutes. Yield: 12 servings (serving size: 2 muffins).

CALORIES 102 (37% from fat); FAT 4g (sat 0.6g, mono 2g, poly 0.8g); PROTEIN 2.2g; CARB 13.8g; FIBER 0.6g; CHOL 4mg; IRON 0.4mg; SODIUM 147mg; CALC 29mg

A tagine is a Moroccan dish named after the cooking vessel it is prepared in. These braised stews contain meat, poultry, or fish; vegetables; and a combination of spices. Serve with a traditional Moroccan beverage: hot minted tea.

Chicken Tagine
Prep: 4 minutes • Cook: 13 minutes

8 (3-ounce) skinless, boneless chicken thighs
1½ teaspoons salt-free Moroccan spice blend (such as The Spice Hunter)
¼ teaspoon salt
¼ teaspoon black pepper
2 teaspoons olive oil
1 (16-ounce) can chickpeas (garbanzo beans), rinsed and drained
1 (14.5-ounce) can diced tomatoes with garlic and onion, undrained
¾ cup uncooked couscous
Plain fat-free yogurt (optional)
Chopped fresh mint (optional)

1. Sprinkle both sides of chicken evenly with spice blend, salt, and pepper. Heat oil in a large nonstick skillet over medium-high heat; add chicken. Cook 2 to 3 minutes on each side or until browned. Add chickpeas and tomatoes; bring to a boil. Cover, reduce heat, and simmer 8 minutes or until chicken is done.
2. While chicken simmers, cook couscous according to package directions, omitting salt and fat. Serve chicken thighs and vegetable mixture over couscous. Top with yogurt and mint, if desired. Yield: 4 servings (serving size: 2 chicken thighs, ⅔ cup vegetables, and about ¾ cup couscous).

CALORIES 510 (30% from fat); FAT 17g (sat 4g, mono 6.8g, poly 3.7g); PROTEIN 40g; CARB 48.7g; FIBER 5.8g; CHOL 112mg; IRON 4.4mg; SODIUM 884mg; CALC 63mg

Thai seasoning blend is packed with flavor, but isn't spicy. Look for it in the Asian section of your supermarket. Prepare the filling ahead, if desired, but assemble the rolls just before serving.

Turkey-Basil Rolls

Prep: 10 minutes • Cook: 5 minutes

Cooking spray
¾ pound ground turkey
½ teaspoon salt-free Thai seasoning blend (such as Frontier)
¼ teaspoon freshly ground black pepper
⅛ teaspoon salt

¾ cup cabbage-and-carrot coleslaw
6 (8-inch) round sheets rice paper
12 basil leaves
6 tablespoons light sesame-ginger dressing (such as Newman's Own)

1. Heat a large nonstick skillet over medium-high heat. Coat with cooking spray. Add turkey and next 3 ingredients; cook 5 minutes or until done. Combine turkey mixture and coleslaw in a medium bowl.

2. Add hot water to a large, shallow dish to a depth of 1 inch. Place 1 rice paper sheet in dish; let stand 30 seconds or just until soft. Place sheet on a flat surface. Arrange 2 basil leaves on top third of sheet. Arrange ⅓ cup turkey mixture on bottom third of sheet. Folding sides of sheet over filling and starting with filled side, roll up jelly-roll fashion. Gently press seam to seal. Place roll, seam side down, on a serving platter (cover to keep from drying).

3. Repeat procedure with remaining sheets, basil, and turkey mixture. Slice each roll in half diagonally. Serve rolls with dressing as a dipping sauce. Yield: 3 servings (serving size: 2 rolls and 2 tablespoons dipping sauce).

CALORIES 263 (30% from fat); FAT 9g (sat 2g, mono 4.5g, poly 2.3g); PROTEIN 24.5g; CARB 20.8g; FIBER 0.4g; CHOL 65mg; IRON 2.3mg; SODIUM 589mg; CALC 9mg

serve with
Mandarin Oranges with Grand Marnier and Mascarpone

Prep: 8 minutes

¼ cup reduced-fat sour cream
2 tablespoons mascarpone cheese
4 teaspoons sugar
1 (15-ounce) can mandarin oranges in light syrup, drained

1½ tablespoons Grand Marnier (orange-flavored liqueur)
Mint leaves (optional)

1. Combine first 3 ingredients in a small bowl, stirring with a whisk until sugar dissolves.

2. Combine oranges and liqueur; spoon evenly into 3 wine glasses or dessert dishes. Spoon sour cream mixture over oranges; garnish with mint leaves, if desired. Yield: 3 servings (serving size: about 2½ tablespoons oranges and 1 tablespoon sour cream topping).

CALORIES 200 (50% from fat); FAT 11g (sat 6.2g, mono 0g, poly 0g); PROTEIN 3g; CARB 19.9g; FIBER 0.8g; CHOL 34mg; IRON 0.3mg; SODIUM 28mg; CALC 72mg

Browning intensifies the smokiness of the sausage, allowing you to use less sausage while achieving maximum results in this simple-to-prepare frittata.

Smoked Sausage and Corn Frittata
Prep: 3 minutes • Cook: 16 minutes • Other: 2 minutes

Cooking spray
4 ounces smoked turkey sausage, quartered lengthwise and diced
1½ cups frozen shoepeg white corn, thawed
¼ teaspoon ground red pepper (optional)
1 large egg

4 large egg whites
½ cup (2 ounces) reduced-fat shredded sharp cheddar cheese
3 tablespoons chopped fresh cilantro, divided

1. Heat a medium nonstick skillet over medium-high heat. Coat pan with cooking spray. Add sausage; sauté 4 minutes or until browned. Stir in corn and, if desired, red pepper; reduce heat to medium-low.
2. Combine egg and egg whites in a small bowl; stir with a whisk. Drizzle evenly over sausage mixture. Cover and cook 8 minutes or until almost set. Remove pan from heat; sprinkle evenly with cheese and 1½ tablespoons cilantro. Cover and let stand 2 minutes. Sprinkle with 1½ tablespoons cilantro. Cut into 4 wedges. Yield: 4 servings (serving size: 1 wedge).

CALORIES 174 (31% from fat); FAT 6g (sat 2.9g, mono 0.5g, poly 0.2g); PROTEIN 13.8g; CARB 14.5g; FIBER 1.6g; CHOL 76mg; IRON 0.6mg; SODIUM 472mg; CALC 121mg

serve with
Sweet Lemon-Splashed Melon
Prep: 3 minutes

1 tablespoon sugar
½ teaspoon grated lemon rind

1 tablespoon fresh lemon juice
3 cups cubed peeled cantaloupe

1. Combine all ingredients in a medium bowl; toss gently to coat. Yield: 4 servings (serving size: ¾ cup).

CALORIES 54 (3% from fat); FAT 0g (sat 0.1g, mono 0g, poly 0.1g); PROTEIN 1g; CARB 13.3g; FIBER 0g; CHOL 0mg; IRON 0.3mg; SODIUM 19mg; CALC 11mg

Popular fast-food "all-in-one" bowls are loaded with fat and sodium. Our quick alternative is much healthier.

Smoked Sausage-and-Vegetable Pile-Up

Prep: 4 minutes • Cook: 11 minutes

Cooking spray
7 ounces smoked turkey sausage, diagonally sliced
1 cup refrigerated prechopped onion
1 cup refrigerated prechopped tricolor bell pepper

1 cup refrigerated presliced zucchini
1 (20-ounce) package refrigerated garlic mashed potatoes (such as Simply Potatoes)
2 cups frozen whole-kernel corn

1. Heat a large nonstick skillet over medium-high heat. Coat pan with cooking spray. Add sausage; sauté 2 minutes or until browned. Remove from skillet; keep warm.
2. Return pan to heat; coat with cooking spray. Add onion, bell pepper, and zucchini. Coat vegetables with cooking spray; sauté 5 minutes or until tender and beginning to brown.
3. While vegetables cook, heat potatoes according to package directions.
4. Add corn and cooked sausage to onion mixture. Sauté 4 minutes or until thoroughly heated. Serve sausage mixture over mashed potatoes. Yield: 4 servings (serving size: 1 cup sausage and vegetables and ½ cup mashed potatoes).

CALORIES 306 (26% from fat); FAT 9g (sat 4.6g, mono 1.1g, poly 3.3g); PROTEIN 12.9g; CARB 46.2g; FIBER 6g; CHOL 37mg; IRON 1.8mg; SODIUM 434mg; CALC 77mg

Zucchini This summer squash has thin, edible skin and soft seeds. In peak form from June through late August, zucchini can be used in almost anything from salads and breads to gratins. Zucchini will keep in the refrigerator for about five days.

kitchen secrets

When working with short ingredient lists and straightforward proce-
dures, recipes depend on quality ingredients. Choose your ingredients
carefully, follow a few simple strategies, and you, too, can master the art
of Fresh Food Fast. First, start with fresh, quick-cooking proteins, such
as fish fillets, pork chops, lamb chops, ground beef, and chicken breast
halves. Combine these with fresh fruits, vegetables, and herbs, plus a few
high-quality, high-flavor convenience foods (see "The 15-Minute Pantry"
on the facing page). Rely on cooking methods that can produce flavorful results fast, such as sautéing or broiling. Finally, pair the dish with a
simple side (see "Speedy Sides," page 358) or even an easy dessert.

8 Super Shortcuts

1 Purchase prepared ingredients such
as sliced mushrooms, prechopped
vegetable mixes, or bagged salad mixes.

2 Use a food processor to chop onions
or shred cabbage.

3 Slice larger cuts of meat like pork
tenderloin into medallions or thin
strips to shorten cooking times.

4 Choose dual-duty ingredients such as
olives, capers, or sun-dried tomatoes.
Capers, for example, impart acid and a
briny saltiness, allowing you to use fewer
ingredients to achieve robust results.

5 Gather all the ingredients before you
begin to cook.

6 To bring water to a boil more quickly,
preheat the pan on the stove, start
with hot tap water, and cover the pot
until the water reaches the boiling point.

7 While you wait for the oven to
preheat or water to boil, prep the
ingredients.

8 Pay a little extra at the fish counter
to have your shrimp peeled and
deveined.

The 15-Minute Pantry

We use these ingredients and convenience products to shave time from recipes. Keep them on hand, and your next meal is only minutes away.

Staple Pantry Items
- ❏ Alcohol and liqueurs: beer, bourbon, Grand Marnier (orange-flavored liqueur), rum, and wine
- ❏ Anchovy paste
- ❏ Balsamic glaze
- ❏ Bottled roasted red bell peppers
- ❏ Breadcrumbs: dry and panko
- ❏ Broth: low-fat low-sodium beef, chicken, and vegetable
- ❏ Canned beans: black, cannellini, garbanzo, kidney, and navy
- ❏ Canned or packaged tuna
- ❏ Capers
- ❏ Chili paste and curry paste
- ❏ Chipotle chiles in adobo sauce
- ❏ Chutneys
- ❏ Cooking spray: regular, butter-flavored, and olive oil–flavored
- ❏ Dried fruits and vegetables: cranberries, figs, raisins, and sun-dried tomatoes
- ❏ Dried herbs, spices, and spice blends
- ❏ Extracts: almond, vanilla
- ❏ Grains: barley, bulgur, quick-cooking oats, grits, and polenta
- ❏ Honey and syrups: regular and lavender honey; chocolate and maple syrup
- ❏ Jams, jellies, and preserves
- ❏ Ketchup
- ❏ Mayonnaise: light and reduced-fat
- ❏ Mustard: Dijon, prepared, and whole-grain Dijon
- ❏ Nuts: almonds, hazelnuts, peanuts, pecans, pistachios, pine nuts, and walnuts
- ❏ Oil: canola, dark sesame, extra-virgin olive, and olive
- ❏ Olives: black, green, and kalamata

- ❏ Pastas: angel hair, couscous, farfalle, orzo, penne, rotini, soba, and spaghetti
- ❏ Pasta sauce
- ❏ Relishes: dill pickle and sweet pickle
- ❏ Rice: Arborio, basmati, brown, jasmine, long-grain, white, and wild
- ❏ Salad dressings
- ❏ Sauces: barbecue, chili, fish, hoisin, low-sodium soy, picante, and Worcestershire
- ❏ Sugars: dark and light brown, granulated, and turbinado
- ❏ Tomato products, canned
- ❏ Vinegars: balsamic, cider, Champagne, red wine, rice, sherry, white balsamic, and white wine

Produce Department
- ❏ Bagged salad and salad mixes
- ❏ Fresh fruits, vegetables, and herbs
- ❏ Fresh garlic and ginger
- ❏ Fresh salsa
- ❏ Lemons, limes, and oranges
- ❏ Pesto
- ❏ Prechopped vegetables and vegetable mixes
- ❏ Tofu, extra-firm

Dairy Case
- ❏ Butter
- ❏ Cheeses: Asiago, blue, cheddar, cheddar-Jack, cream cheese, feta, Fontina, goat, Jarlsberg, mascarpone, Mexican blend, Monterey Jack, mozzarella, Muenster, Parmesan, pepper-Jack, provolone, queso fresco, and Swiss
- ❏ Milk: low-fat and nonfat buttermilk, fat-free, half-and-half, 1% low-fat, whole
- ❏ Sour cream: light and reduced-fat
- ❏ Yogurt-based spread
- ❏ Yogurt: lemon meringue light, nonfat Greek, plain fat-free, and vanilla fat-free

Refrigerated Section
- ❏ Fresh pasta
- ❏ Fresh pasta sauce
- ❏ Eggs
- ❏ Egg substitute

Deli, Meat, and Seafood Counter
- ❏ Deli Meats: ham, roast beef, and turkey
- ❏ Bacon
- ❏ Sausage: hot turkey Italian sausage and turkey breakfast sausage
- ❏ Beef: ground, roasts, steaks, and tenderloin
- ❏ Lamb: ground and loin chops
- ❏ Pork: chops and tenderloin
- ❏ Chicken: breast cutlets, drumsticks, rotisserie, skinless breast halves, tenders, and thighs
- ❏ Turkey, ground
- ❏ Fresh fish and shellfish: catfish, flounder, grouper, halibut, littleneck clams, lump crab meat, orange roughy, red snapper, salmon, sea scallops, shrimp, tilapia, trout, and tuna steaks

Freezer Case
- ❏ Frozen fish and seafood
- ❏ Frozen fruits and vegetables
- ❏ Ice cream

Speedy Sides

The perfect accompaniment can take a meal from mediocre to mouth-watering. Yet our readers tell us that side dishes are the first item they eliminate when they're in a time crunch. Here are creative side-dish solutions when time is of the essence.

Combine vegetables and starches in one side dish.
Double-duty side dishes like Sweet Pea and Fresh Mint Couscous (page 293) pair both in a simple preparation. The combination makes the dish more interesting and allows one side dish to do the work of two at mealtime. Add chopped chicken, pork, or beef to leftovers for a one-dish meal another night.

Use familiar vegetables and starches in different ways.
Even your favorite side dishes may begin to pall if prepared in the same way time after time, but applying new flavors or cooking techniques keeps them interesting. Low-sodium soy sauce, rice vinegar, and dark sesame oil in Spicy-Sweet Broccoli (page 341) put an Asian twist on a standard green vegetable, for instance.

Create vegetable medleys.
Combining two or three vegetables into one dish, such as Grilled Zucchini and Red Bell Pepper with Corn (page 199), adds appeal. Mix vegetables like peppers, onions, and spinach in a simple sauté, or roast a few with chopped herbs, shallots, and garlic. Vary the shape, color, taste, and texture of ingredients to boost interest.

Try new ingredients. Using dried figs to pep up Fig, Carrot, and Ginger Rice Pilaf (page 218) provides a fresh look and texture to a plain rice dish. If edamame, horned melons, pine nuts, or heirloom tomatoes are unfamiliar to you, try them. Experiment with one new ingredient a week. Each new food you enjoy broadens your options.

Sauce it. Veggies and grains can change personality with the addition of vinaigrettes or ethnic condiments. Spice up potato or rice sides with a tablespoon or two of chutney.

Side Staples

When it comes to rounding out your plate, reach for wholesome, satisfying options. This short list includes the choices we turn to time and again:

- Frozen mashed potatoes
- Refrigerated mashed sweet potatoes
- Presliced refrigerated potato wedges
- Fresh pasta
- Boil-in-bag rice
- Couscous
- Quick-cooking grits or polenta
- Bulgur
- Rice sticks or cellophane noodles
- Quick-cooking fresh vegetables such as green beans, zucchini, etc.

4 Fail-safe Sauces

Quick homemade sauces dress up sautéed chicken breasts, grilled steaks, or pork chops any night of the week. The vinaigrette and pesto also pair well with pasta or rice. While these sauces can be made in mere minutes, they add incredible depth and intensity of flavor.

Horseradish mayonnaise: Combine ⅓ cup light mayonnaise, 1½ tablespoons fresh lemon juice, 1 tablespoon Dijon mustard, 2 teaspoons prepared horseradish, and ¼ teaspoon salt, stirring well.

Basic herb vinaigrette: Combine 2 tablespoons chopped shallots, 1 tablespoon chopped fresh chives, 2 tablespoons white wine vinegar, 1 teaspoon chopped fresh thyme, 2 teaspoons Dijon mustard, ¼ teaspoon salt, and ⅛ teaspoon black pepper, stirring well. Stir in 1½ tablespoons extra-virgin olive oil.

Arugula pesto: Combine 2 cups trimmed arugula, 3 tablespoons shredded Parmesan cheese, 2 tablespoons fat-free, less-sodium chicken broth, 1 tablespoon extra-virgin olive oil, 2 teaspoons fresh lemon juice, 1 teaspoon bottled minced garlic, and ¼ teaspoon salt in a food processor; process until smooth.

Sweet-and-spicy pan sauce: Heat a nonstick skillet over medium-high heat. Coat pan with cooking spray. Add 1 teaspoon bottled minced garlic and ½ teaspoon bottled ground fresh ginger to pan; sauté 1 minute. Stir in 1 cup fat-free, less-sodium chicken broth and ¼ cup apricot preserves; bring to a boil. Cook 2 minutes or until slightly thick.

HOW TO USE IT AND WHY Glance at the end of any *Cooking Light* recipe, and you'll see how committed we are to helping you make the best of today's light cooking. With chefs, registered dietitians, home economists, and a computer system that analyzes every ingredient we use, *Cooking Light* gives you authoritative dietary detail like no other magazine. We go to such lengths so you can see how our recipes fit into your healthful eating plan. If you're trying to lose weight, the calorie and fat figures will probably help most. But if you're keeping a close eye on the sodium, cholesterol, and saturated fat in your diet, we provide those numbers, too. And because many women don't get enough iron or calcium, we can also help there, as well. Finally, there's a fiber analysis for those of us who don't get enough roughage.

Here's a helpful guide to put our nutrition analysis numbers into perspective. Remember, one size doesn't fit all, so take your lifestyle, age, and circumstances into consideration when determining your nutrition needs. For example, pregnant or breast-feeding women need more protein, calories, and calcium. And men older than 50 need 1,200mg of calcium daily, 200mg more than the amount recommended for younger men.

IN OUR NUTRITIONAL ANALYSIS, WE USE THESE ABBREVIATIONS:

sat	saturated fat	CHOL	cholesterol
mono	monounsaturated fat	CALC	calcium
poly	polyunsaturated fat	g	gram
CARB	carbohydrates	mg	milligram

DAILY NUTRITION GUIDE

	WOMEN AGES 25 TO 50	WOMEN OVER 50	MEN OVER 24
Calories	2,000	2,000 or less	2,700
Protein	50g	50g or less	63g
Fat	65g or less	65g or less	88g or less
Saturated Fat	20g or less	20g or less	27g or less
Carbohydrates	304g	304g	410g
Fiber	25g to 35g	25g to 35g	25g to 35g
Cholesterol	300mg or less	300mg or less	300mg or less
Iron	18mg	8mg	8mg
Sodium	2,300mg or less	1,500mg or less	2,300mg or less
Calcium	1,000mg	1,200mg	1,000mg

The nutritional values used in our calculations either come from The Food Processor, Version 7.5 (ESHA Research), or are provided by food manufacturers.

The information in the following charts is provided to help cooks outside the United States successfully use the recipes in this book. All equivalents are approximate.

Equivalents for Different Types of Ingredients

Standard Cup	Fine Powder (ex. flour)	Grain (ex. rice)	Granular (ex. sugar)	Liquid Solids (ex. butter)	Liquid (ex. milk)
1	140 g	150 g	190 g	200 g	240 ml
3/4	105 g	113 g	143 g	150 g	180 ml
2/3	93 g	100 g	125 g	133 g	160 ml
1/2	70 g	75 g	95 g	100 g	120 ml
1/3	47 g	50 g	63 g	67 g	80 ml
1/4	35 g	38 g	48 g	50 g	60 ml
1/8	18 g	19 g	24 g	25 g	30 ml

Liquid Ingredients by Volume

1/4 tsp					=	1 ml	
1/2 tsp					=	2 ml	
1 tsp					=	5 ml	
3 tsp	=	1 tbl		=	1/2 fl oz	=	15 ml
		2 tbls	= 1/8 cup	=	1 fl oz	=	30 ml
		4 tbls	= 1/4 cup	=	2 fl oz	=	60 ml
		5 1/3 tbls	= 1/3 cup	=	3 fl oz	=	80 ml
		8 tbls	= 1/2 cup	=	4 fl oz	=	120 ml
		10 2/3 tbls	= 2/3 cup	=	5 fl oz	=	160 ml
		12 tbls	= 3/4 cup	=	6 fl oz	=	180 ml
		16 tbls	= 1 cup	=	8 fl oz	=	240 ml
		1 pt	= 2 cups	=	16 fl oz	=	480 ml
		1 qt	= 4 cups	=	32 fl oz	=	960 ml
					33 fl oz	= 1000 ml	= 1 l

Dry Ingredients by Weight

(To convert ounces to grams, multiply the number of ounces by 30.)

1 oz	=	1/16 lb =	30 g
4 oz	=	1/4 lb =	120 g
8 oz	=	1/2 lb =	240 g
12 oz	=	3/4 lb =	360 g
16 oz	=	1 lb =	480 g

Length

(To convert inches to centimeters, multiply the number of inches by 2.5.)

1 in	=			2.5 cm
6 in	= 1/2 ft		=	15 cm
12 in	= 1 ft		=	30 cm
36 in	= 3 ft	= 1 yd	=	90 cm
40 in	=			100 cm = 1 m

Cooking/Oven Temperatures

	Fahrenheit	Celsius	Gas Mark
Freeze Water	32° F	0° C	
Room Temperature	68° F	20° C	
Boil Water	212° F	100° C	
Bake	325° F	160° C	3
	350° F	180° C	4
	375° F	190° C	5
	400° F	200° C	6
	425° F	220° C	7
	450° F	230° C	8
Broil			Grill

index